TURE FOUNDATION

UNIFIED FIELD THEORY: STAN LEE & JACK KIRBY

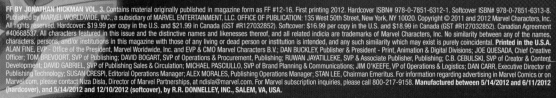

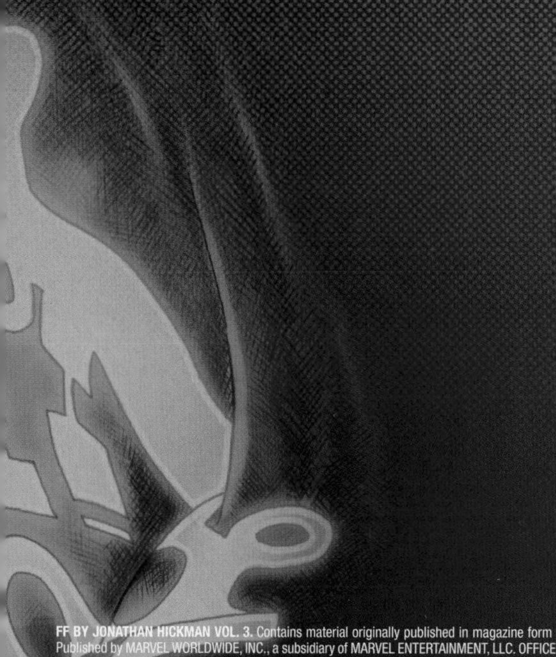

FF BY JONATHAN HICKMAN VOL. 3. Contains material originally published in magazine form as FF #12-16. First printing 2012. Hardcover ISBN# 978-0-7851-6312-1. Softcover ISBN# 978-0-7851-6313-8. Published by MARVEL WORLDWIDE, INC., a subsidiary of MARVEL ENTERTAINMENT, LLC. OFFICE OF PUBLICATION: 135 West 50th Street, New York, NY 10020. Copyright © 2011 and 2012 Marvel Characters, Inc. All rights reserved. Hardcover: $19.99 per copy in the U.S. and $21.99 in Canada (GST #R127032852). Softcover: $16.99 per copy in the U.S. and $18.99 in Canada (GST #R127032852). Canadian Agreement #40668537. All characters featured in this issue and the distinctive names and likenesses thereof, and all related indicia are trademarks of Marvel Characters, Inc. No similarity between any of the names, characters, persons, and/or institutions in this magazine with those of any living or dead person or institution is intended, and any such similarity which may exist is purely coincidental. **Printed in the U.S.A.** ALAN FINE, EVP - Office of the President, Marvel Worldwide, Inc. and EVP & CMO Marvel Characters B.V.; DAN BUCKLEY, Publisher & President - Print, Animation & Digital Divisions; JOE QUESADA, Chief Creative Officer; TOM BREVOORT, SVP of Publishing; DAVID BOGART, SVP of Operations & Procurement, Publishing; RUWAN JAYATILLEKE, SVP & Associate Publisher, Publishing; C.B. CEBULSKI, SVP of Creator & Content Development; DAVID GABRIEL, SVP of Publishing Sales & Circulation; MICHAEL PASCIULLO, SVP of Brand Planning & Communications; JIM O'KEEFE, VP of Operations & Logistics; DAN CARR, Executive Director of Publishing Technology; SUSAN CRESPI, Editorial Operations Manager; ALEX MORALES, Publishing Operations Manager; STAN LEE, Chairman Emeritus. For information regarding advertising in Marvel Comics or on Marvel.com, please contact Niza Disla, Director of Marvel Partnerships, at ndisla@marvel.com. For Marvel subscription inquiries, please call 800-217-9158. **Manufactured between 5/14/2012 and 6/11/2012 (hardcover), and 5/14/2012 and 12/10/2012 (softcover), by R.R. DONNELLEY, INC., SALEM, VA, USA.**

10 9 8 7 6 5 4 3 2 1

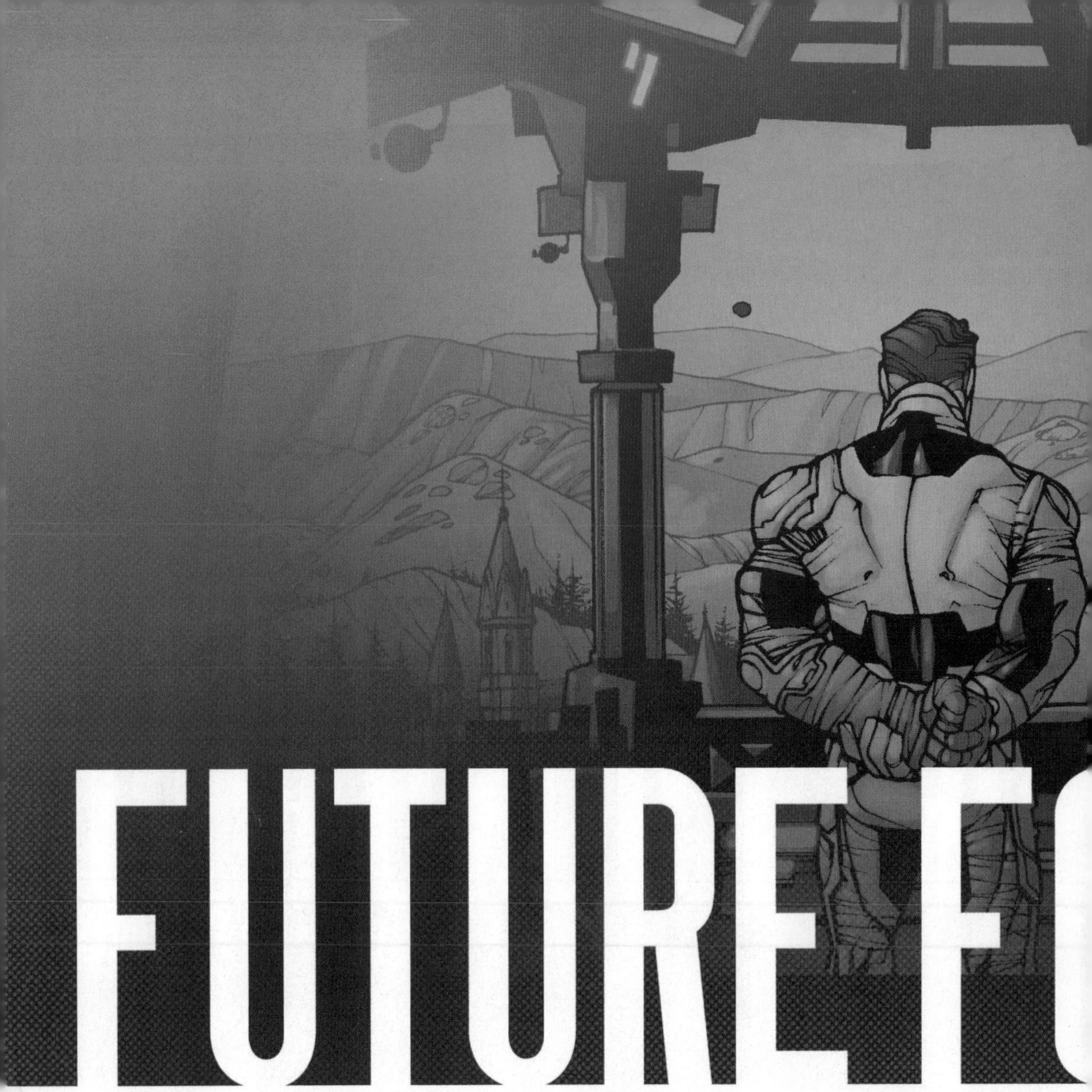
FUTURE FO

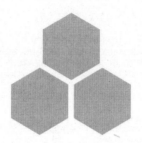

WRITER: **JONATHAN HICKMAN**

ARTISTS: **JUAN BOBILLO** [#12-14] & **NICK DRAGOTTA** [#15-16] WITH **STEVE EPTING** [#16]

INKER, ISSUES #12-14: **MARCELO SOSA**

COLOR ARTIST: **CHRIS SOTOMAYOR** WITH **SOTOCOLOR** [#12-16] & **PAUL MOUNTS** [#16]

LETTERER: **VIRTUAL CALLIGRAPHY'S CLAYTON COWLES**

COVER ARTISTS: **STEVE EPTING** [#12] AND **MIKE CHOI & GURU-EFX** [#13-16]

ASSISTANT EDITOR: **JOHN DENNING**

ASSOCIATE EDITOR: **LAUREN SANKOVITCH**

EDITOR: **TOM BREVOORT**

COLLECTION EDITOR: **JENNIFER GRÜNWALD**
ASSISTANT EDITORS: **ALEX STARBUCK & NELSON RIBEIRO**
EDITOR, SPECIAL PROJECTS: **MARK D. BEAZLEY**
SENIOR EDITOR, SPECIAL PROJECTS: **JEFF YOUNGQUIST**
SENIOR VICE PRESIDENT OF SALES: **DAVID GABRIEL**
SVP OF BRAND PLANNING & COMMUNICATIONS: **MICHAEL PASCIULLO**

EDITOR IN CHIEF: **AXEL ALONSO**
CHIEF CREATIVE OFFICER: **JOE QUESADA**
PUBLISHER: **DAN BUCKLEY**
EXECUTIVE PRODUCER: **ALAN FINE**

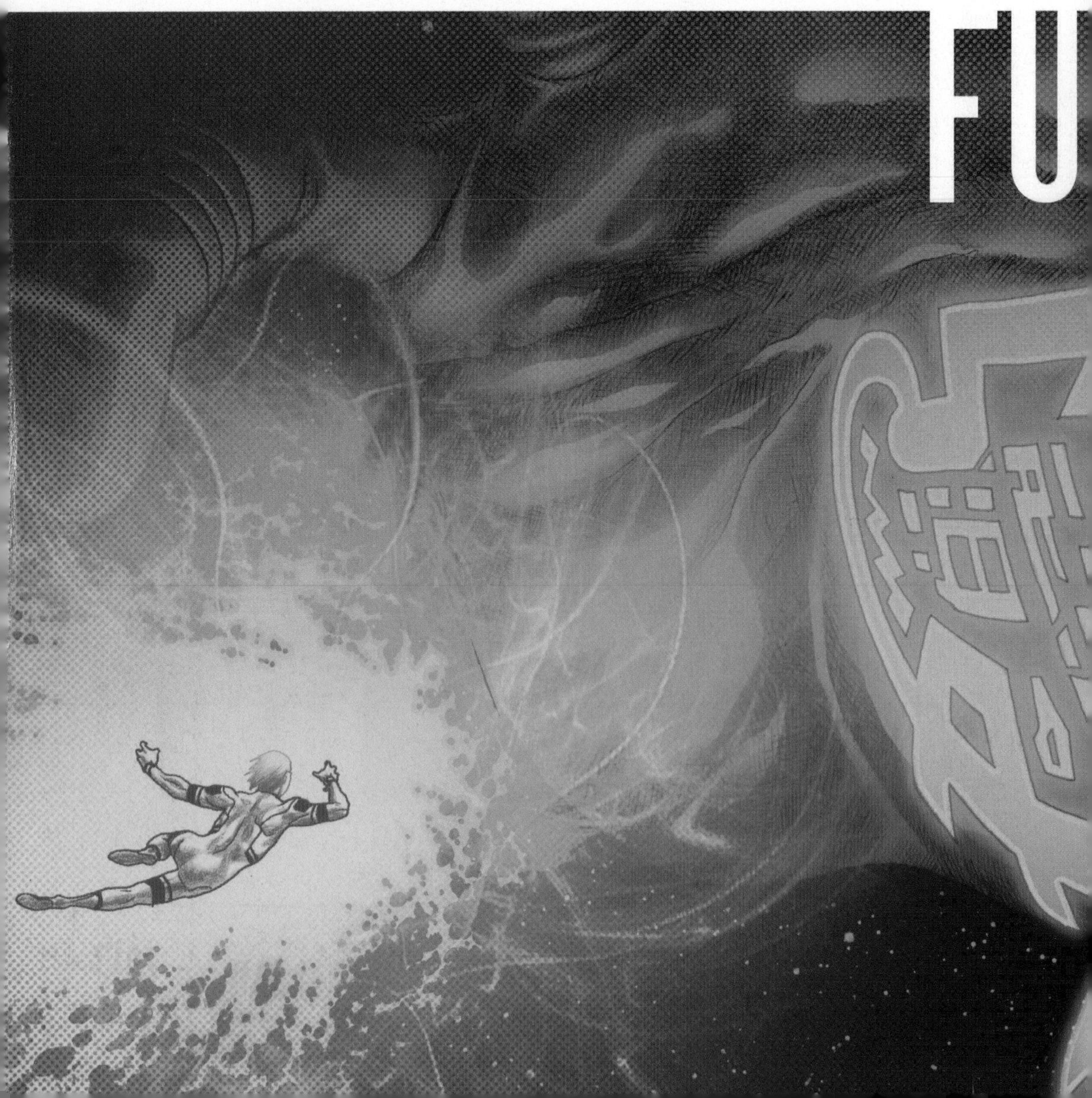

OUNDATION

VOL **THREE** ALL HOPE LIES IN DOOM

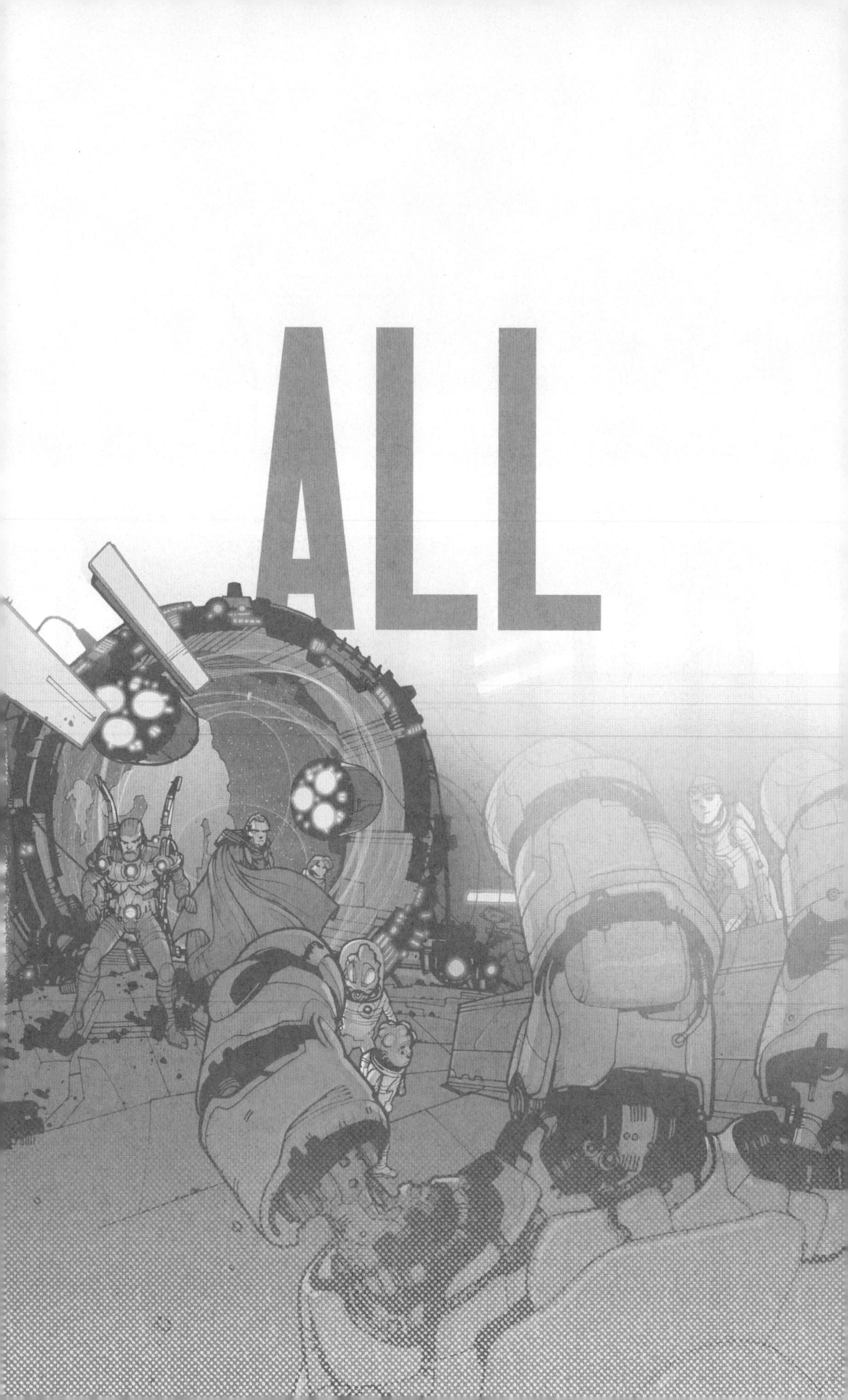
ALL

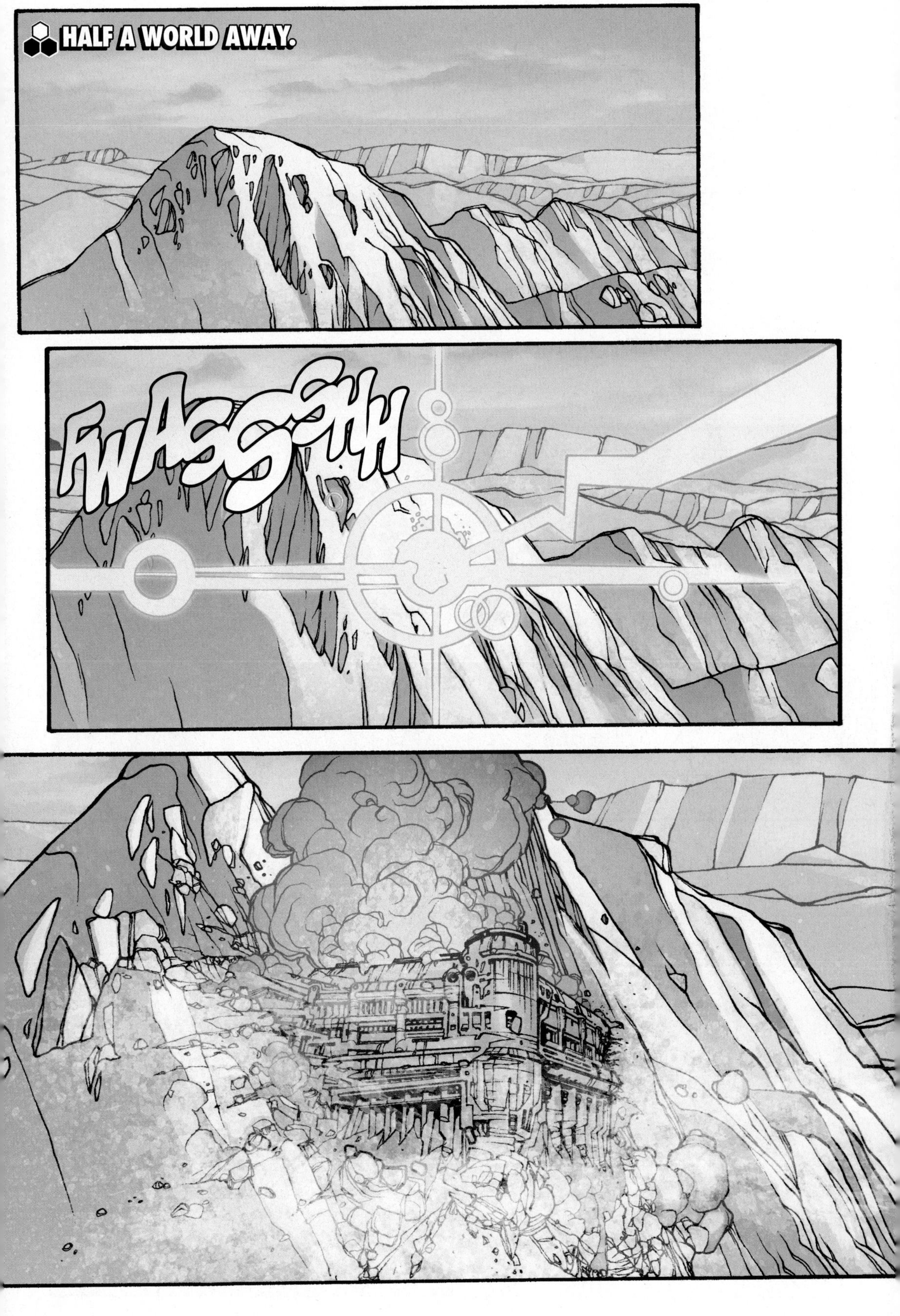
HALF A WORLD AWAY.
FWASSHH

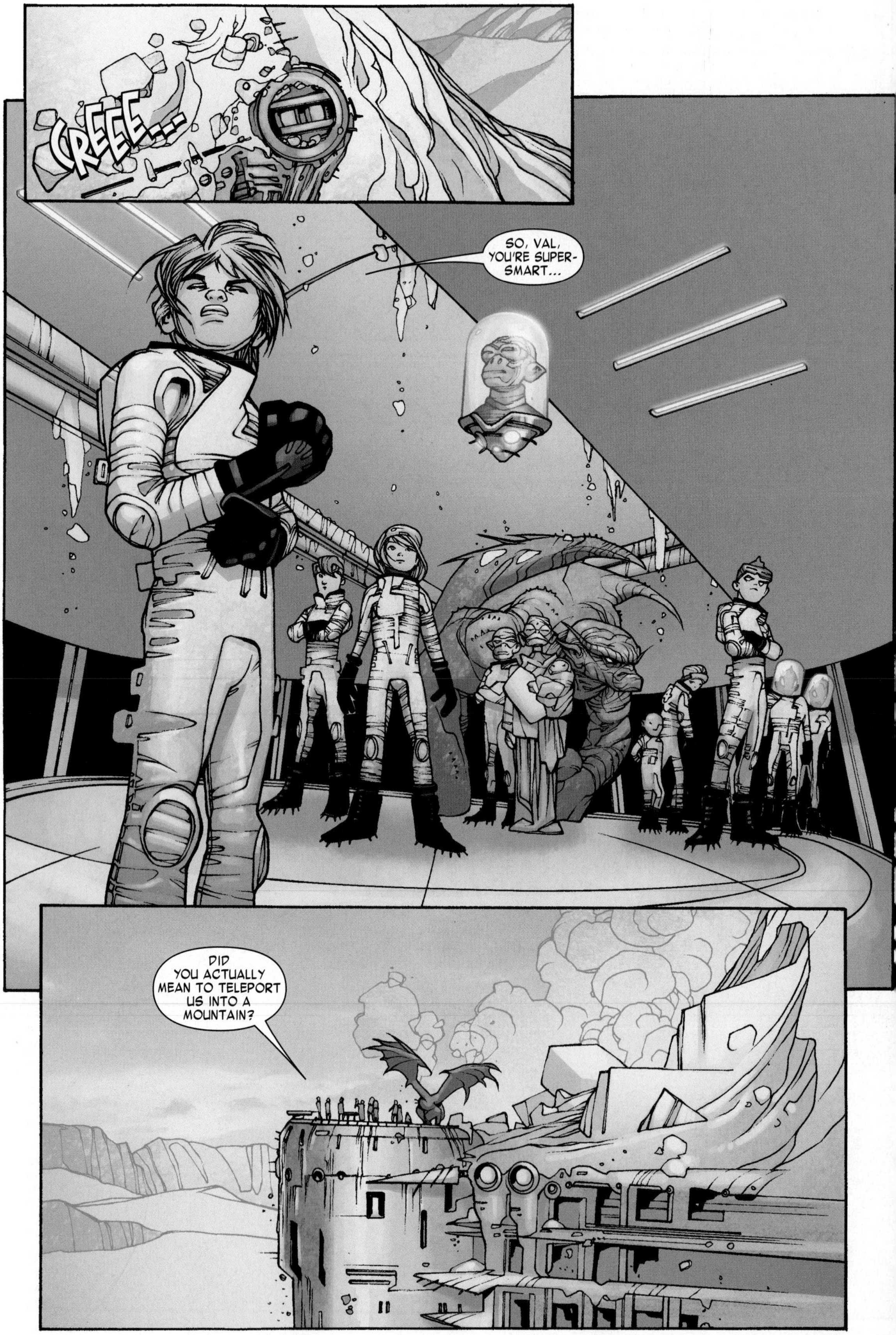
CREEE...
SO, VAL, YOU'RE SUPER-SMART...
DID YOU ACTUALLY MEAN TO TELEPORT US INTO A MOUNTAIN?

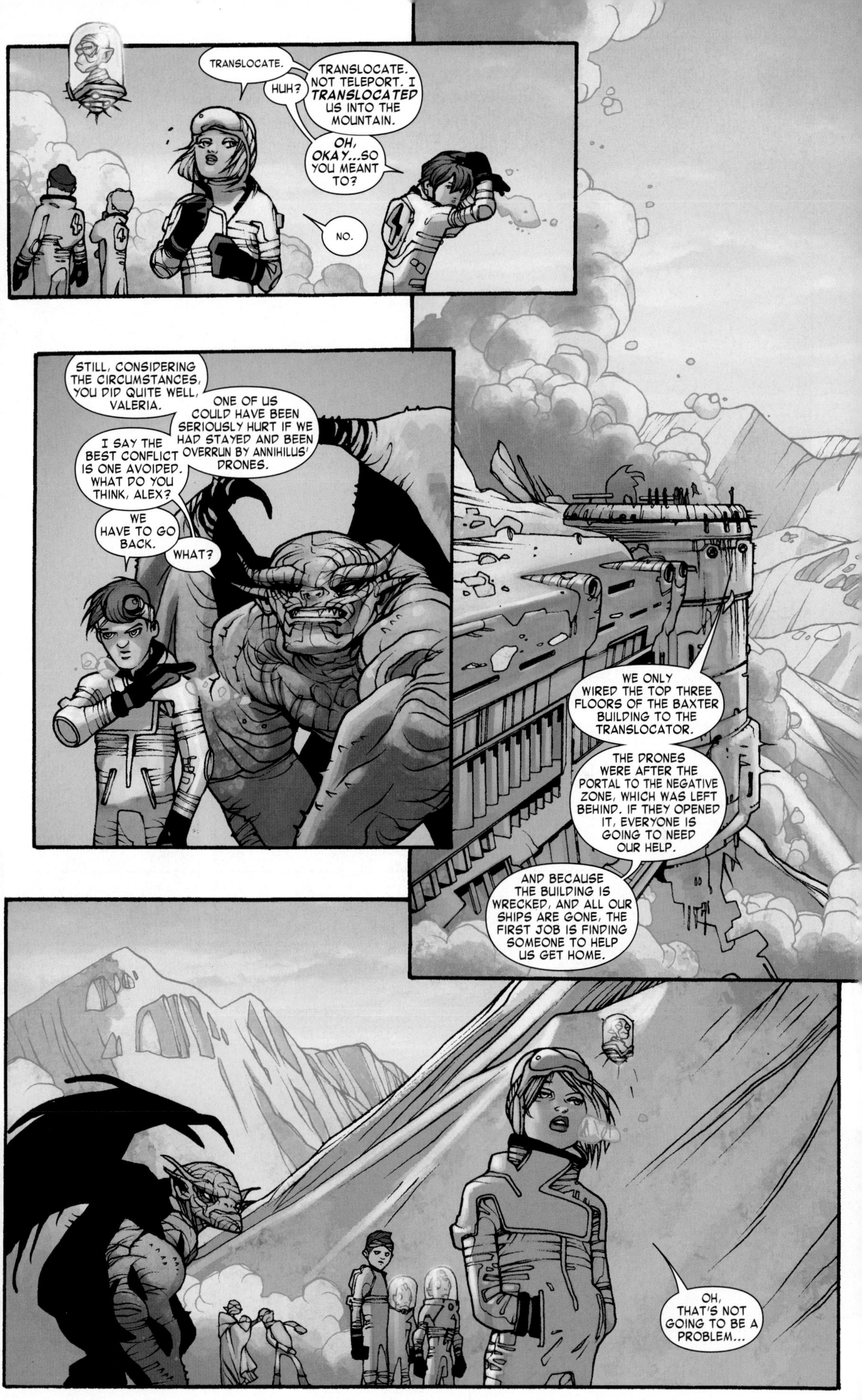
TRANSLOCATE.
HUH?
TRANSLOCATE. NOT TELEPORT. I *TRANSLOCATED* US INTO THE MOUNTAIN.
*OH, OKAY...*SO YOU MEANT TO?
NO.
STILL, CONSIDERING THE CIRCUMSTANCES, YOU DID QUITE WELL, VALERIA.
ONE OF US COULD HAVE BEEN SERIOUSLY HURT IF WE HAD STAYED AND BEEN OVERRUN BY ANNIHILUS' DRONES.
I SAY THE BEST CONFLICT IS ONE AVOIDED. WHAT DO YOU THINK, ALEX?
WE HAVE TO GO BACK.
WHAT?
WE ONLY WIRED THE TOP THREE FLOORS OF THE BAXTER BUILDING TO THE TRANSLOCATOR.
THE DRONES WERE AFTER THE PORTAL TO THE NEGATIVE ZONE, WHICH WAS LEFT BEHIND. IF THEY OPENED IT, EVERYONE IS GOING TO NEED OUR HELP.
AND BECAUSE THE BUILDING IS WRECKED, AND ALL OUR SHIPS ARE GONE, THE FIRST JOB IS FINDING SOMEONE TO HELP US GET HOME.
OH, THAT'S NOT GOING TO BE A PROBLEM...

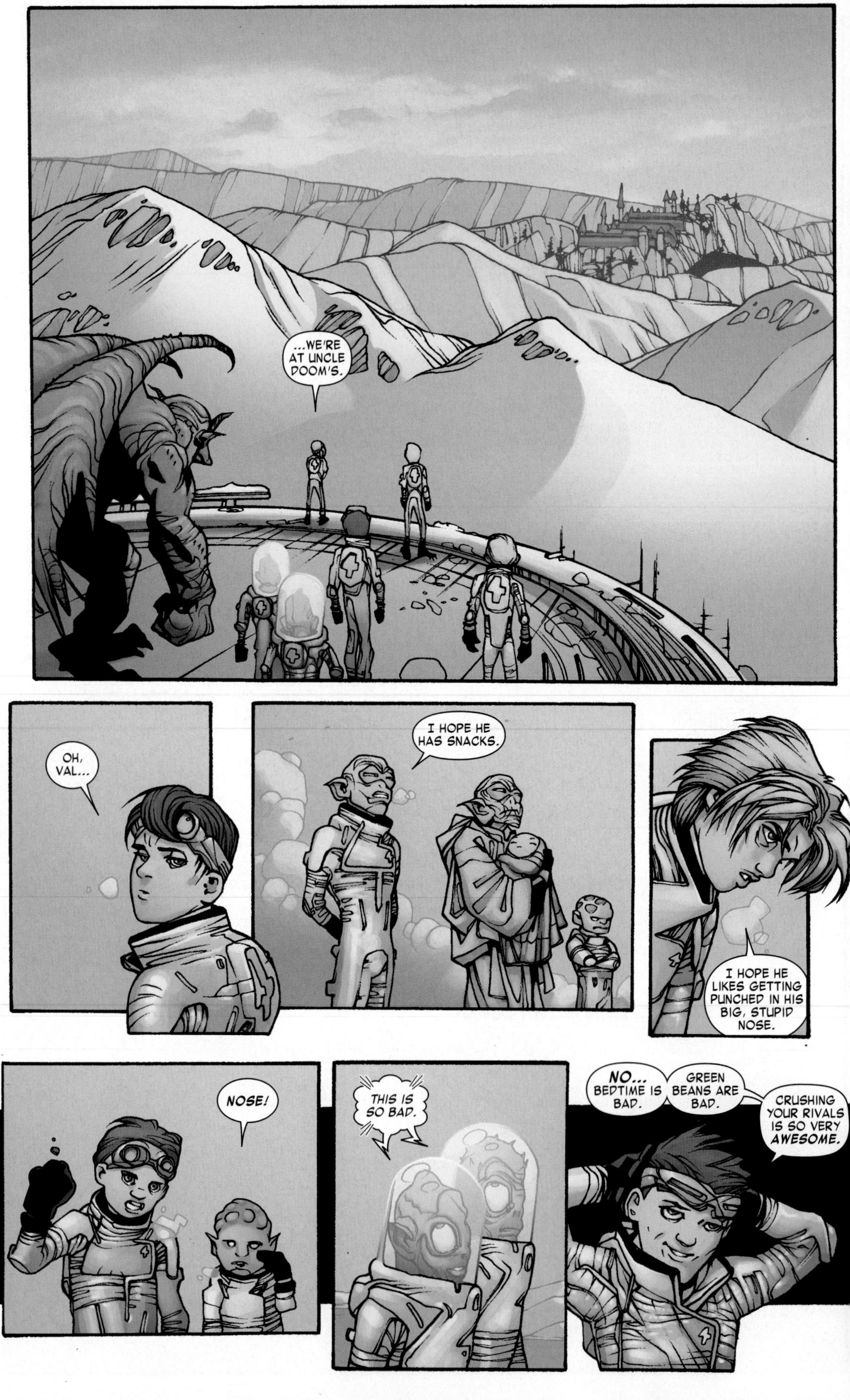
...WE'RE AT UNCLE DOOM'S.
OH, VAL...
I HOPE HE HAS SNACKS.
I HOPE HE LIKES GETTING PUNCHED IN HIS BIG, STUPID NOSE.
NOSE!
THIS IS SO BAD.
NO... BEDTIME IS BAD.
GREEN BEANS ARE BAD.
CRUSHING YOUR RIVALS IS SO VERY AWESOME.

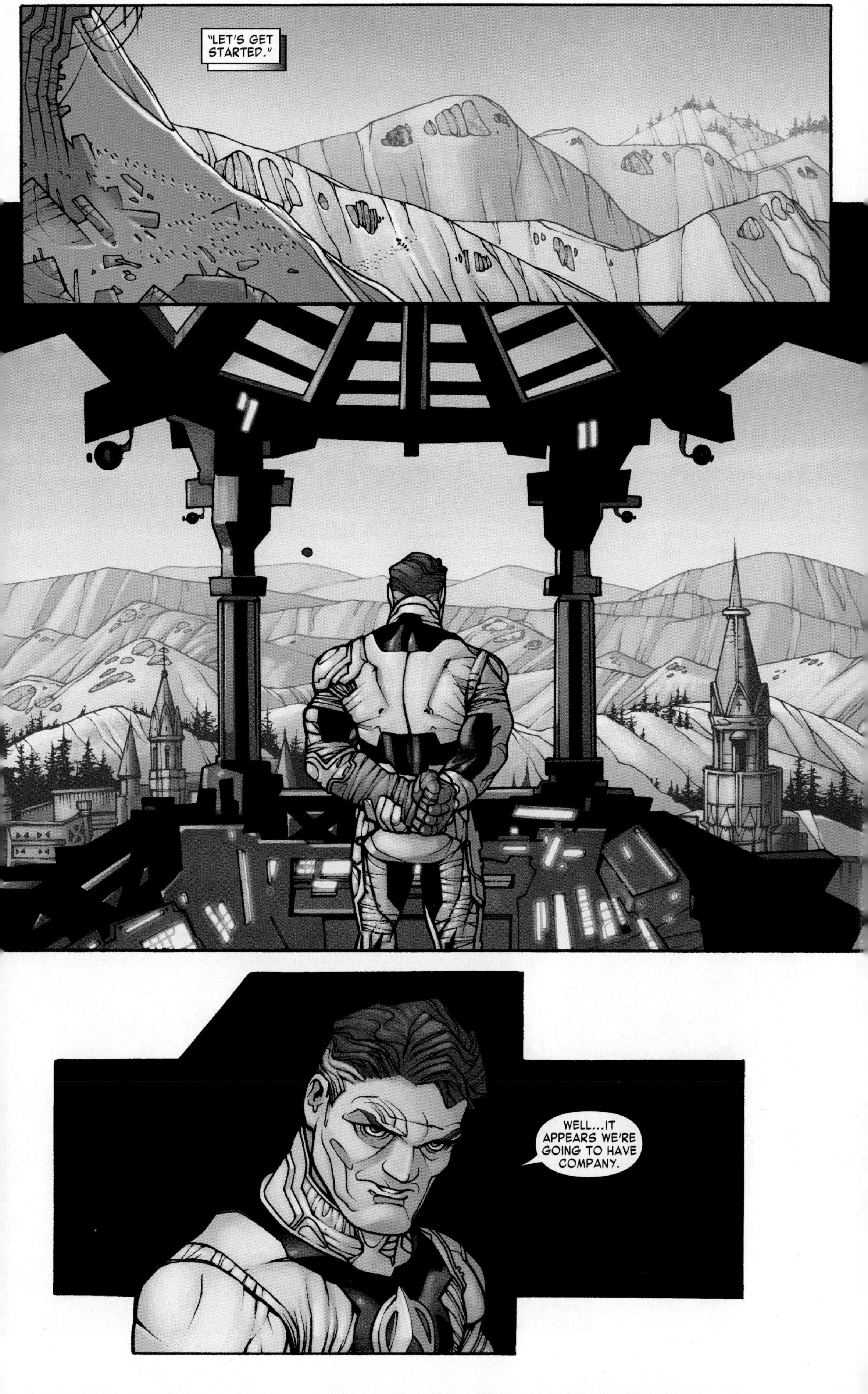
"LET'S GET STARTED."
WELL...IT APPEARS WE'RE GOING TO HAVE COMPANY.

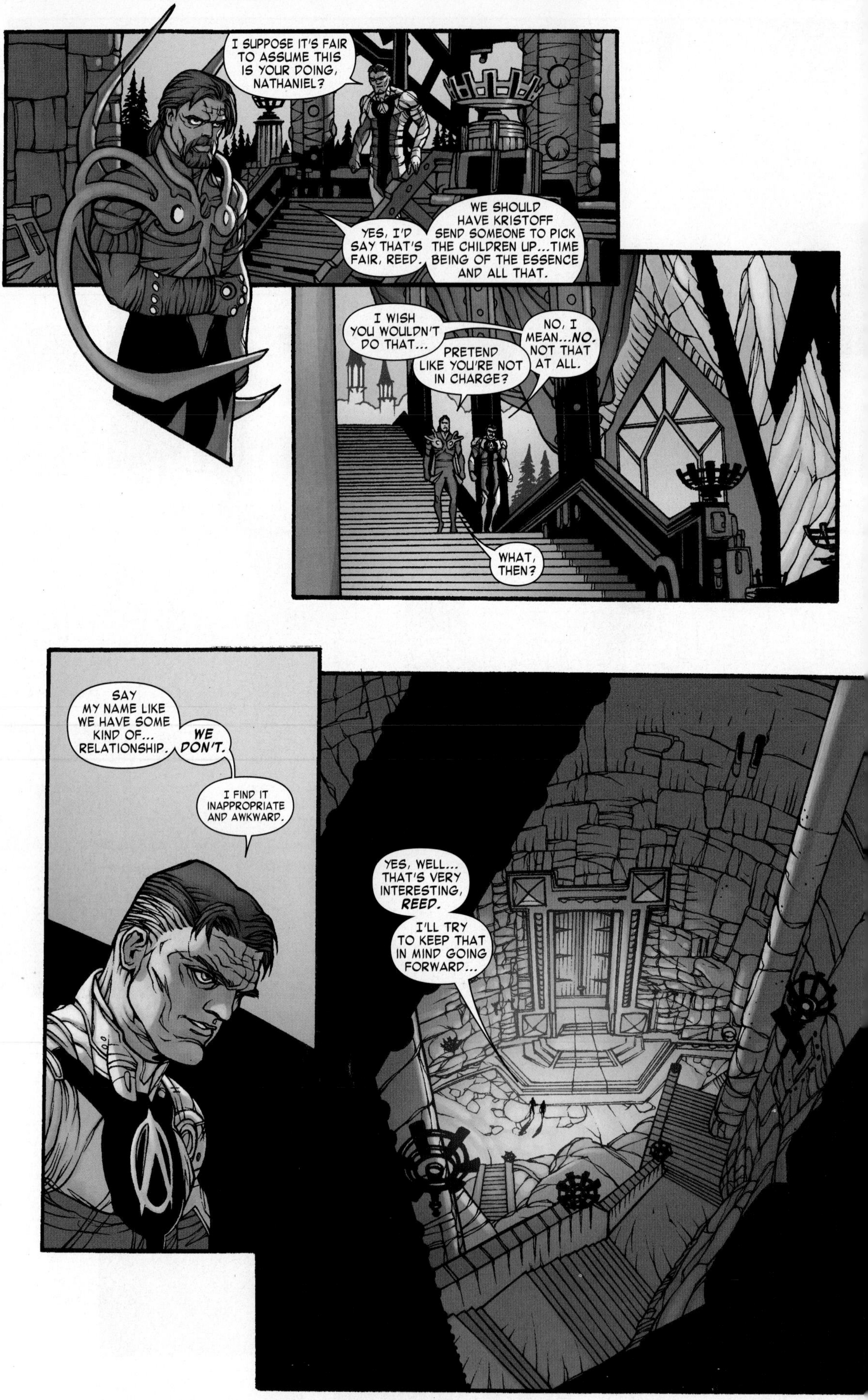
I SUPPOSE IT'S FAIR TO ASSUME THIS IS YOUR DOING, NATHANIEL?
YES, I'D SAY THAT'S FAIR, REED.
WE SHOULD HAVE KRISTOFF SEND SOMEONE TO PICK THE CHILDREN UP...TIME BEING OF THE ESSENCE AND ALL THAT.
I WISH YOU WOULDN'T DO THAT...
PRETEND LIKE YOU'RE NOT IN CHARGE?
NO, I MEAN...NO. NOT THAT AT ALL.
WHAT, THEN?
SAY MY NAME LIKE WE HAVE SOME KIND OF... RELATIONSHIP.
WE DON'T.
I FIND IT INAPPROPRIATE AND AWKWARD.
YES, WELL... THAT'S VERY INTERESTING, REED.
I'LL TRY TO KEEP THAT IN MIND GOING FORWARD...

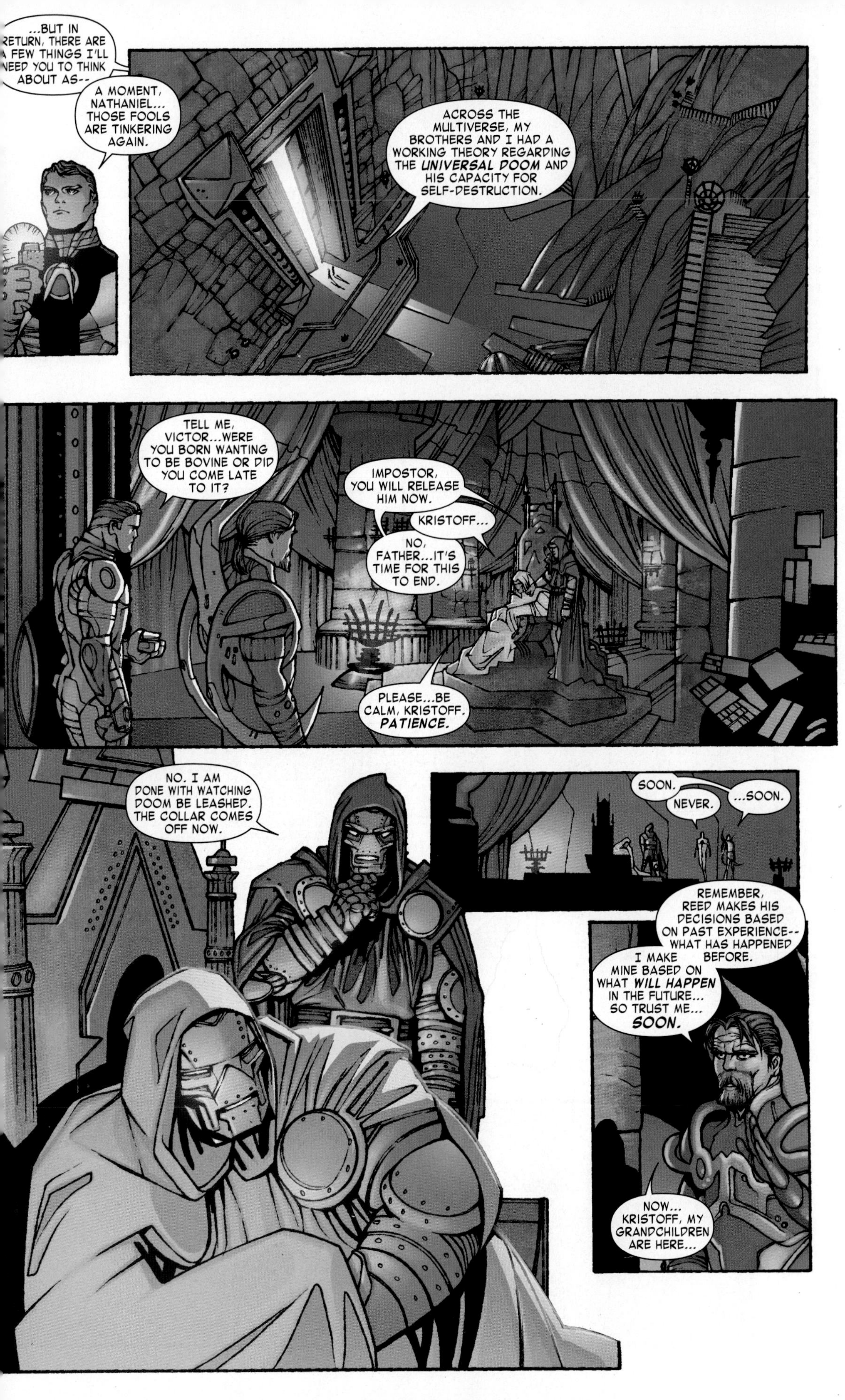
...BUT IN RETURN, THERE ARE A FEW THINGS I'LL NEED YOU TO THINK ABOUT AS--
A MOMENT, NATHANIEL... THOSE FOOLS ARE TINKERING AGAIN.
ACROSS THE MULTIVERSE, MY BROTHERS AND I HAD A WORKING THEORY REGARDING THE UNIVERSAL DOOM AND HIS CAPACITY FOR SELF-DESTRUCTION.
TELL ME, VICTOR...WERE YOU BORN WANTING TO BE BOVINE OR DID YOU COME LATE TO IT?
IMPOSTOR, YOU WILL RELEASE HIM NOW.
KRISTOFF...
NO, FATHER...IT'S TIME FOR THIS TO END.
PLEASE...BE CALM, KRISTOFF. PATIENCE.
NO. I AM DONE WITH WATCHING DOOM BE LEASHED. THE COLLAR COMES OFF NOW.
SOON.
NEVER.
...SOON.
REMEMBER, REED MAKES HIS DECISIONS BASED ON PAST EXPERIENCE-- WHAT HAS HAPPENED BEFORE.
I MAKE MINE BASED ON WHAT WILL HAPPEN IN THE FUTURE... SO TRUST ME... SOON.
NOW... KRISTOFF, MY GRANDCHILDREN ARE HERE...

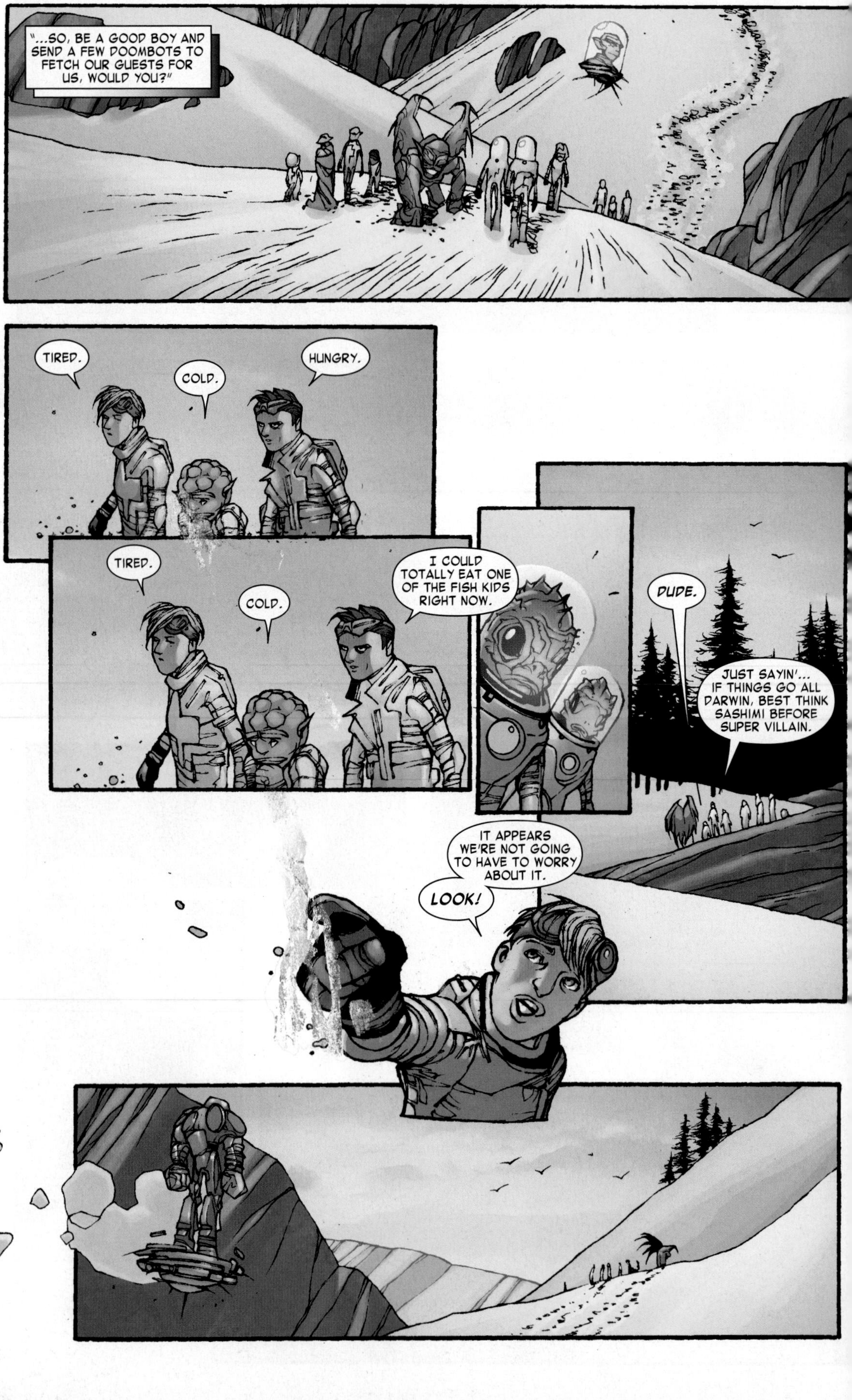
"...SO, BE A GOOD BOY AND SEND A FEW DOOMBOTS TO FETCH OUR GUESTS FOR US, WOULD YOU?"
TIRED.
COLD.
HUNGRY.
TIRED.
COLD.
I COULD TOTALLY EAT ONE OF THE FISH KIDS RIGHT NOW.
DUDE.
JUST SAYIN'... IF THINGS GO ALL DARWIN, BEST THINK SASHIMI BEFORE SUPER VILLAIN.
IT APPEARS WE'RE NOT GOING TO HAVE TO WORRY ABOUT IT.
LOOK!

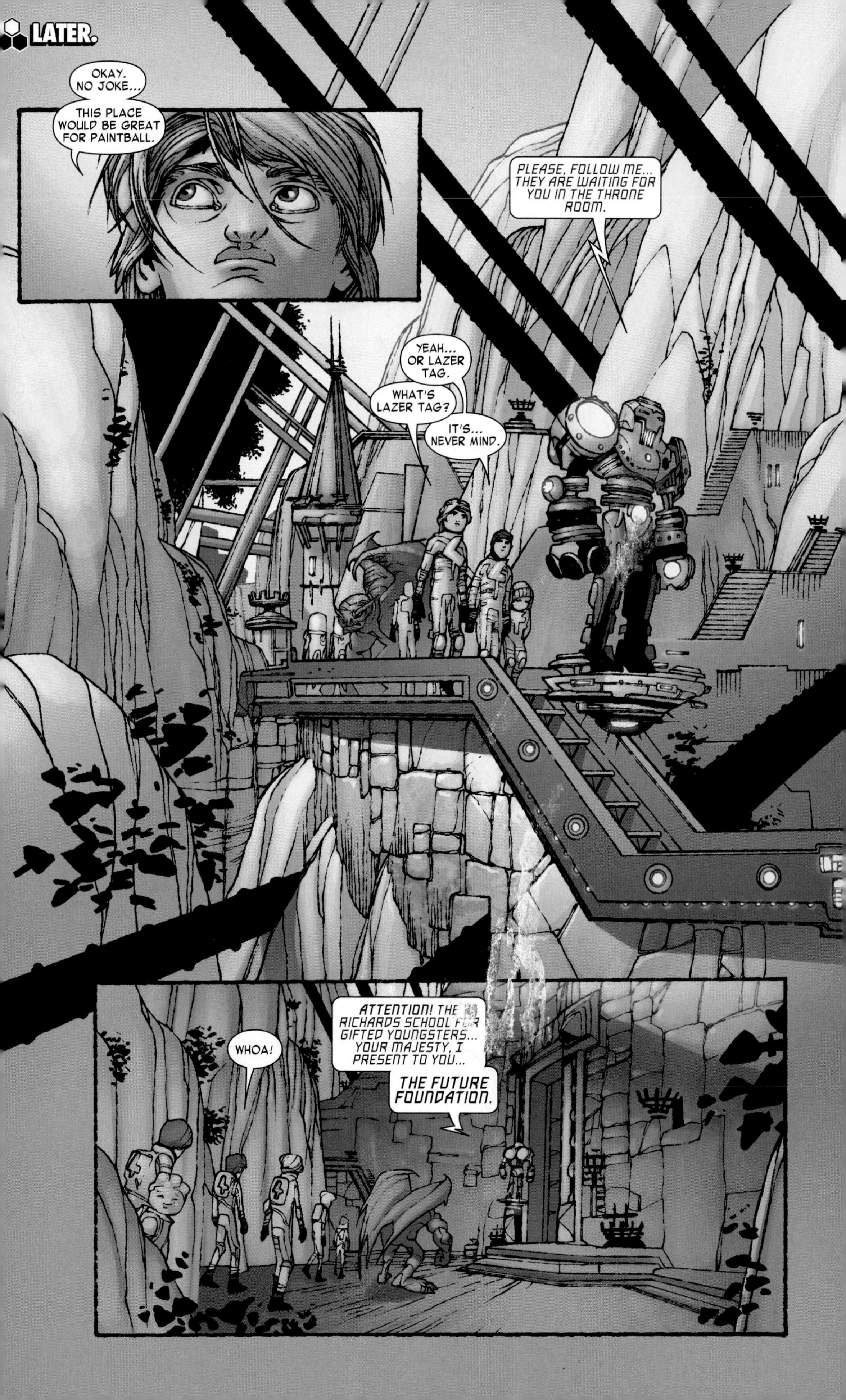
LATER.
OKAY. NO JOKE...
THIS PLACE WOULD BE GREAT FOR PAINTBALL.
PLEASE, FOLLOW ME... THEY ARE WAITING FOR YOU IN THE THRONE ROOM.
YEAH... OR LAZER TAG.
WHAT'S LAZER TAG?
IT'S... NEVER MIND.
WHOA!
ATTENTION! THE RICHARDS SCHOOL FOR GIFTED YOUNGSTERS... YOUR MAJESTY, I PRESENT TO YOU...
THE FUTURE FOUNDATION.

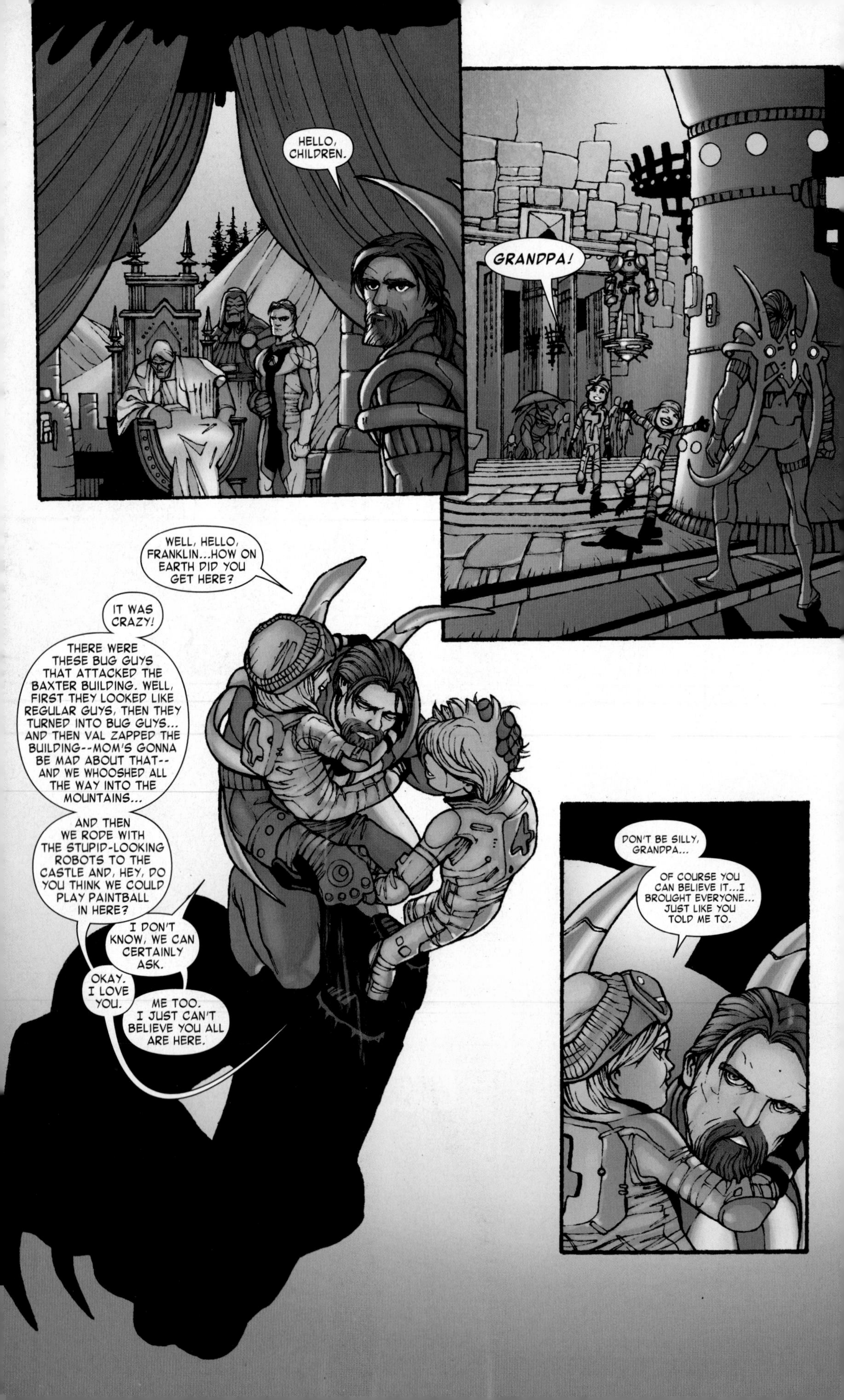
HELLO, CHILDREN.
GRANDPA!
WELL, HELLO, FRANKLIN...HOW ON EARTH DID YOU GET HERE?
IT WAS CRAZY!
THERE WERE THESE BUG GUYS THAT ATTACKED THE BAXTER BUILDING. WELL, FIRST THEY LOOKED LIKE REGULAR GUYS, THEN THEY TURNED INTO BUG GUYS... AND THEN VAL ZAPPED THE BUILDING--MOM'S GONNA BE MAD ABOUT THAT-- AND WE WHOOSHED ALL THE WAY INTO THE MOUNTAINS...
AND THEN WE RODE WITH THE STUPID-LOOKING ROBOTS TO THE CASTLE AND, HEY, DO YOU THINK WE COULD PLAY PAINTBALL IN HERE?
I DON'T KNOW, WE CAN CERTAINLY ASK.
OKAY. I LOVE YOU.
ME TOO. I JUST CAN'T BELIEVE YOU ALL ARE HERE.
DON'T BE SILLY, GRANDPA...
OF COURSE YOU CAN BELIEVE IT...I BROUGHT EVERYONE... JUST LIKE YOU TOLD ME TO.

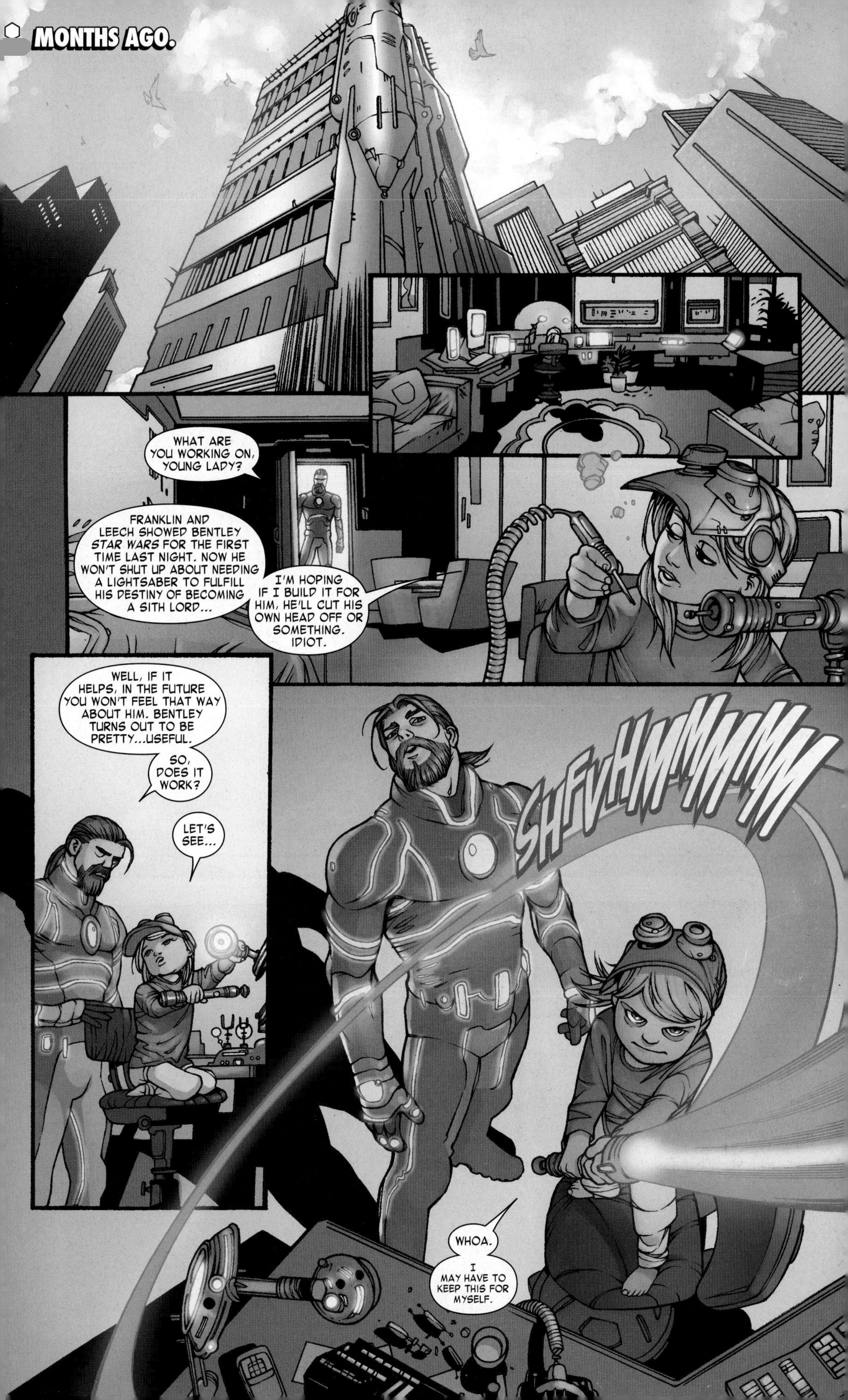
MONTHS AGO.
WHAT ARE YOU WORKING ON, YOUNG LADY?
FRANKLIN AND LEECH SHOWED BENTLEY *STAR WARS* FOR THE FIRST TIME LAST NIGHT. NOW HE WON'T SHUT UP ABOUT NEEDING A LIGHTSABER TO FULFILL HIS DESTINY OF BECOMING A SITH LORD...
I'M HOPING IF I BUILD IT FOR HIM, HE'LL CUT HIS OWN HEAD OFF OR SOMETHING. IDIOT.
WELL, IF IT HELPS, IN THE FUTURE YOU WON'T FEEL THAT WAY ABOUT HIM. BENTLEY TURNS OUT TO BE PRETTY...USEFUL.
SO, DOES IT WORK?
LET'S SEE...
SHFVHMMMMM
WHOA.
I MAY HAVE TO KEEP THIS FOR MYSELF.

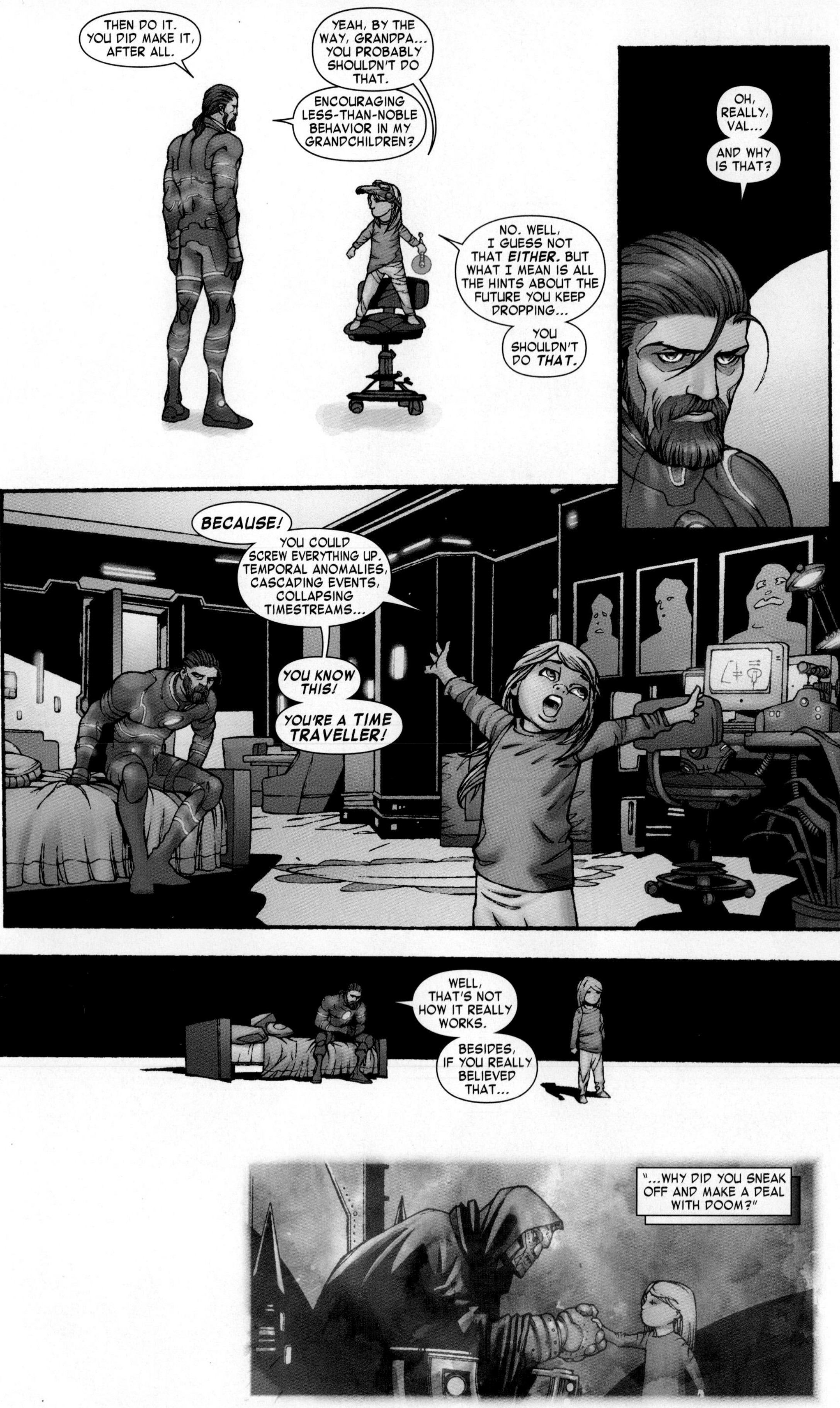
THEN DO IT. YOU DID MAKE IT, AFTER ALL.
YEAH, BY THE WAY, GRANDPA... YOU PROBABLY SHOULDN'T DO THAT.
ENCOURAGING LESS-THAN-NOBLE BEHAVIOR IN MY GRANDCHILDREN?
NO. WELL, I GUESS NOT THAT EITHER. BUT WHAT I MEAN IS ALL THE HINTS ABOUT THE FUTURE YOU KEEP DROPPING...
YOU SHOULDN'T DO THAT.
OH, REALLY, VAL...
AND WHY IS THAT?
BECAUSE!
YOU COULD SCREW EVERYTHING UP. TEMPORAL ANOMALIES, CASCADING EVENTS, COLLAPSING TIMESTREAMS...
YOU KNOW THIS!
YOU'RE A TIME TRAVELLER!
WELL, THAT'S NOT HOW IT REALLY WORKS.
BESIDES, IF YOU REALLY BELIEVED THAT...
"...WHY DID YOU SNEAK OFF AND MAKE A DEAL WITH DOOM?"

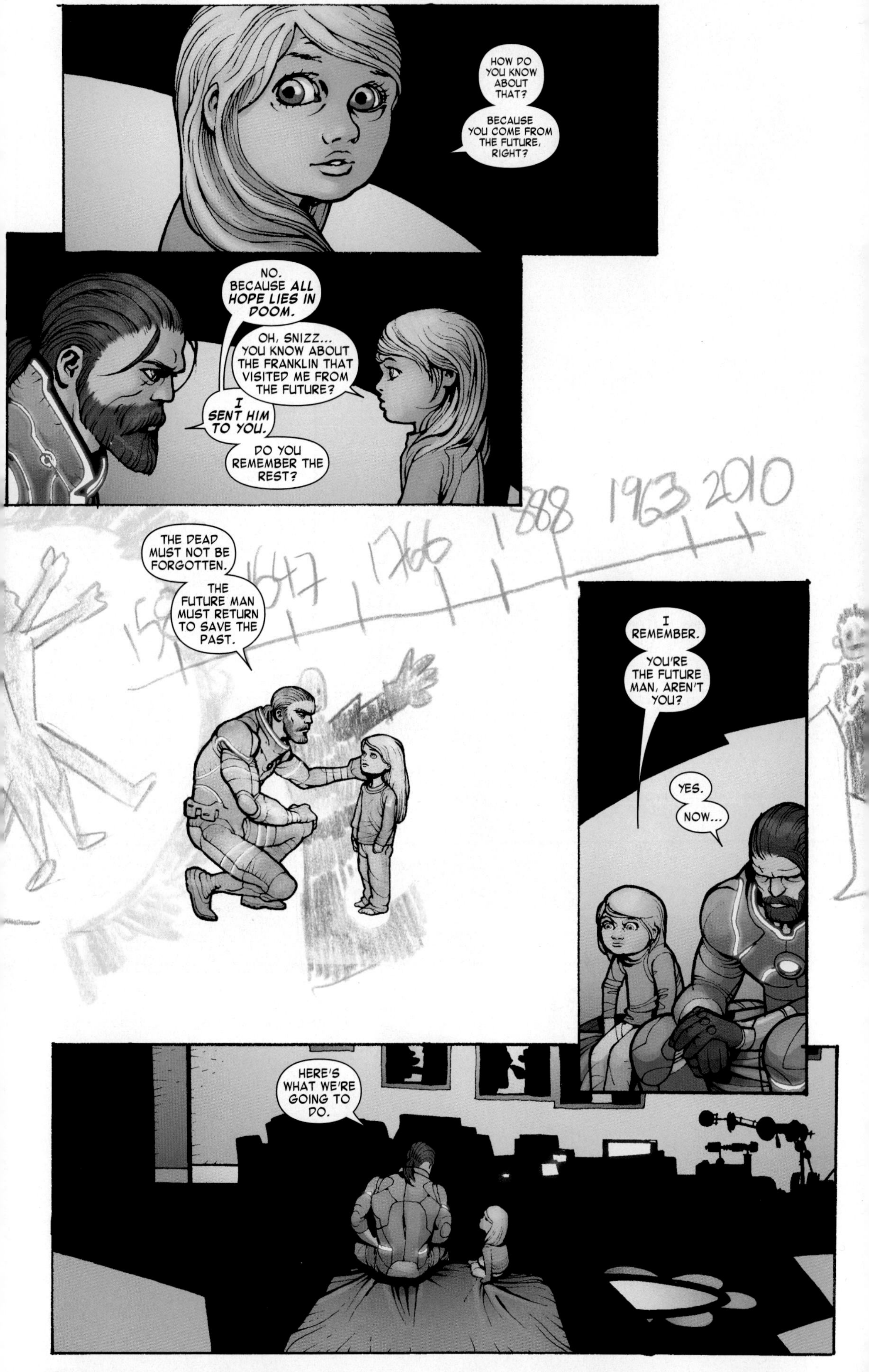
HOW DO YOU KNOW ABOUT THAT?
BECAUSE YOU COME FROM THE FUTURE, RIGHT?
NO. BECAUSE *ALL HOPE LIES IN DOOM.*
OH, SNIZZ... YOU KNOW ABOUT THE FRANKLIN THAT VISITED ME FROM THE FUTURE?
I SENT HIM TO YOU.
DO YOU REMEMBER THE REST?
THE DEAD MUST NOT BE FORGOTTEN.
THE FUTURE MAN MUST RETURN TO SAVE THE PAST.
1647
1766
1888
1963
2010
I REMEMBER.
YOU'RE THE FUTURE MAN, AREN'T YOU?
YES.
NOW...
HERE'S WHAT WE'RE GOING TO DO.

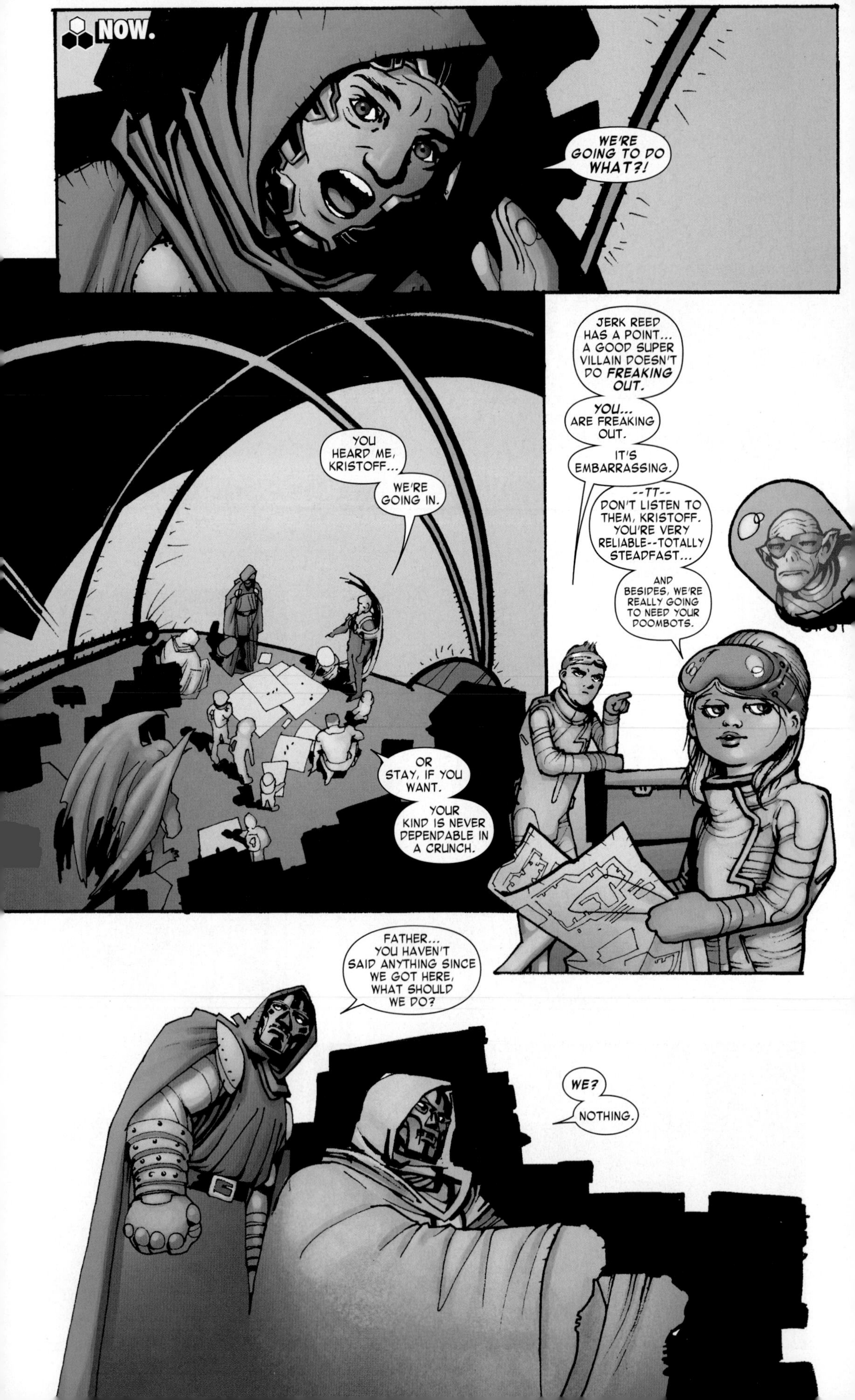
NOW.
WE'RE GOING TO DO WHAT?!
YOU HEARD ME, KRISTOFF...
WE'RE GOING IN.
JERK REED HAS A POINT... A GOOD SUPER VILLAIN DOESN'T DO FREAKING OUT.
YOU... ARE FREAKING OUT.
IT'S EMBARRASSING.
--TT-- DON'T LISTEN TO THEM, KRISTOFF. YOU'RE VERY RELIABLE--TOTALLY STEADFAST...
AND BESIDES, WE'RE REALLY GOING TO NEED YOUR DOOMBOTS.
OR STAY, IF YOU WANT.
YOUR KIND IS NEVER DEPENDABLE IN A CRUNCH.
FATHER... YOU HAVEN'T SAID ANYTHING SINCE WE GOT HERE, WHAT SHOULD WE DO?
WE?
NOTHING.

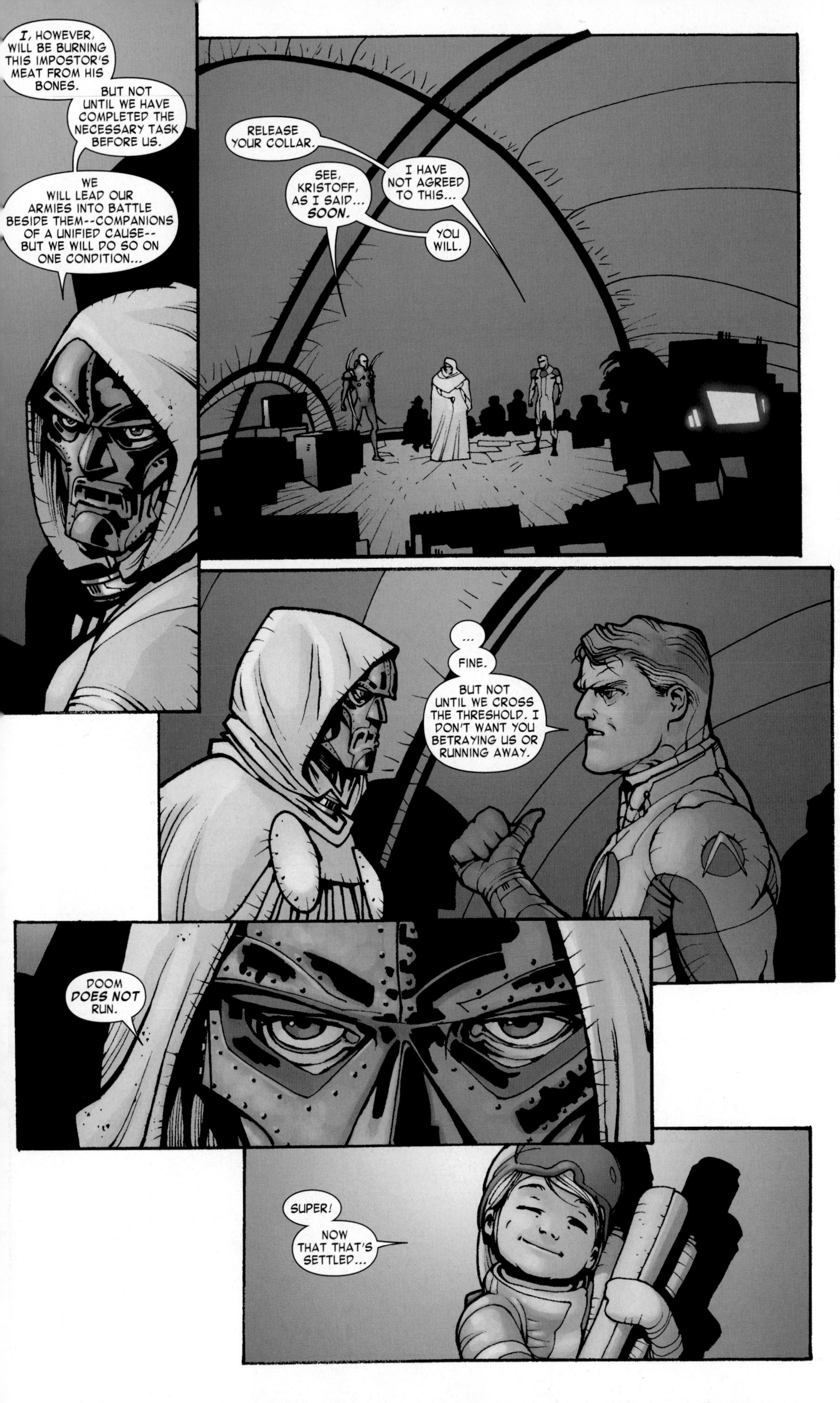
I, HOWEVER, WILL BE BURNING THIS IMPOSTOR'S MEAT FROM HIS BONES.
BUT NOT UNTIL WE HAVE COMPLETED THE NECESSARY TASK BEFORE US.
WE WILL LEAD OUR ARMIES INTO BATTLE BESIDE THEM--COMPANIONS OF A UNIFIED CAUSE--BUT WE WILL DO SO ON ONE CONDITION...
RELEASE YOUR COLLAR.
I HAVE NOT AGREED TO THIS...
SEE, KRISTOFF, AS I SAID... SOON.
YOU WILL.
...
FINE.
BUT NOT UNTIL WE CROSS THE THRESHOLD. I DON'T WANT YOU BETRAYING US OR RUNNING AWAY.
DOOM DOES NOT RUN.
SUPER!
NOW THAT THAT'S SETTLED...

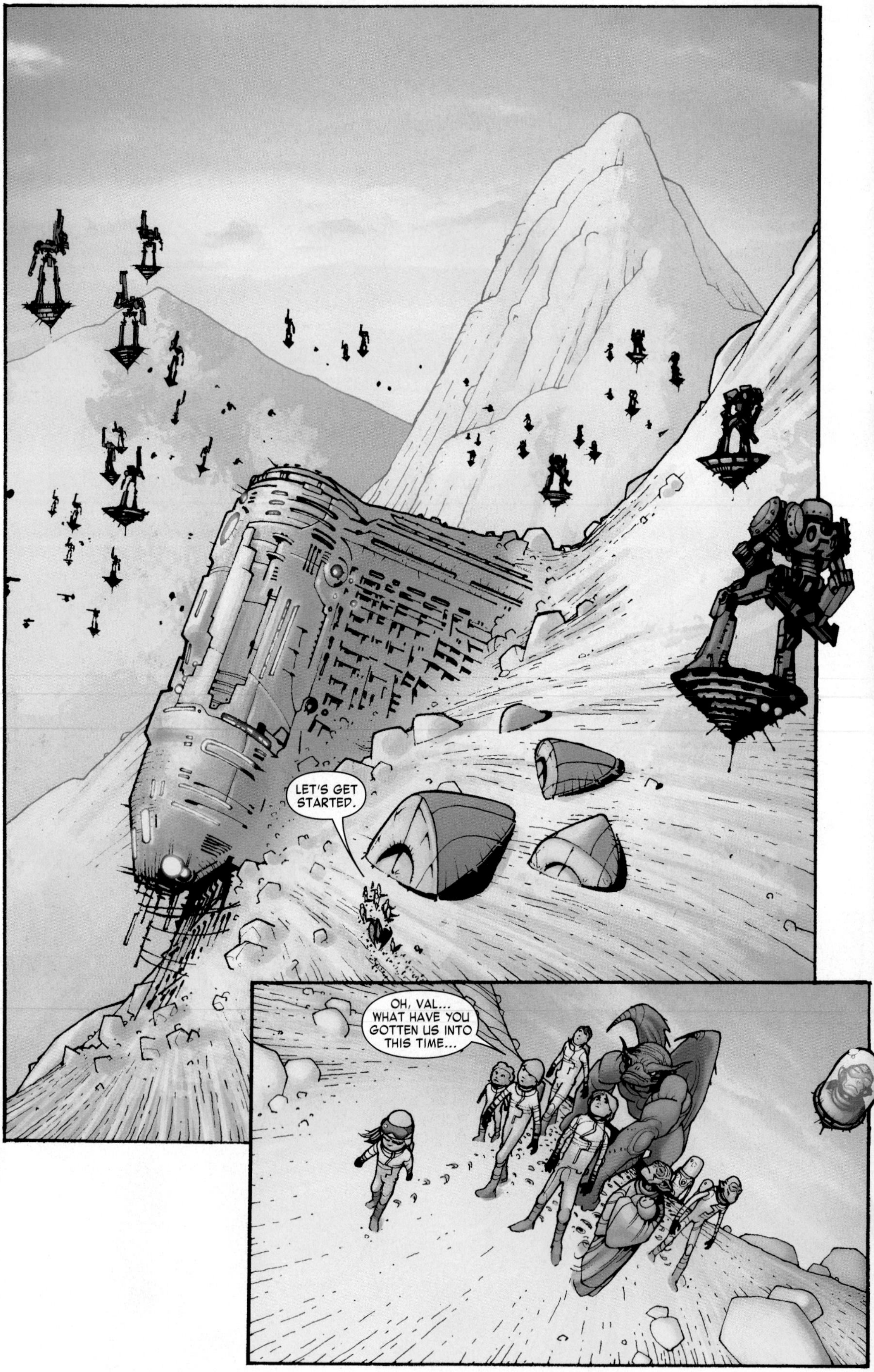
LET'S GET STARTED.
OH, VAL... WHAT HAVE YOU GOTTEN US INTO THIS TIME...

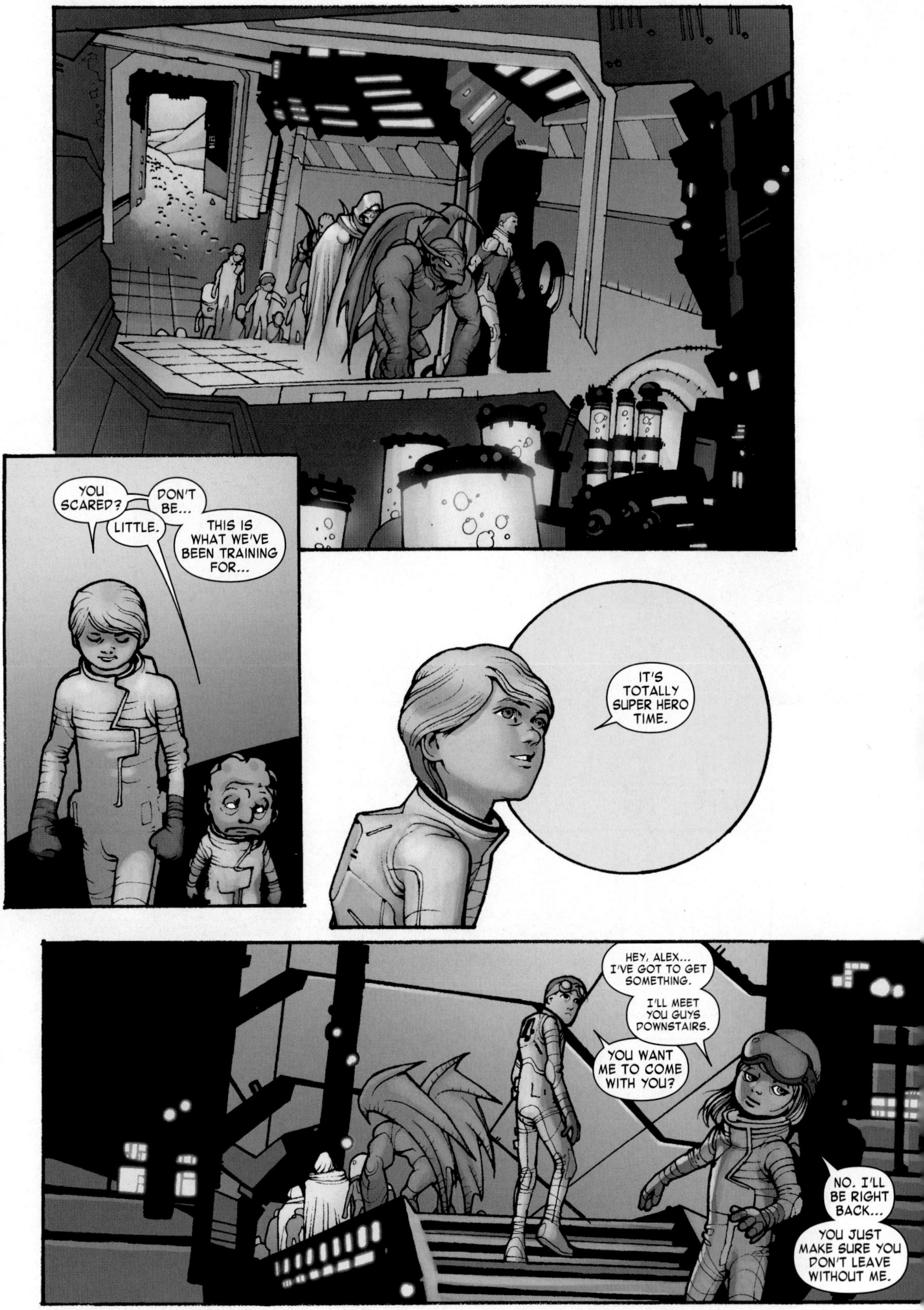
YOU SCARED?
LITTLE.
DON'T BE...
THIS IS WHAT WE'VE BEEN TRAINING FOR...
IT'S TOTALLY SUPER HERO TIME.
HEY, ALEX... I'VE GOT TO GET SOMETHING.
I'LL MEET YOU GUYS DOWNSTAIRS.
YOU WANT ME TO COME WITH YOU?
NO. I'LL BE RIGHT BACK...
YOU JUST MAKE SURE YOU DON'T LEAVE WITHOUT ME.

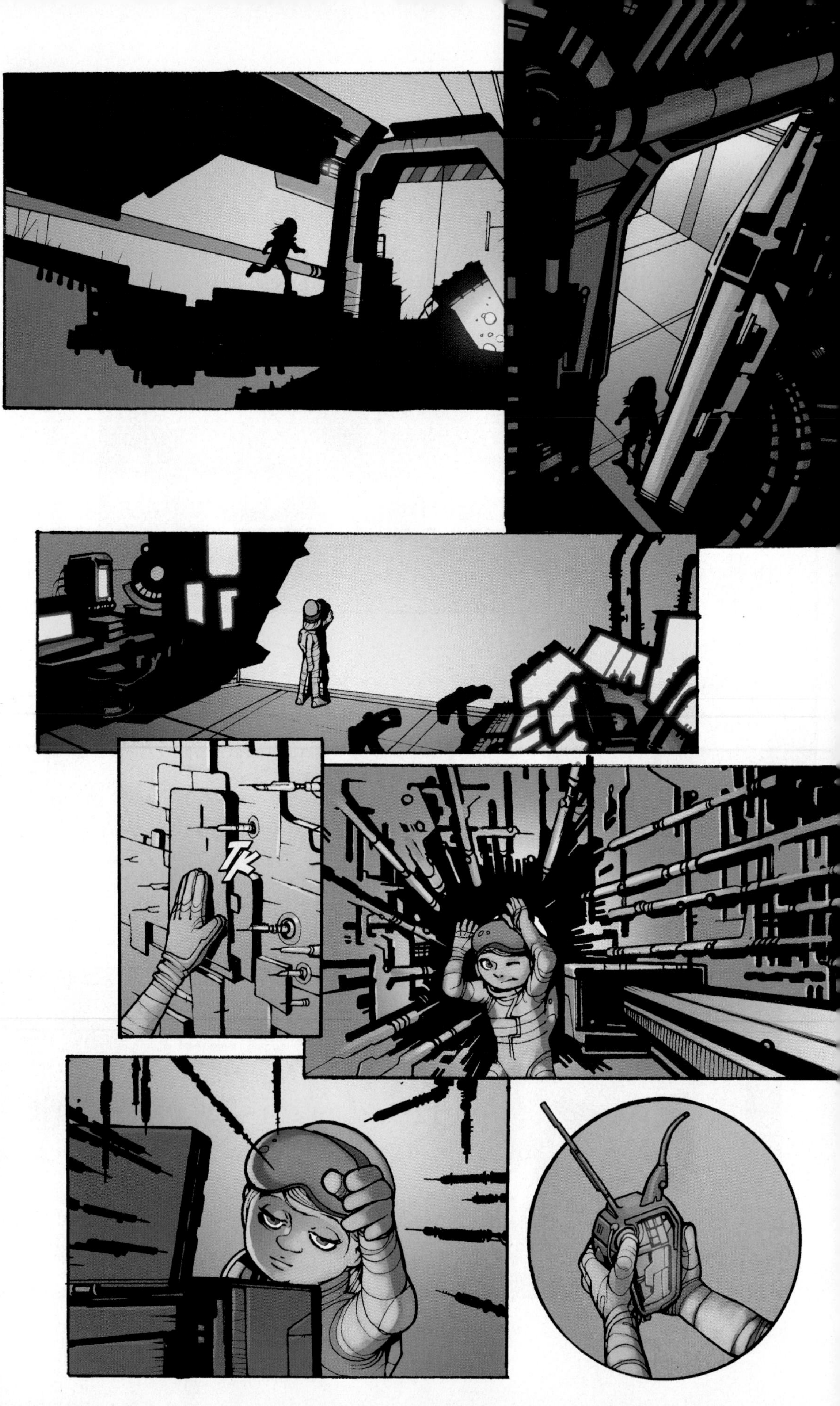
TK

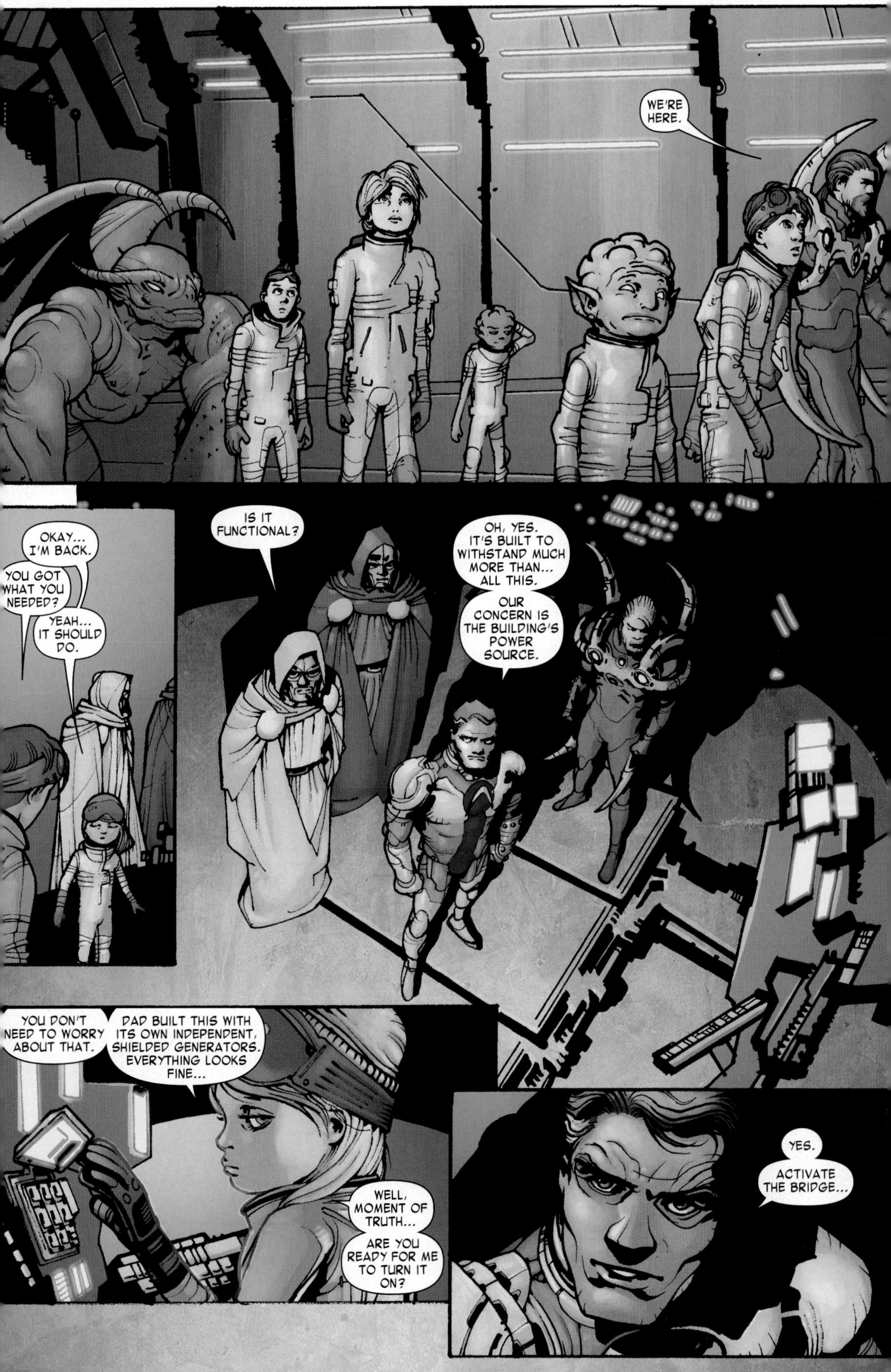
WE'RE HERE.
OKAY... I'M BACK.
YOU GOT WHAT YOU NEEDED?
YEAH... IT SHOULD DO.
IS IT FUNCTIONAL?
OH, YES. IT'S BUILT TO WITHSTAND MUCH MORE THAN... ALL THIS.
OUR CONCERN IS THE BUILDING'S POWER SOURCE.
YOU DON'T NEED TO WORRY ABOUT THAT.
DAD BUILT THIS WITH ITS OWN INDEPENDENT, SHIELDED GENERATORS. EVERYTHING LOOKS FINE...
WELL, MOMENT OF TRUTH...
ARE YOU READY FOR ME TO TURN IT ON?
YES.
ACTIVATE THE BRIDGE...

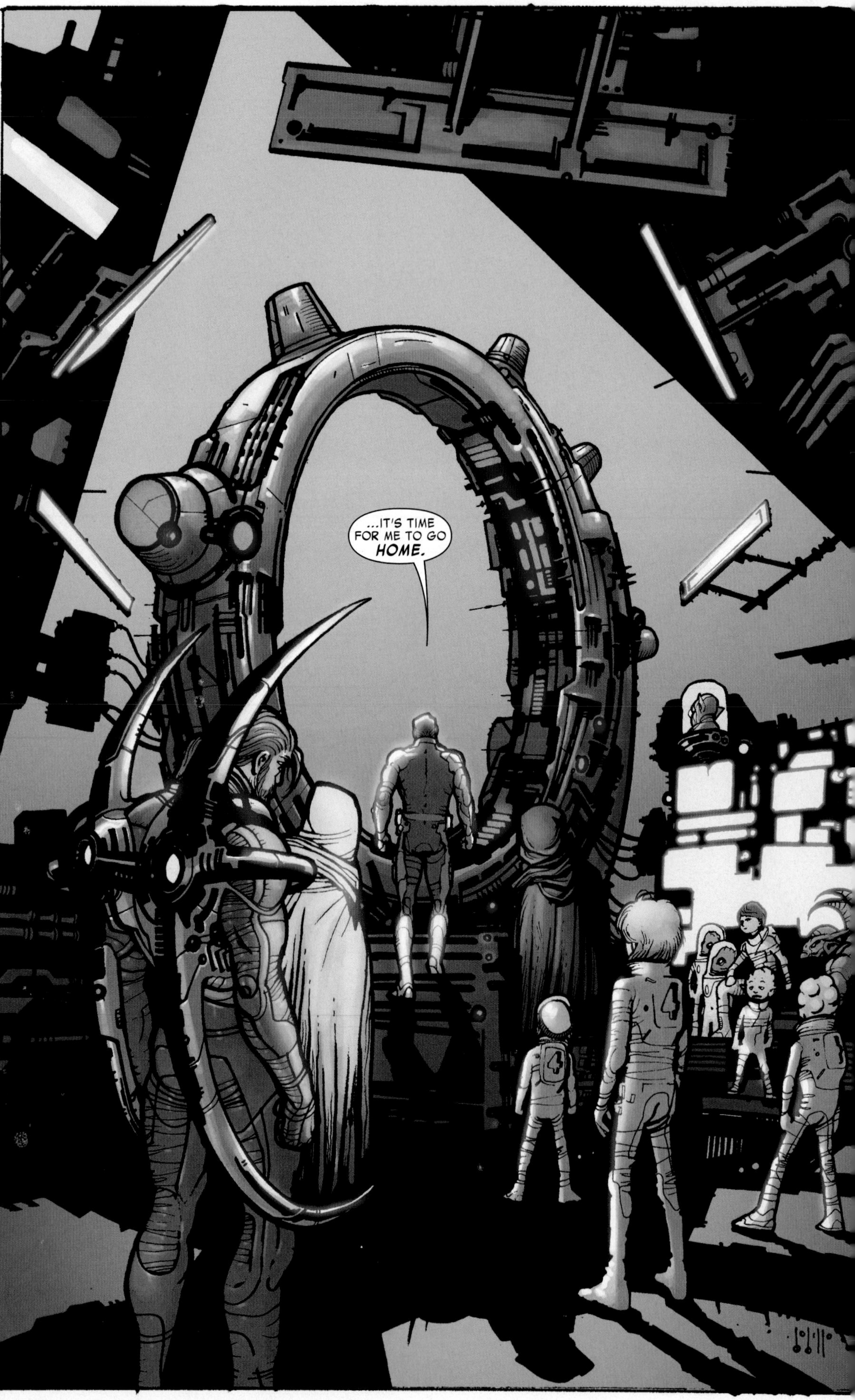
...IT'S TIME FOR ME TO GO HOME.

HOPE

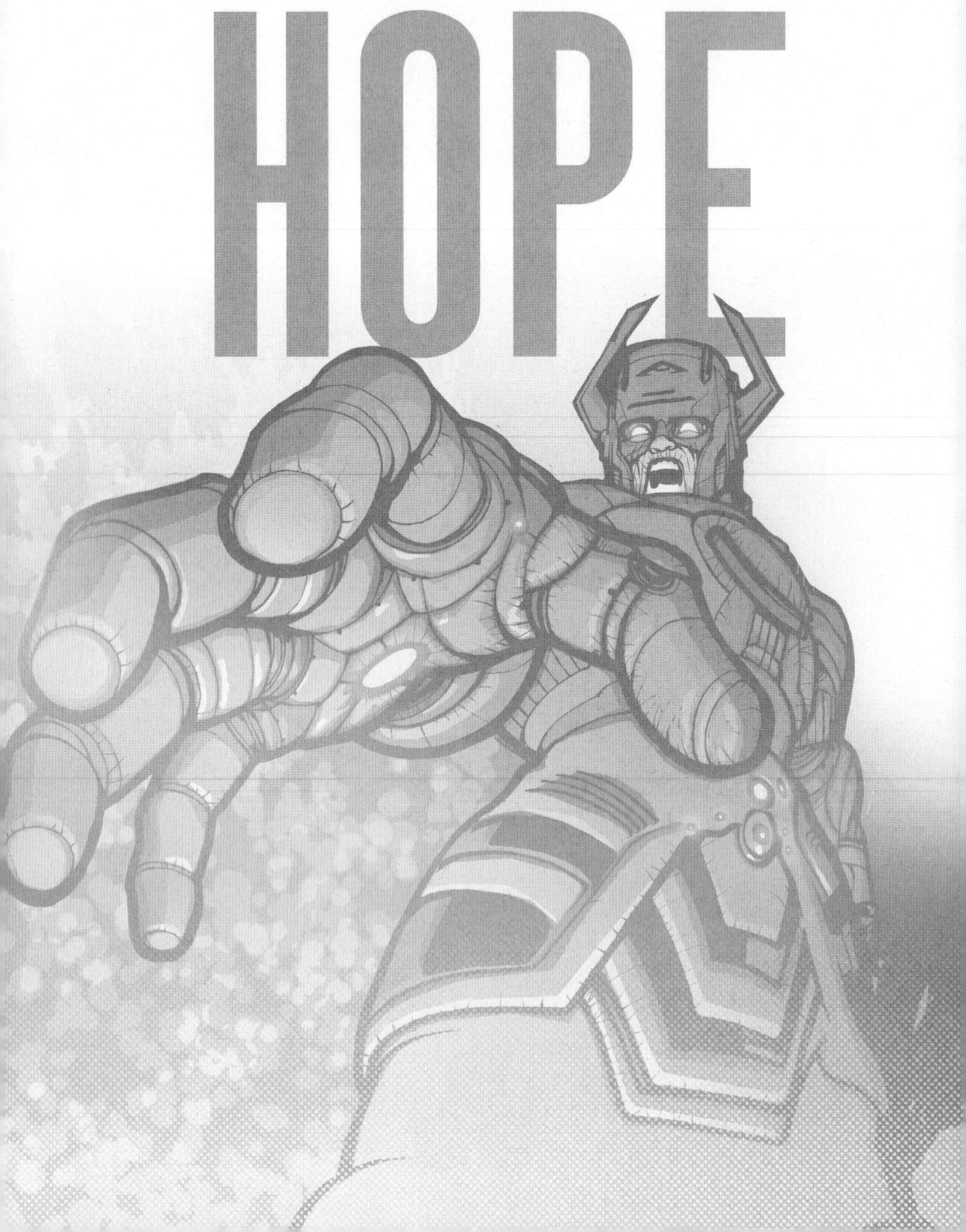

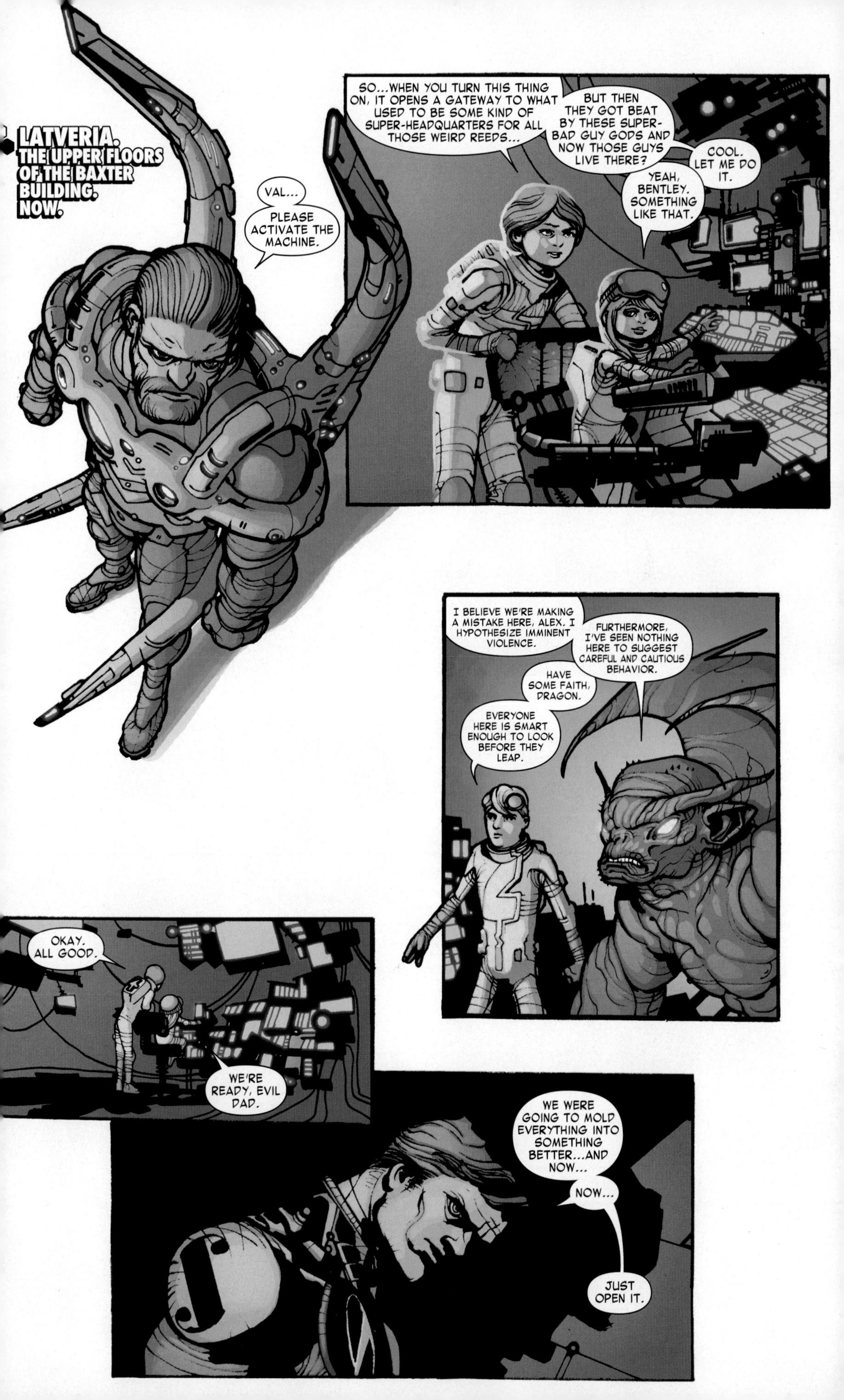
LATVERIA. THE UPPER FLOORS OF THE BAXTER BUILDING. NOW.
VAL...
PLEASE ACTIVATE THE MACHINE.
SO...WHEN YOU TURN THIS THING ON, IT OPENS A GATEWAY TO WHAT USED TO BE SOME KIND OF SUPER-HEADQUARTERS FOR ALL THOSE WEIRD REEDS...
BUT THEN THEY GOT BEAT BY THESE SUPER-BAD GUY GODS AND NOW THOSE GUYS LIVE THERE?
YEAH, BENTLEY. SOMETHING LIKE THAT.
COOL. LET ME DO IT.
I BELIEVE WE'RE MAKING A MISTAKE HERE, ALEX. I HYPOTHESIZE IMMINENT VIOLENCE.
FURTHERMORE, I'VE SEEN NOTHING HERE TO SUGGEST CAREFUL AND CAUTIOUS BEHAVIOR.
HAVE SOME FAITH, DRAGON.
EVERYONE HERE IS SMART ENOUGH TO LOOK BEFORE THEY LEAP.
OKAY. ALL GOOD.
WE'RE READY, EVIL DAD.
WE WERE GOING TO MOLD EVERYTHING INTO SOMETHING BETTER...AND NOW...
NOW...
JUST OPEN IT.

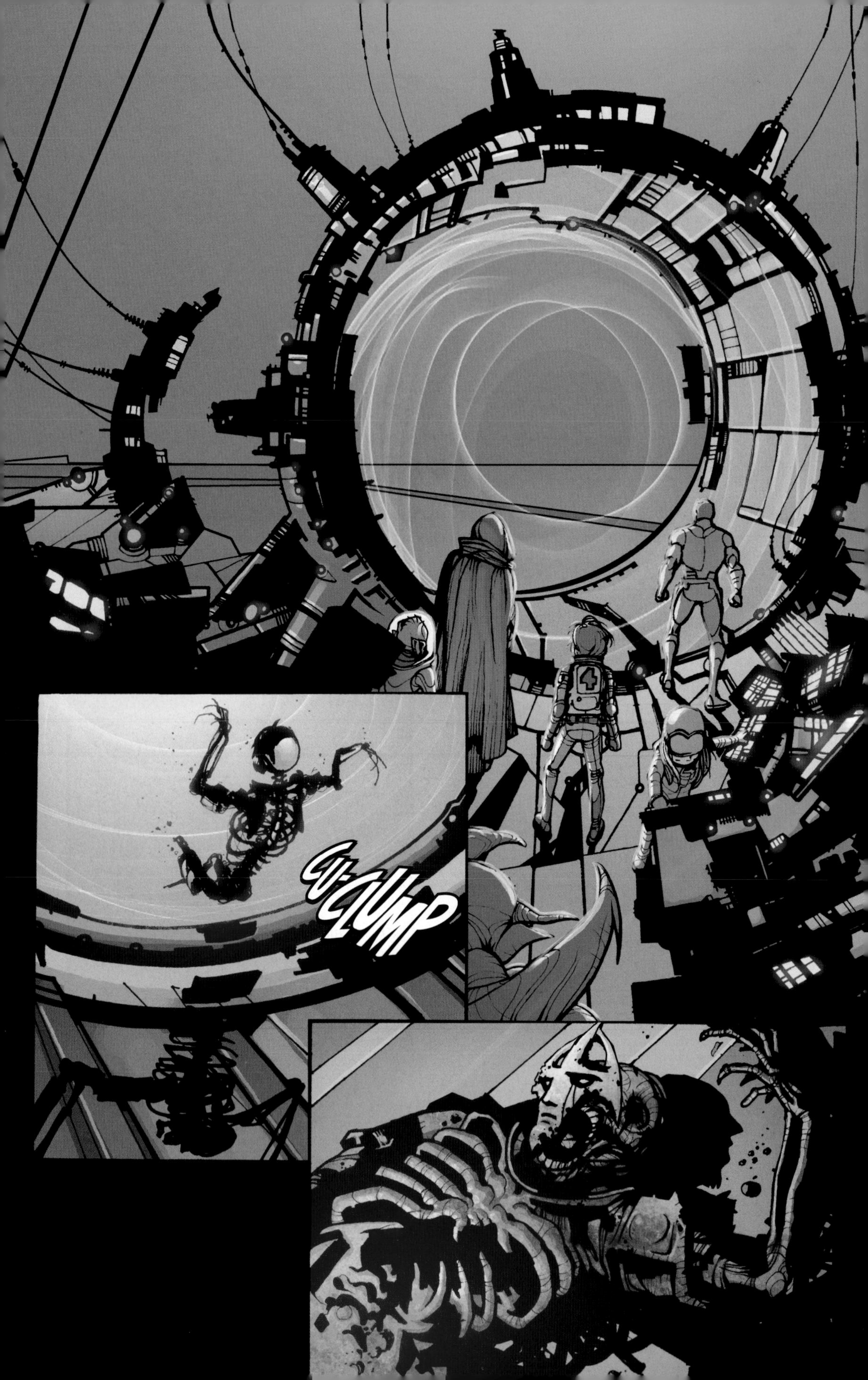
CU-CLUMP

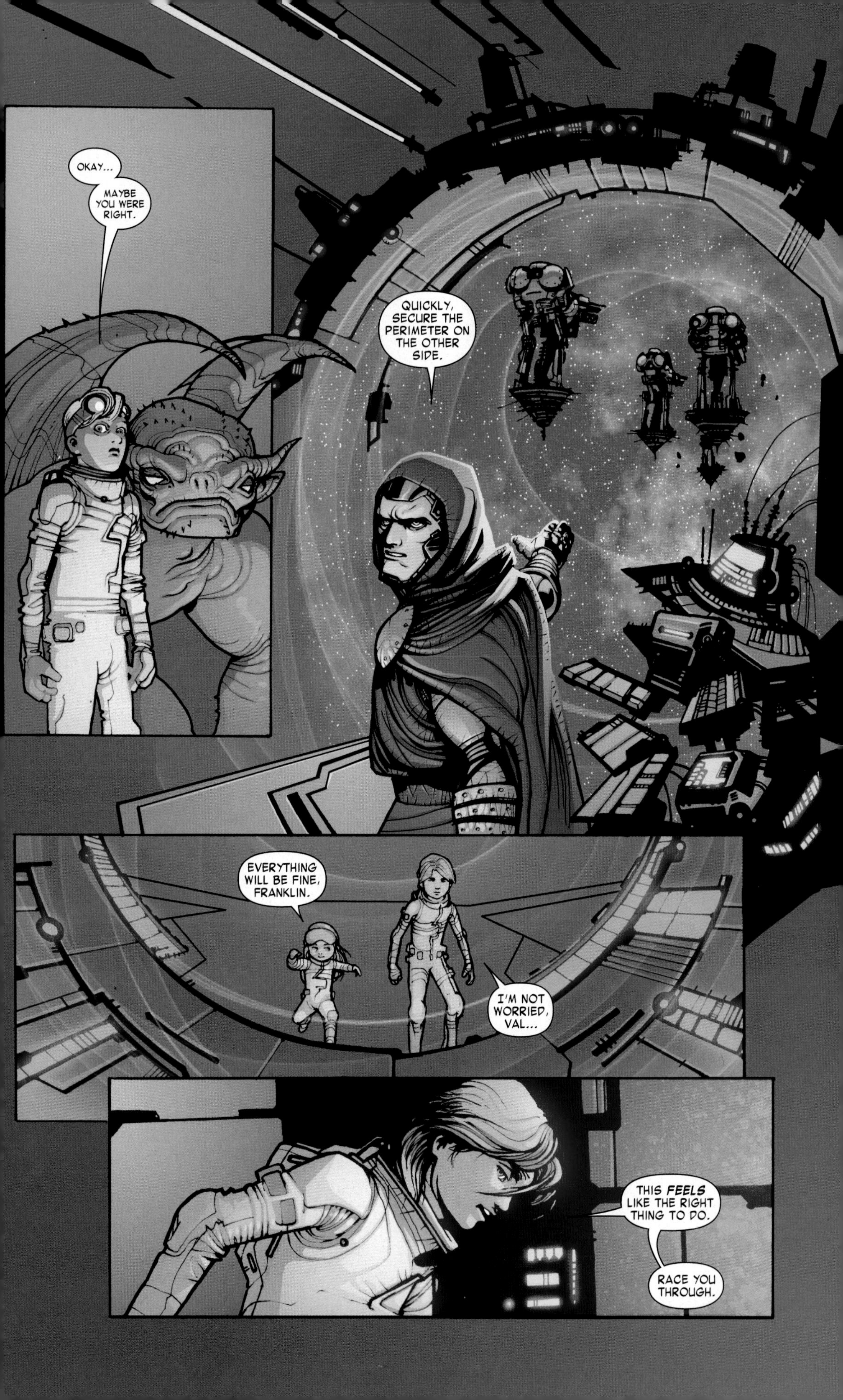
OKAY...
MAYBE YOU WERE RIGHT.
QUICKLY, SECURE THE PERIMETER ON THE OTHER SIDE.
EVERYTHING WILL BE FINE, FRANKLIN.
I'M NOT WORRIED, VAL...
THIS *FEELS* LIKE THE RIGHT THING TO DO.
RACE YOU THROUGH.

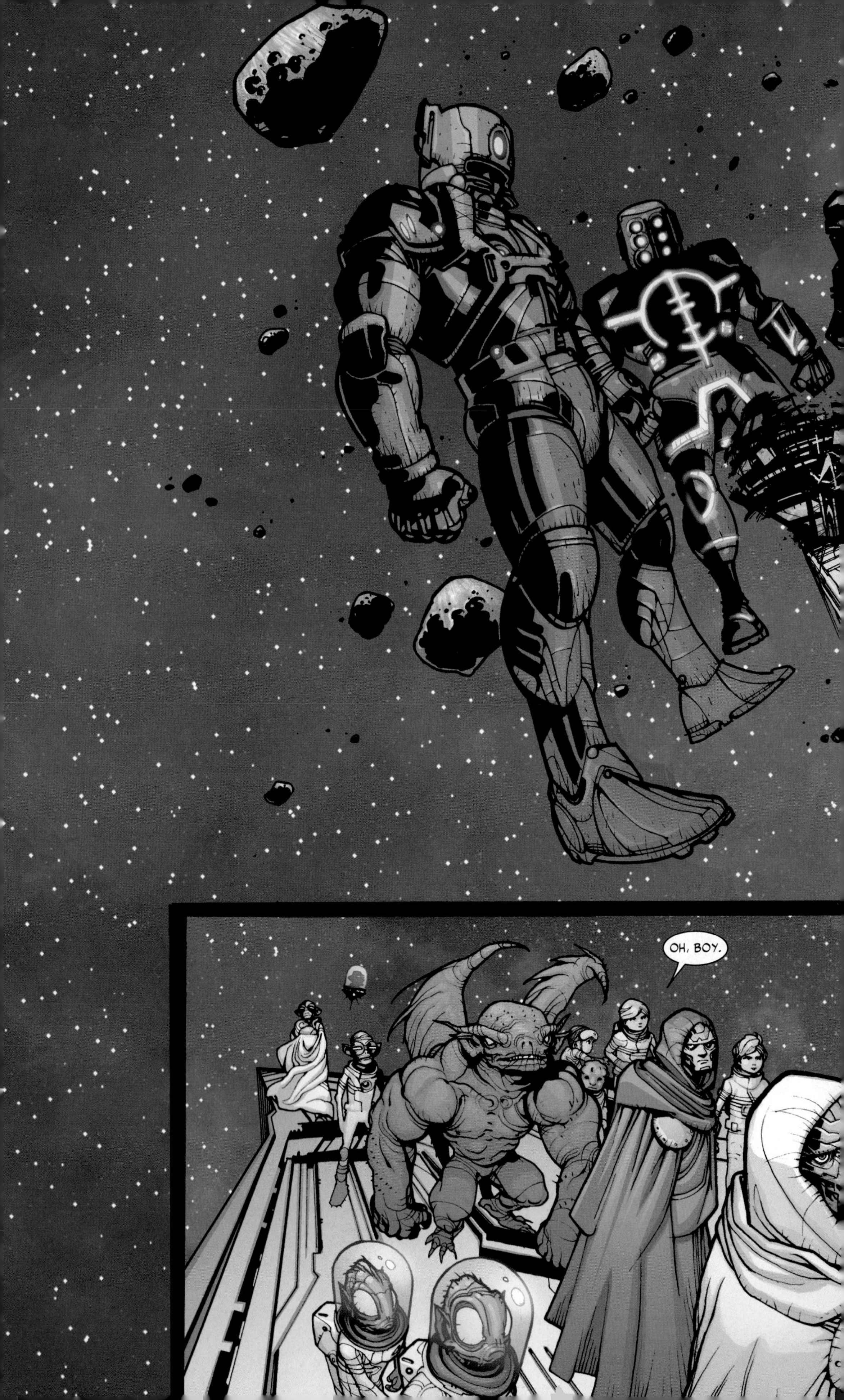
OH, BOY.

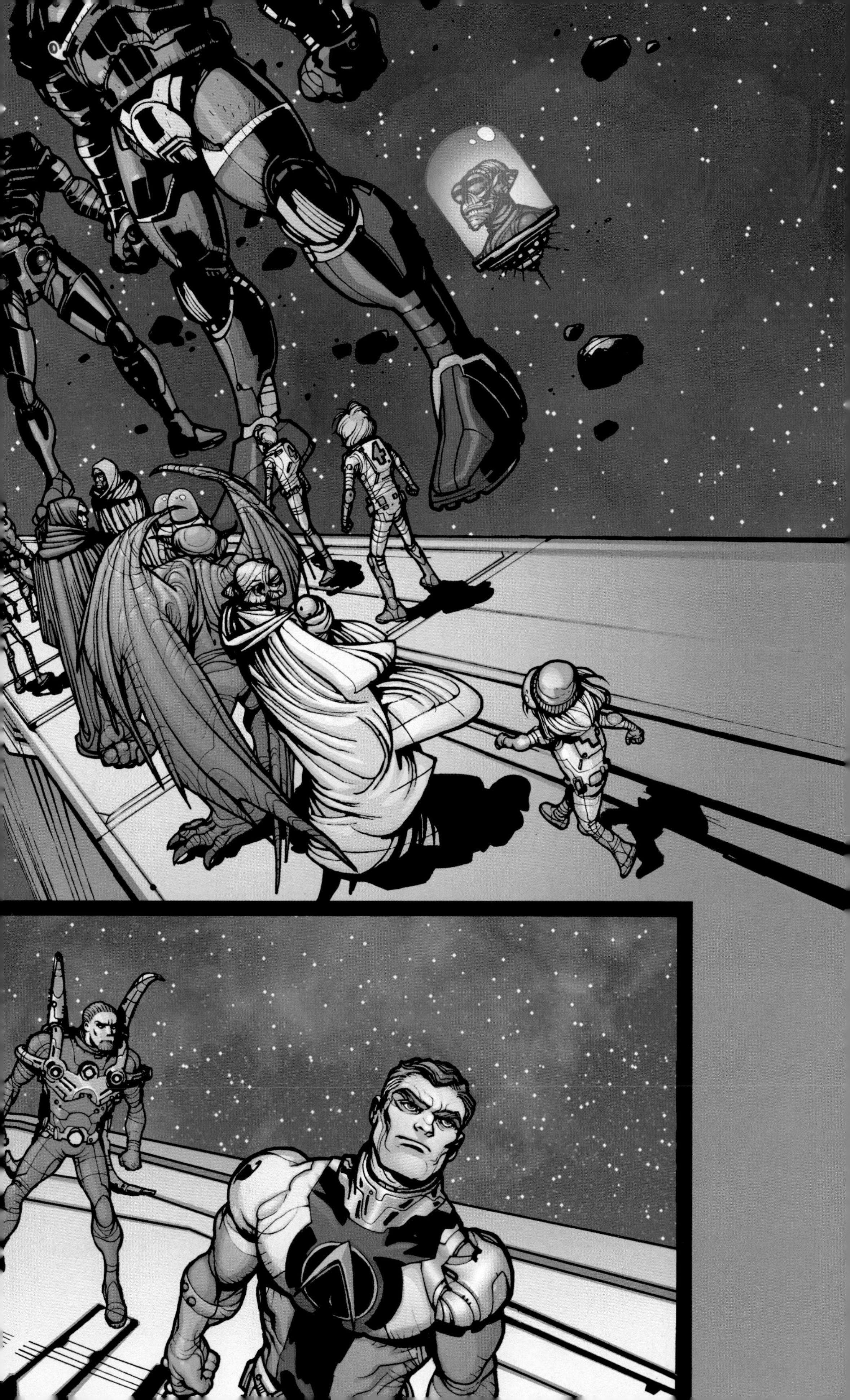

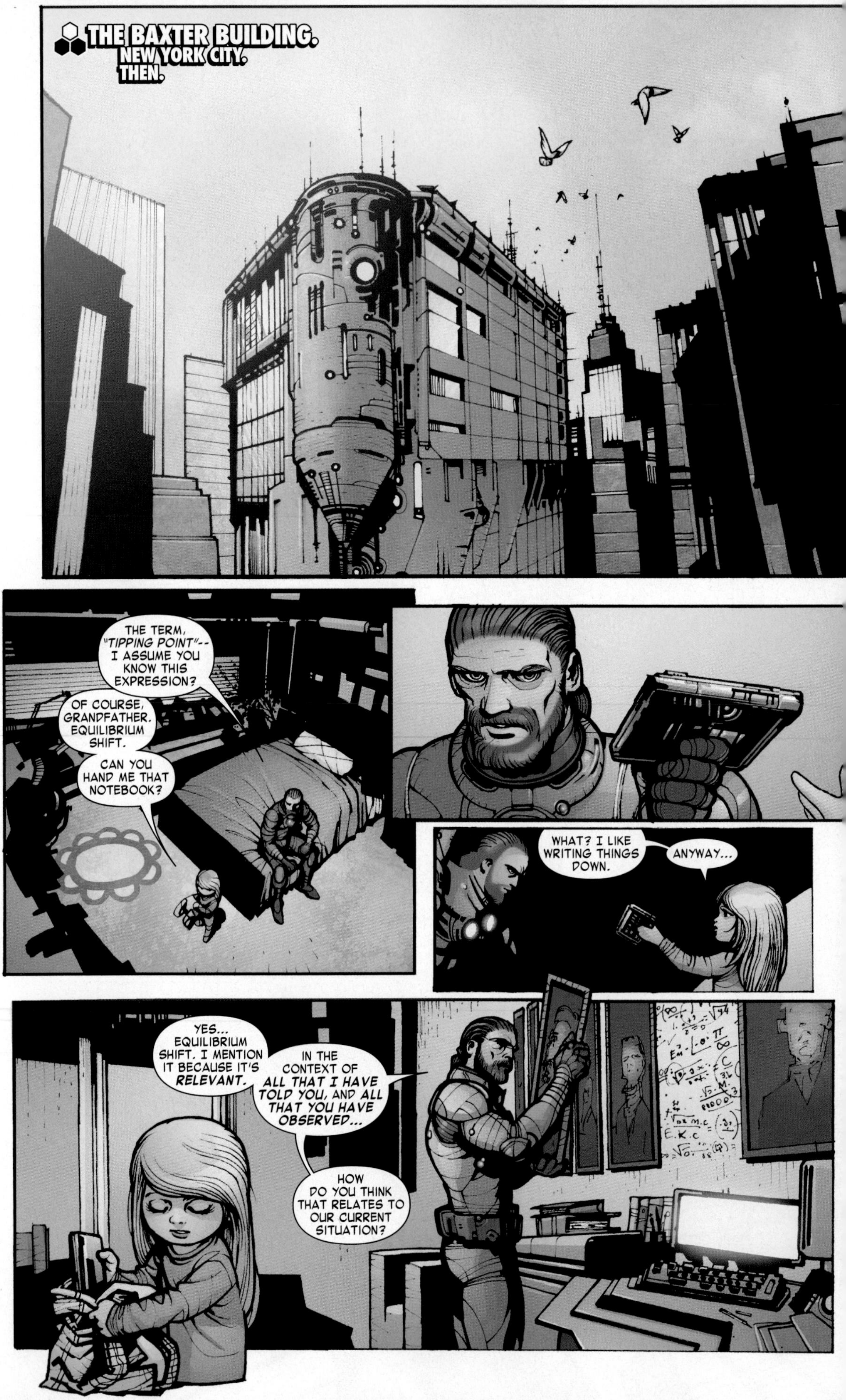
THE BAXTER BUILDING.
NEW YORK CITY.
THEN.
THE TERM, "TIPPING POINT"-- I ASSUME YOU KNOW THIS EXPRESSION?
OF COURSE, GRANDFATHER. EQUILIBRIUM SHIFT.
CAN YOU HAND ME THAT NOTEBOOK?
WHAT? I LIKE WRITING THINGS DOWN.
ANYWAY...
YES... EQUILIBRIUM SHIFT. I MENTION IT BECAUSE IT'S RELEVANT.
IN THE CONTEXT OF ALL THAT I HAVE TOLD YOU, AND ALL THAT YOU HAVE OBSERVED...
HOW DO YOU THINK THAT RELATES TO OUR CURRENT SITUATION?

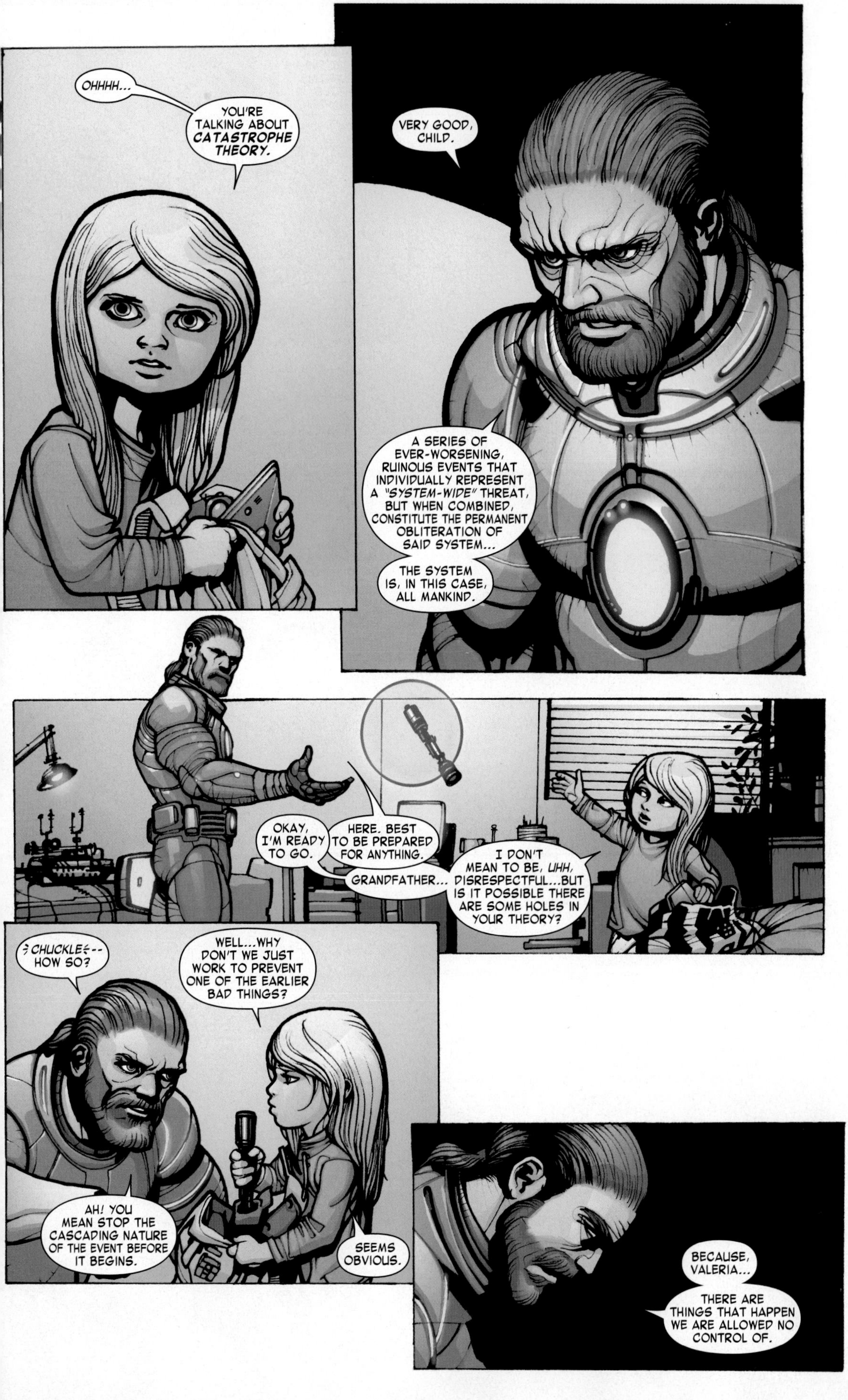
OHHHH...
YOU'RE TALKING ABOUT CATASTROPHE THEORY.
VERY GOOD, CHILD.
A SERIES OF EVER-WORSENING, RUINOUS EVENTS THAT INDIVIDUALLY REPRESENT A "SYSTEM-WIDE" THREAT, BUT WHEN COMBINED, CONSTITUTE THE PERMANENT OBLITERATION OF SAID SYSTEM...
THE SYSTEM IS, IN THIS CASE, ALL MANKIND.
HERE. BEST TO BE PREPARED FOR ANYTHING.
OKAY, I'M READY TO GO.
GRANDFATHER...
I DON'T MEAN TO BE, UHH, DISRESPECTFUL...BUT IS IT POSSIBLE THERE ARE SOME HOLES IN YOUR THEORY?
CHUCKLE --HOW SO?
WELL...WHY DON'T WE JUST WORK TO PREVENT ONE OF THE EARLIER BAD THINGS?
AH! YOU MEAN STOP THE CASCADING NATURE OF THE EVENT BEFORE IT BEGINS.
SEEMS OBVIOUS.
BECAUSE, VALERIA...
THERE ARE THINGS THAT HAPPEN WE ARE ALLOWED NO CONTROL OF.

"THERE WAS NO PREVENTING THE REBIRTH OF THE CELESTIAL REDEEMER, BLACK BOLT.

"AND WHILE IT DOESN'T ALWAYS OCCUR HERE ON EARTH, THE UNIVERSAL RESPONSE--THE REGENESIS OF THE KREE SUPREME INTELLIGENCE--DOES, IN FACT, ALWAYS HAPPEN.

"WAR BETWEEN THE TWO, AND THE EXTERMINATION OF EARTH, IS INEVITABLE, AND CAN ONLY BE HELD AT BAY BY JOHNNY STORM'S ANNIHILATION WAVE.

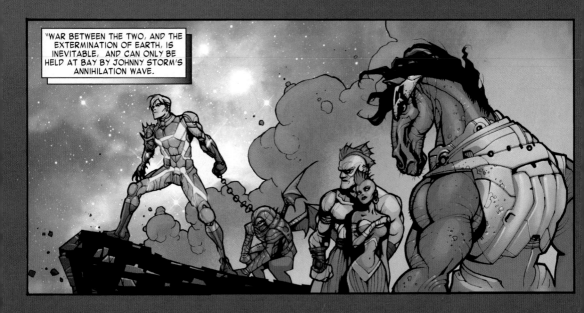

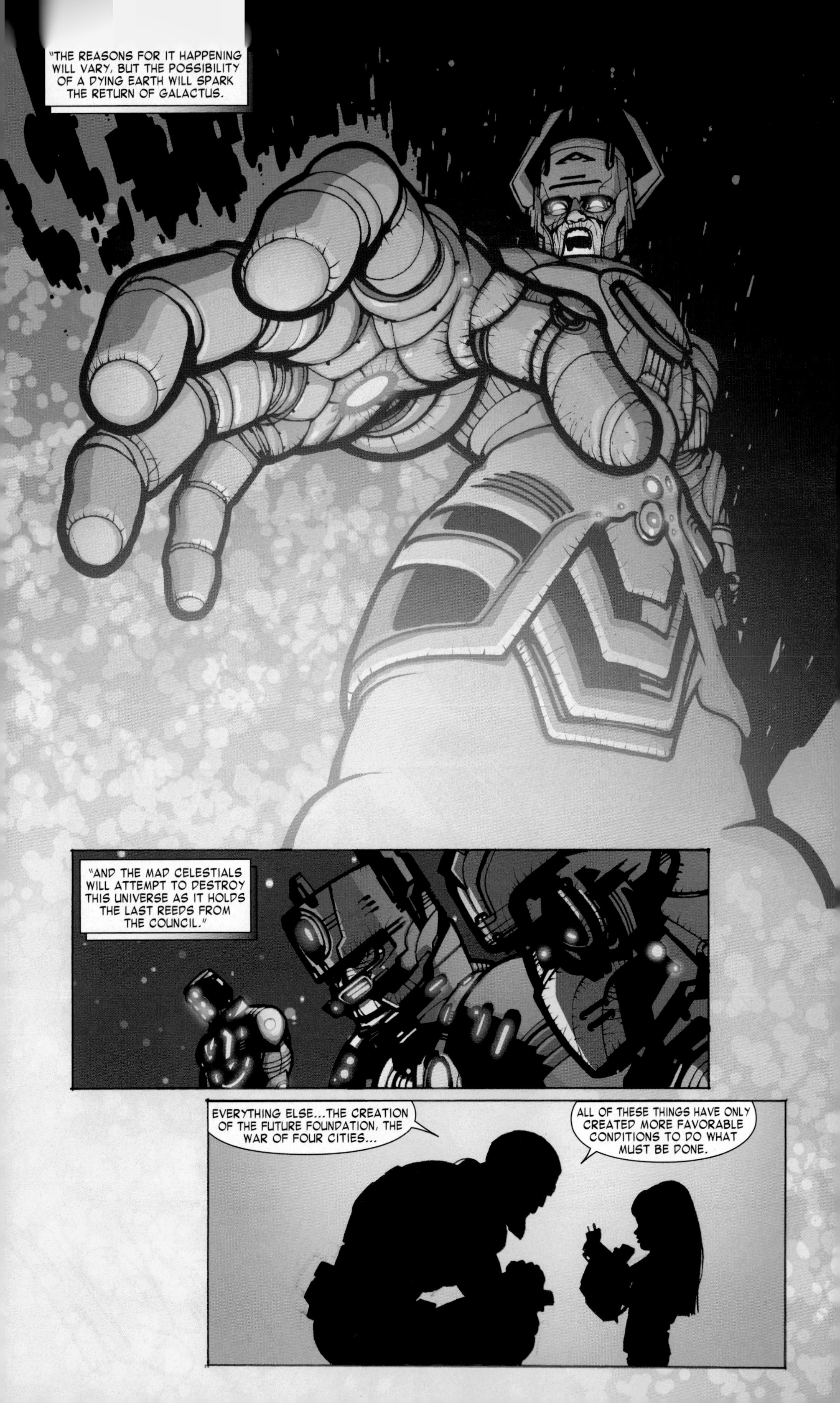
"THE REASONS FOR IT HAPPENING WILL VARY, BUT THE POSSIBILITY OF A DYING EARTH WILL SPARK THE RETURN OF GALACTUS.
"AND THE MAD CELESTIALS WILL ATTEMPT TO DESTROY THIS UNIVERSE AS IT HOLDS THE LAST REEDS FROM THE COUNCIL."
EVERYTHING ELSE...THE CREATION OF THE FUTURE FOUNDATION, THE WAR OF FOUR CITIES...
ALL OF THESE THINGS HAVE ONLY CREATED MORE FAVORABLE CONDITIONS TO DO WHAT MUST BE DONE.

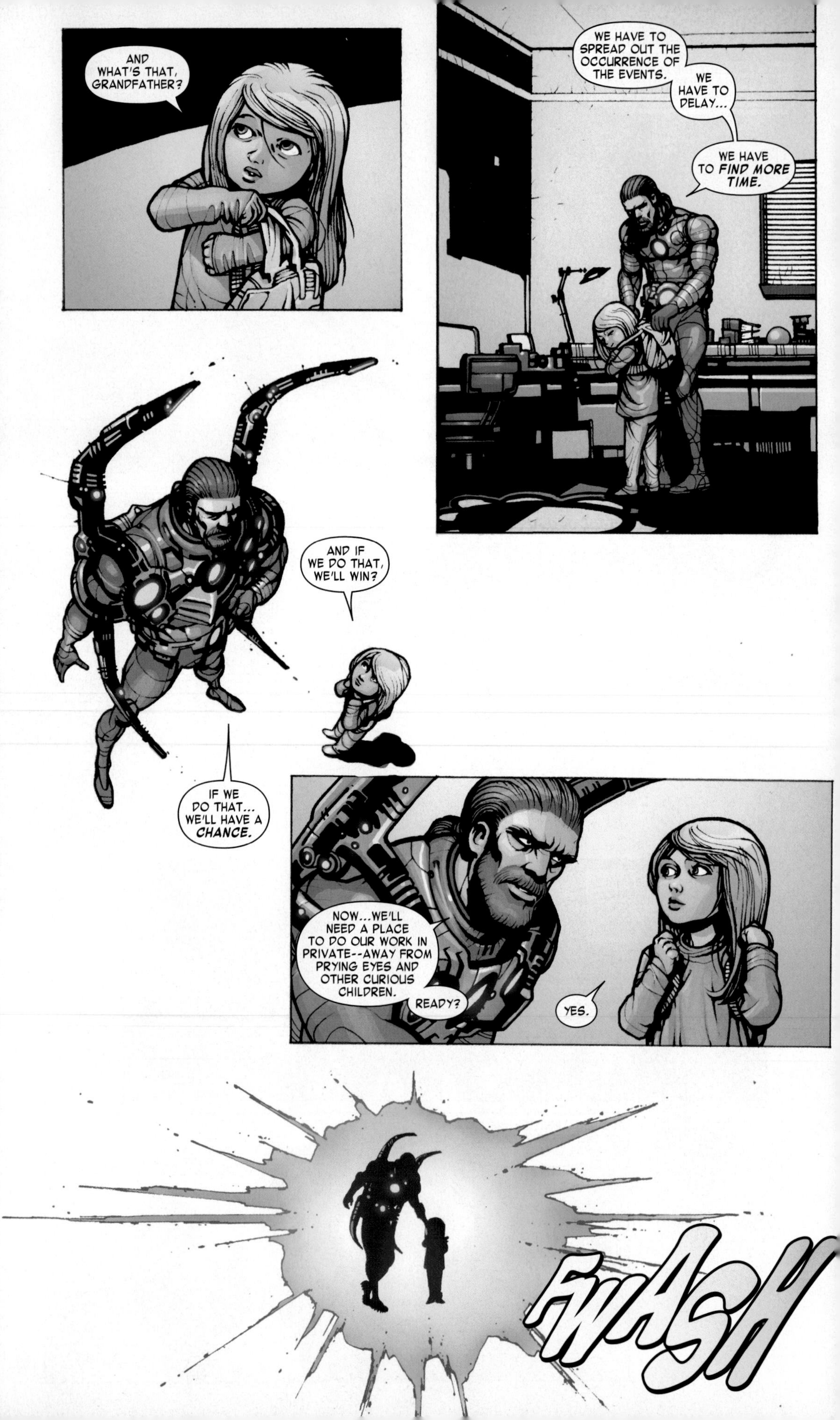

AND WHAT'S THAT, GRANDFATHER?
WE HAVE TO SPREAD OUT THE OCCURRENCE OF THE EVENTS.
WE HAVE TO DELAY...
WE HAVE TO FIND MORE TIME.
AND IF WE DO THAT, WE'LL WIN?
IF WE DO THAT... WE'LL HAVE A CHANCE.
NOW...WE'LL NEED A PLACE TO DO OUR WORK IN PRIVATE--AWAY FROM PRYING EYES AND OTHER CURIOUS CHILDREN.
READY?
YES.
FWASH

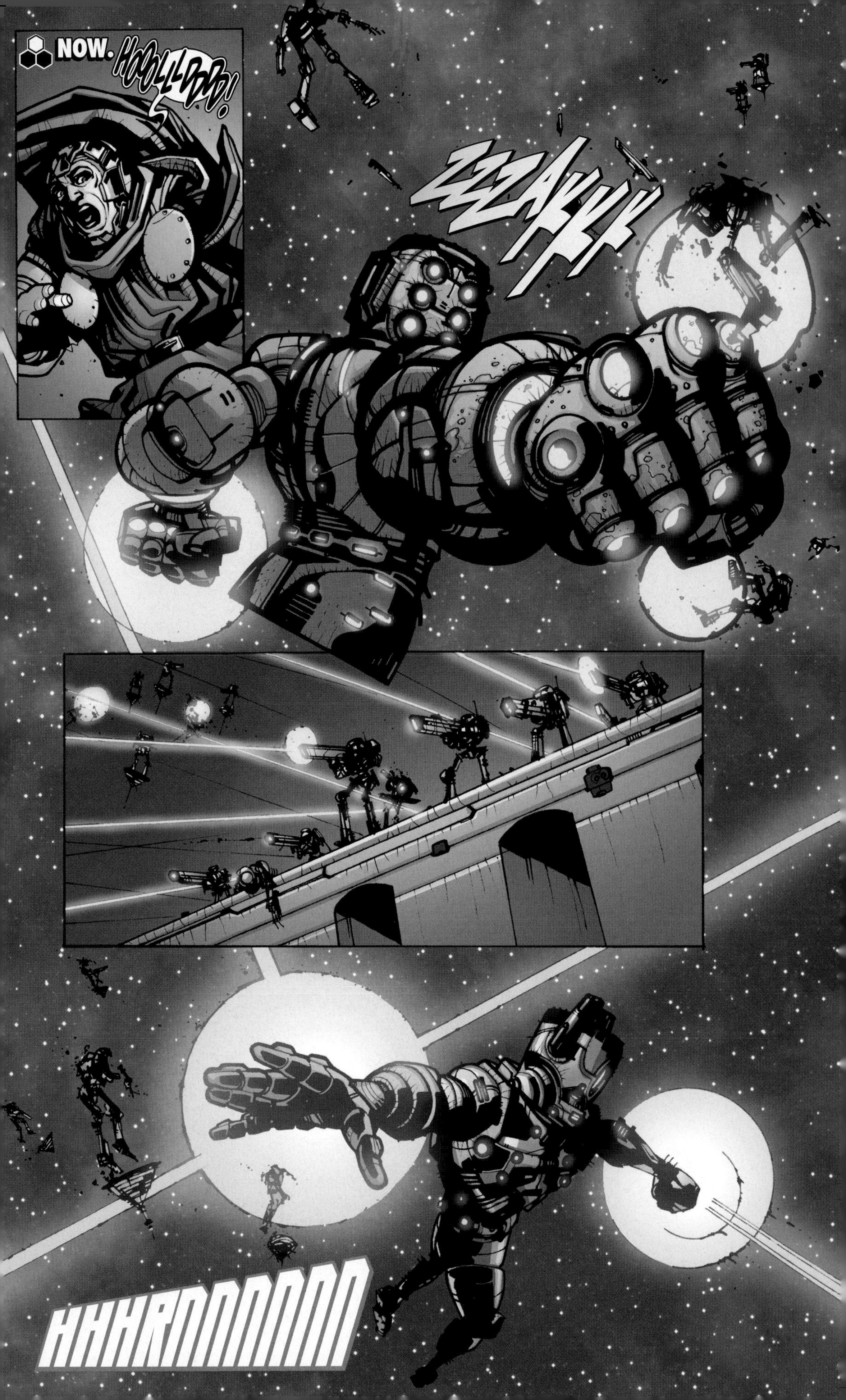
NOW.
HOOOLLLDDDD!
ZZZAKKK
HHHRNNNNNN

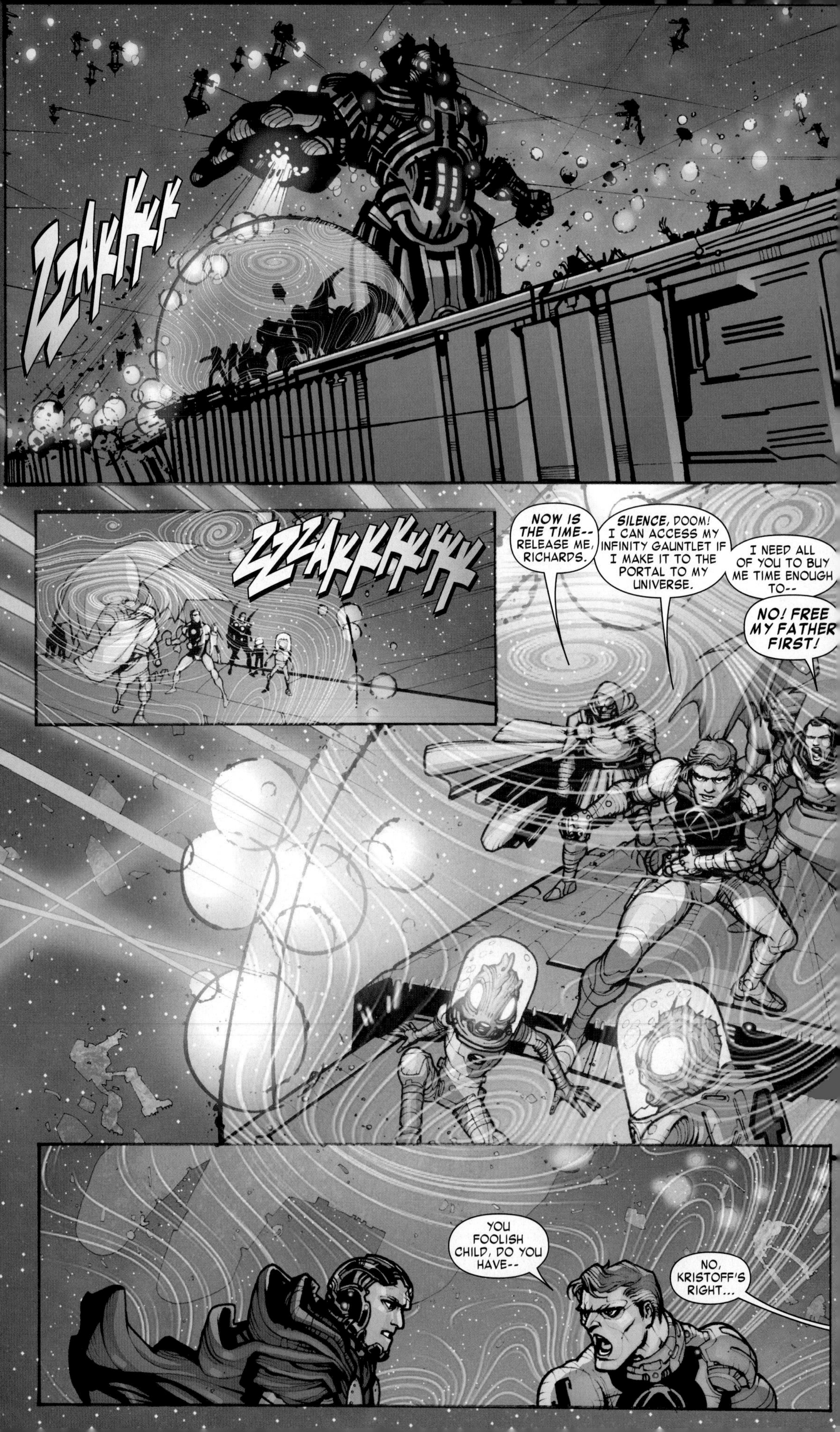
ZZAKKKK
ZZZAKKKKKKK
NOW IS THE TIME-- RELEASE ME, RICHARDS.
SILENCE, DOOM! I CAN ACCESS MY INFINITY GAUNTLET IF I MAKE IT TO THE PORTAL TO MY UNIVERSE.
I NEED ALL OF YOU TO BUY ME TIME ENOUGH TO--
NO! FREE MY FATHER FIRST!
YOU FOOLISH CHILD, DO YOU HAVE--
NO, KRISTOFF'S RIGHT...

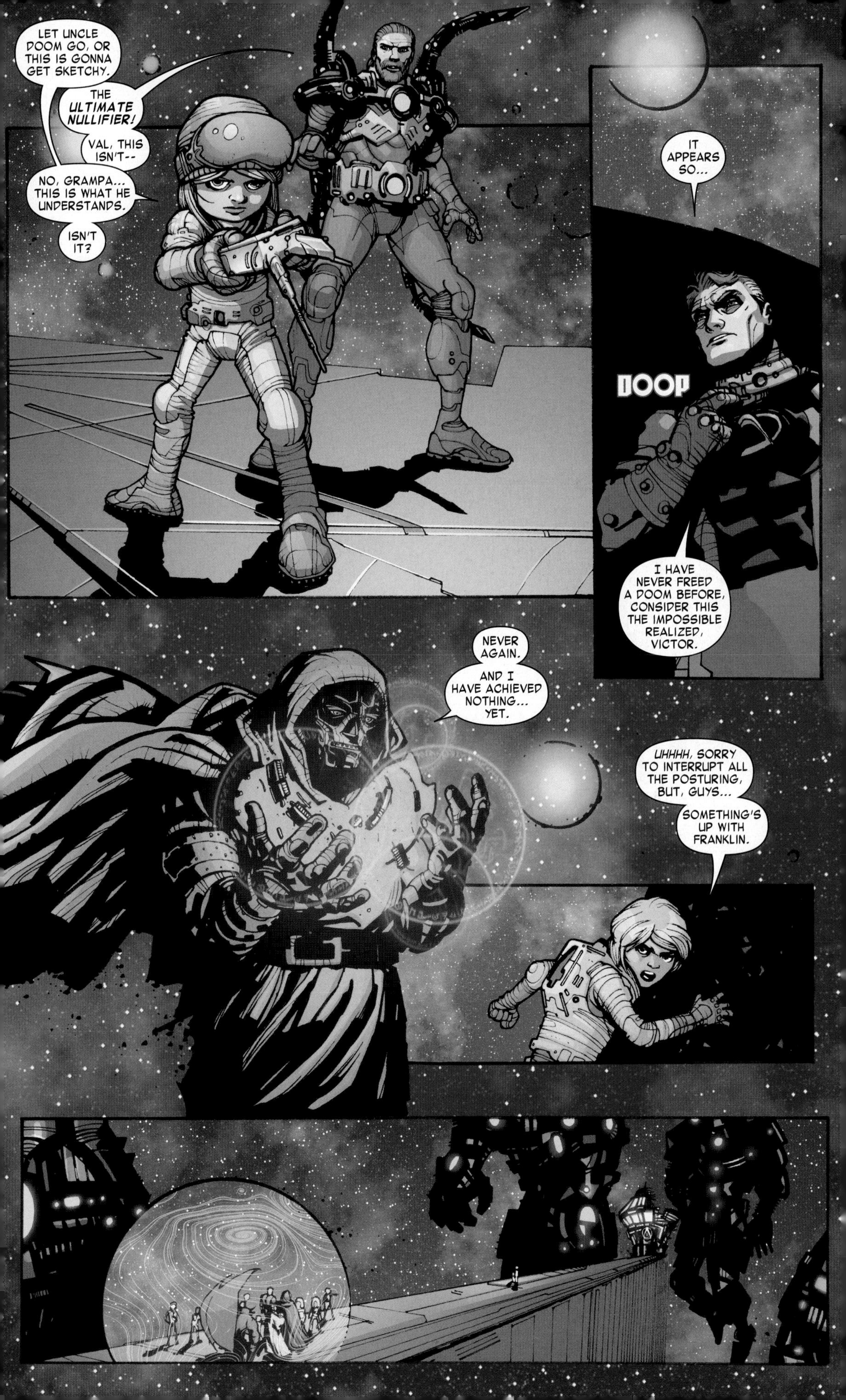
LET UNCLE DOOM GO, OR THIS IS GONNA GET SKETCHY.
THE *ULTIMATE NULLIFIER!*
VAL, THIS ISN'T--
NO, GRAMPA... THIS IS WHAT HE UNDERSTANDS.
ISN'T IT?
IT APPEARS SO...
DOOP
I HAVE NEVER FREED A DOOM BEFORE, CONSIDER THIS THE IMPOSSIBLE REALIZED, VICTOR.
NEVER AGAIN.
AND I HAVE ACHIEVED NOTHING... YET.
UHHHH, SORRY TO INTERRUPT ALL THE POSTURING, BUT, GUYS...
SOMETHING'S UP WITH FRANKLIN.

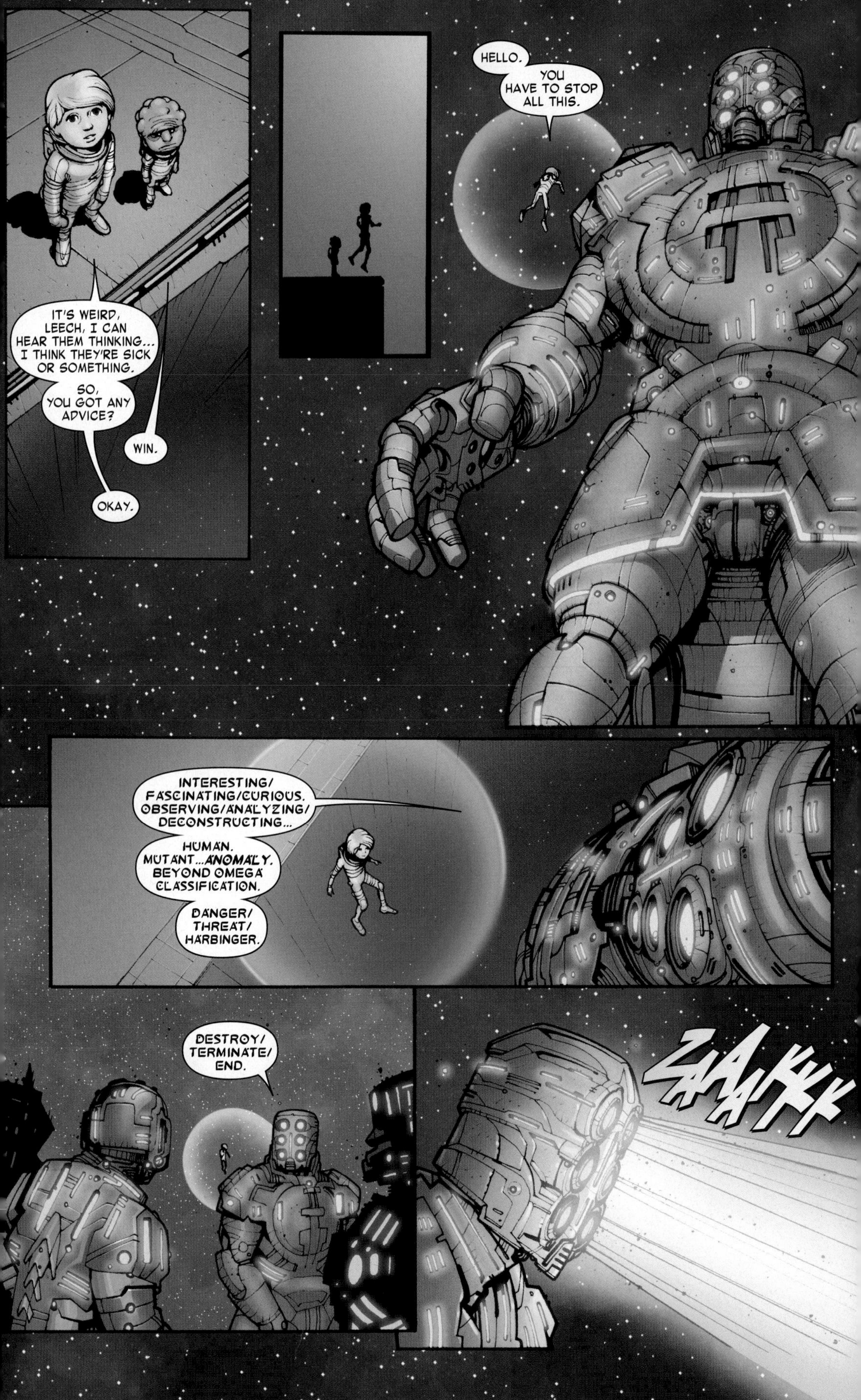
IT'S WEIRD, LEECH, I CAN HEAR THEM THINKING... I THINK THEY'RE SICK OR SOMETHING.
SO, YOU GOT ANY ADVICE?
WIN.
OKAY.
HELLO.
YOU HAVE TO STOP ALL THIS.
INTERESTING/ FASCINATING/CURIOUS. OBSERVING/ANALYZING/ DECONSTRUCTING...
HUMAN. MUTANT...ANOMALY. BEYOND OMEGA CLASSIFICATION.
DANGER/ THREAT/ HARBINGER.
DESTROY/ TERMINATE/ END.
ZAAKKK

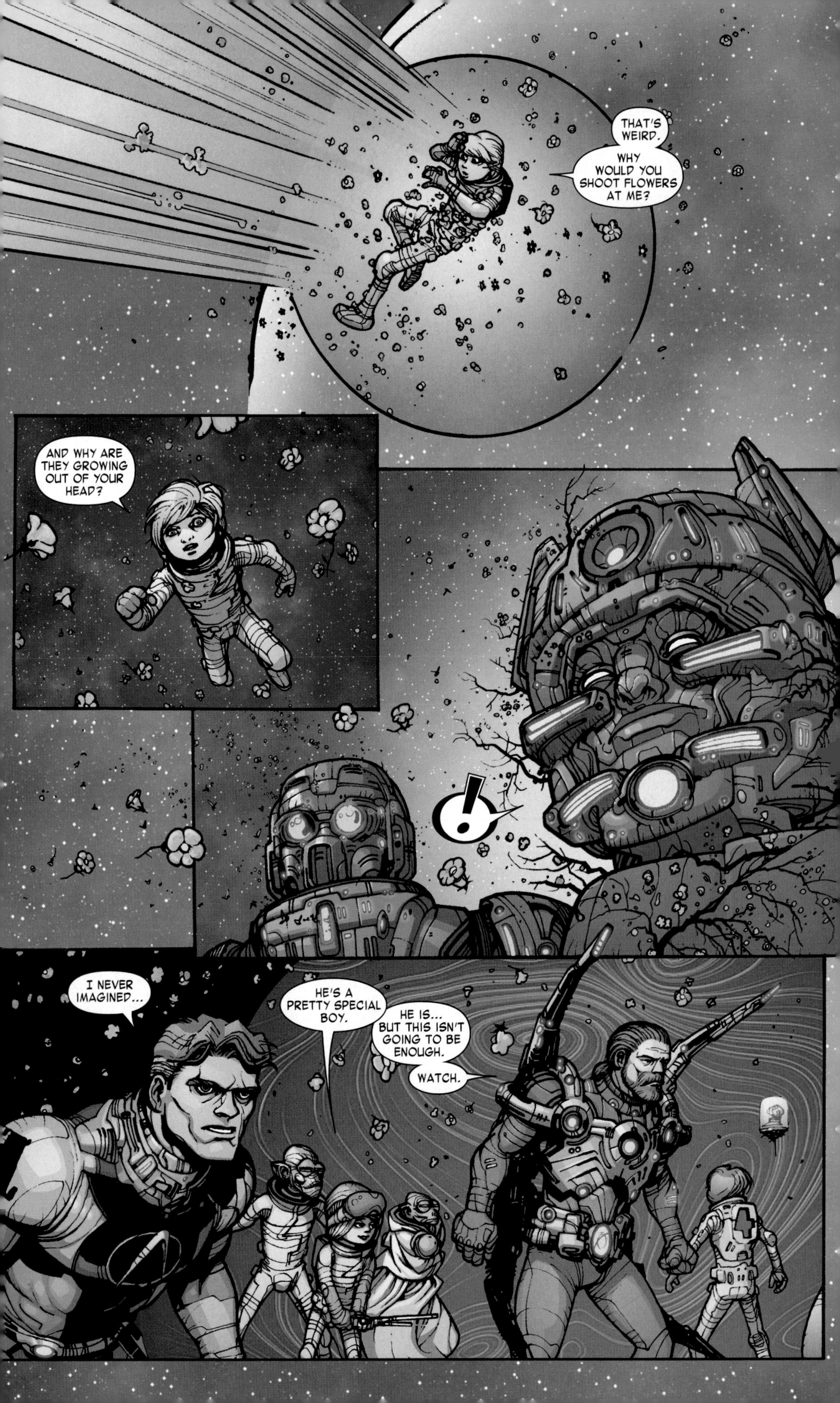
THAT'S WEIRD.
WHY WOULD YOU SHOOT FLOWERS AT ME?
AND WHY ARE THEY GROWING OUT OF YOUR HEAD?
!
I NEVER IMAGINED...
HE'S A PRETTY SPECIAL BOY.
HE IS... BUT THIS ISN'T GOING TO BE ENOUGH.
WATCH.

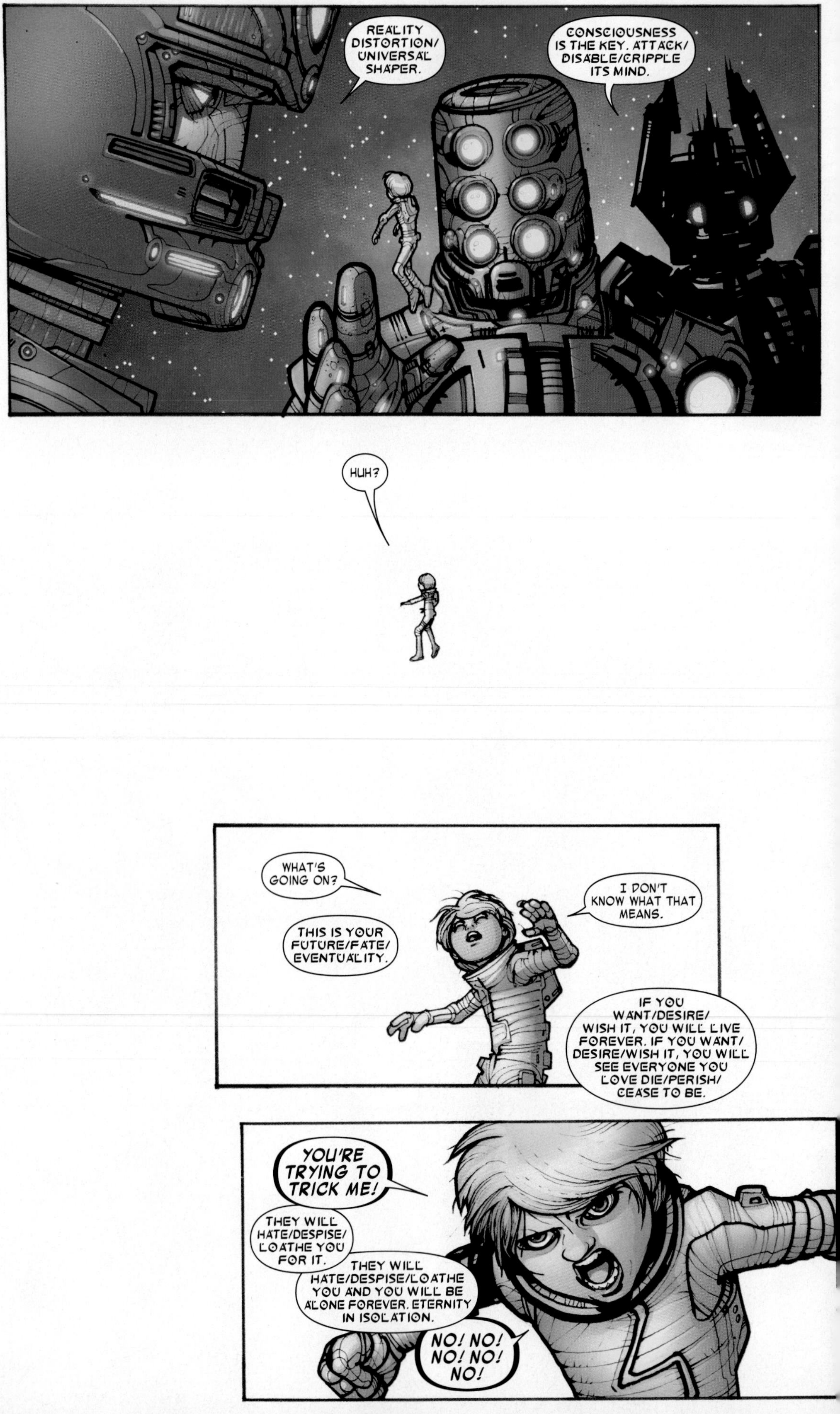
REALITY DISTORTION/ UNIVERSAL SHAPER.
CONSCIOUSNESS IS THE KEY. ATTACK/ DISABLE/CRIPPLE ITS MIND.
HUH?
WHAT'S GOING ON?
I DON'T KNOW WHAT THAT MEANS.
THIS IS YOUR FUTURE/FATE/ EVENTUALITY.
IF YOU WANT/DESIRE/ WISH IT, YOU WILL LIVE FOREVER. IF YOU WANT/ DESIRE/WISH IT, YOU WILL SEE EVERYONE YOU LOVE DIE/PERISH/ CEASE TO BE.
YOU'RE TRYING TO TRICK ME!
THEY WILL HATE/DESPISE/ LOATHE YOU FOR IT.
THEY WILL HATE/DESPISE/LOATHE YOU AND YOU WILL BE ALONE FOREVER. ETERNITY IN ISOLATION.
NO! NO! NO! NO! NO!

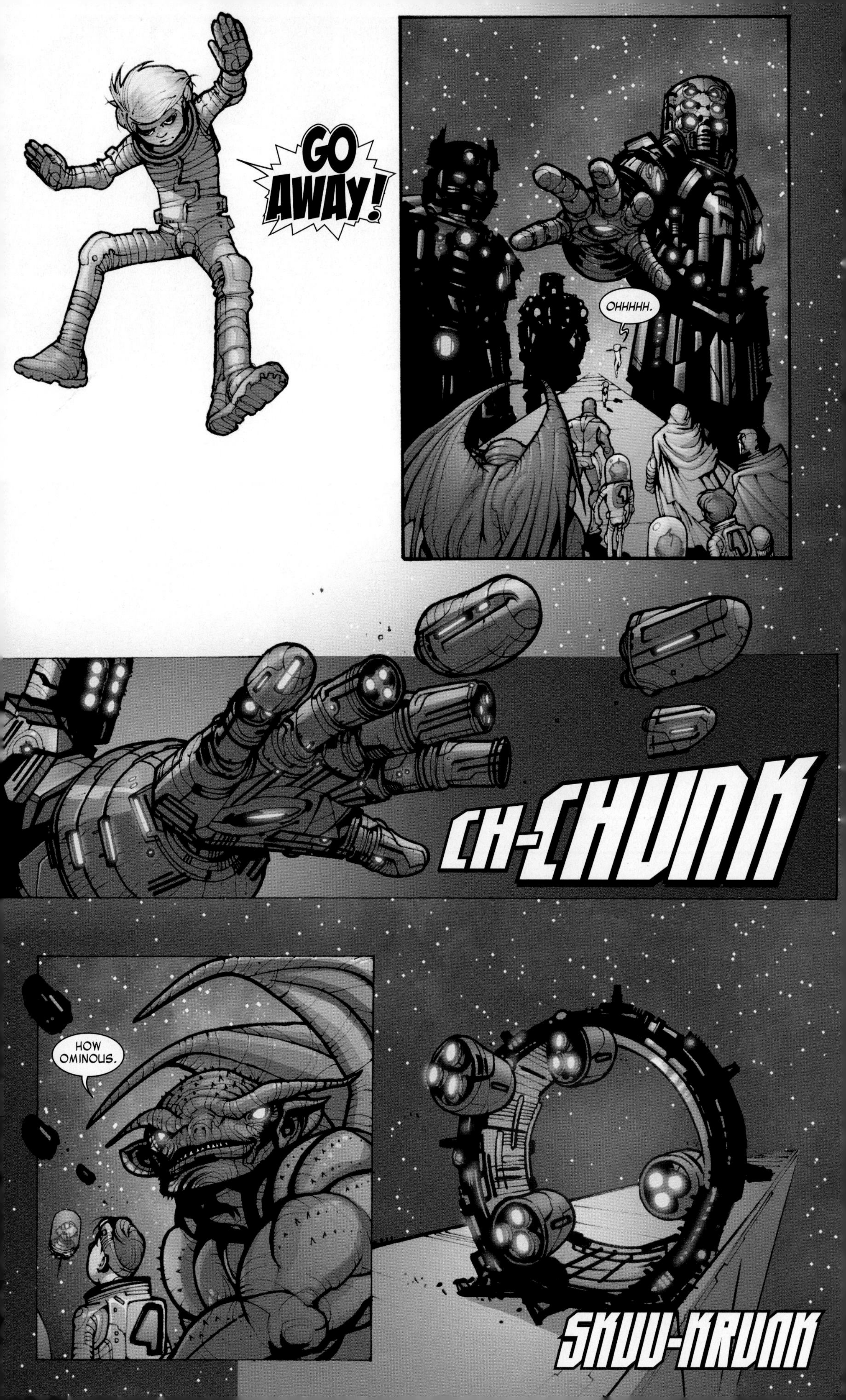
GO AWAY!
OHHHHH.
CH-CHUNK
HOW OMINOUS.
SKUU-KRUNK

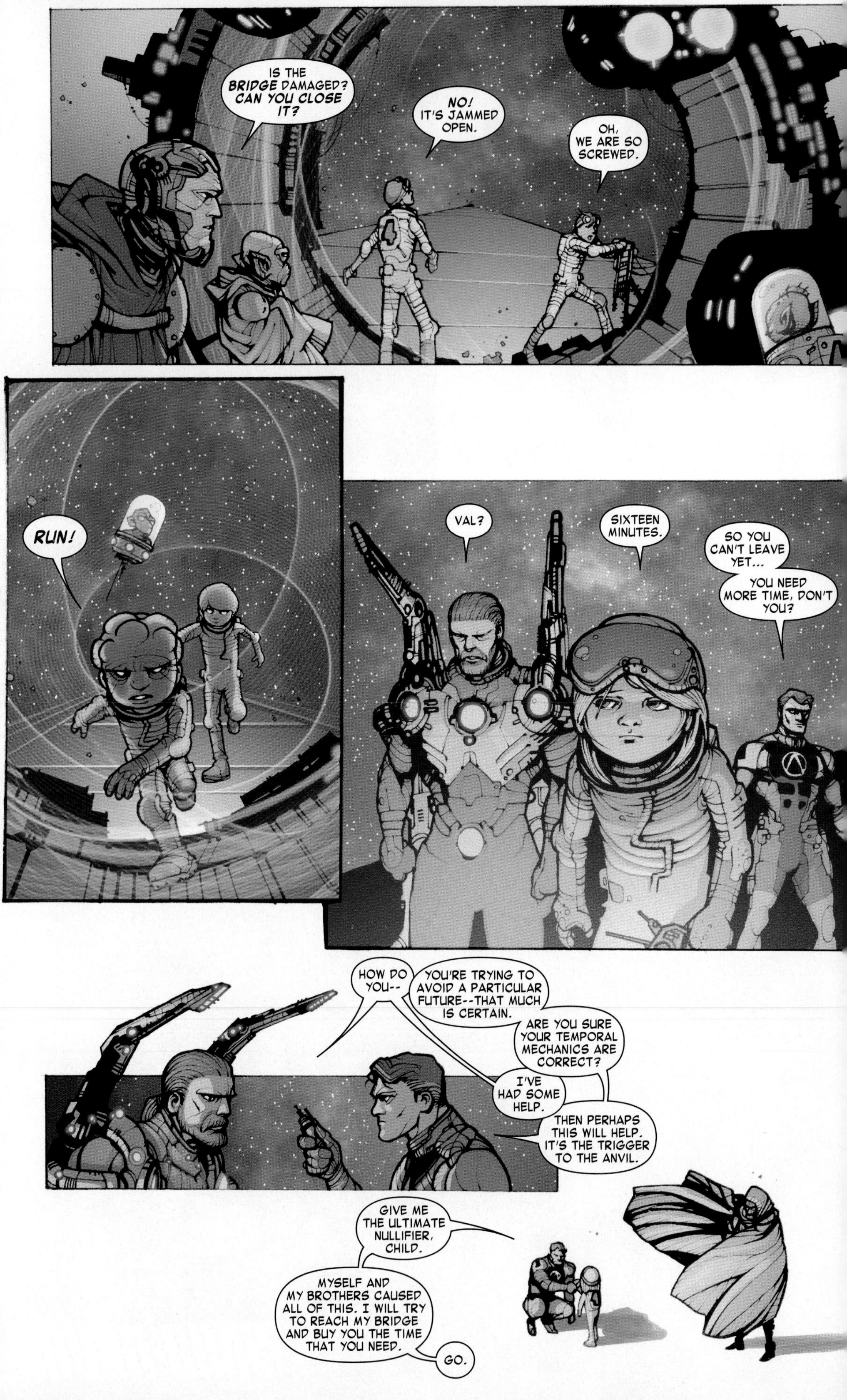
IS THE BRIDGE DAMAGED? CAN YOU CLOSE IT?
NO! IT'S JAMMED OPEN.
OH, WE ARE SO SCREWED.
RUN!
VAL?
SIXTEEN MINUTES.
SO YOU CAN'T LEAVE YET...
YOU NEED MORE TIME, DON'T YOU?
HOW DO YOU--
YOU'RE TRYING TO AVOID A PARTICULAR FUTURE--THAT MUCH IS CERTAIN.
ARE YOU SURE YOUR TEMPORAL MECHANICS ARE CORRECT?
I'VE HAD SOME HELP.
THEN PERHAPS THIS WILL HELP. IT'S THE TRIGGER TO THE ANVIL.
GIVE ME THE ULTIMATE NULLIFIER, CHILD.
MYSELF AND MY BROTHERS CAUSED ALL OF THIS. I WILL TRY TO REACH MY BRIDGE AND BUY YOU THE TIME THAT YOU NEED.
GO.

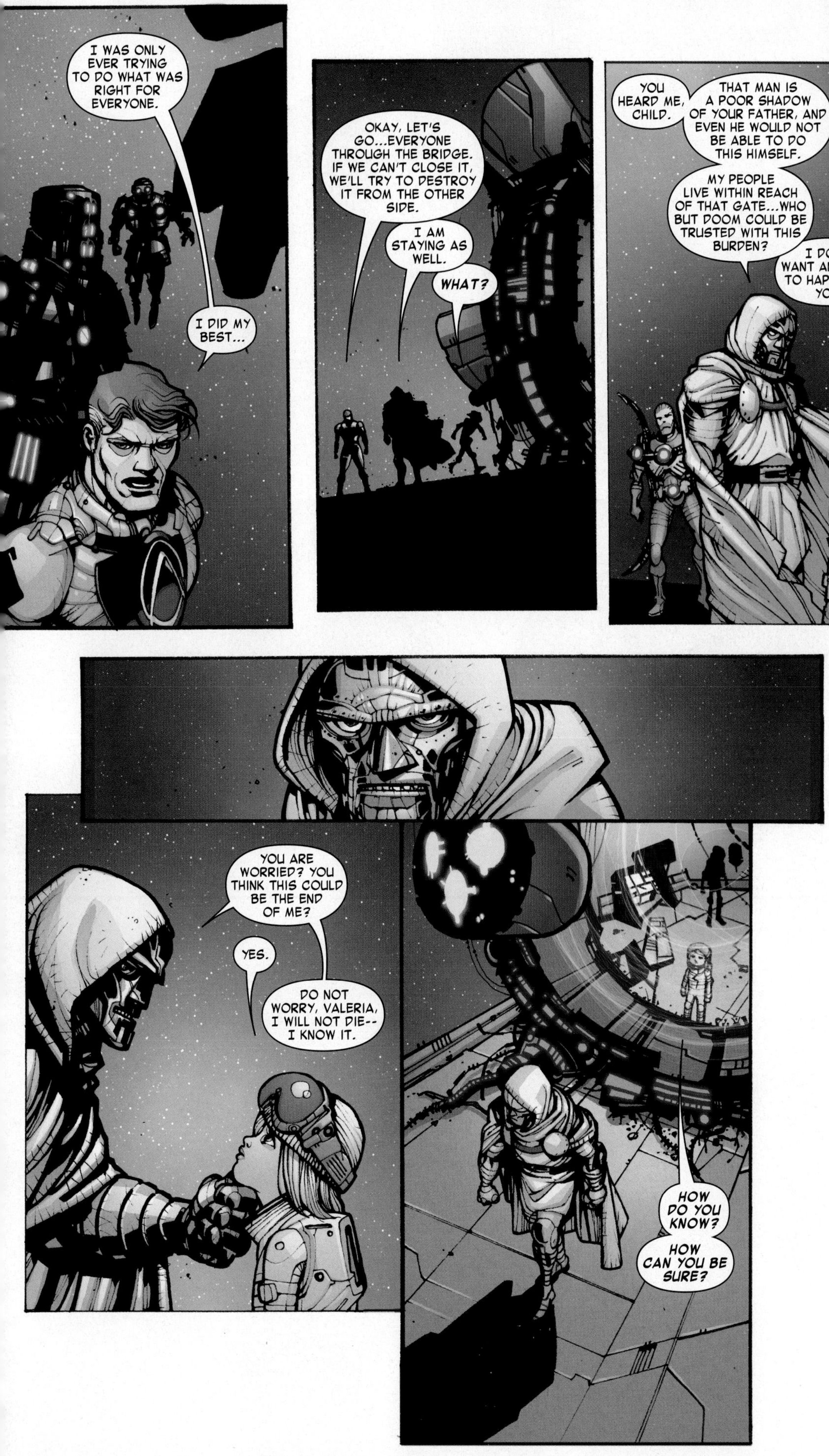
I WAS ONLY EVER TRYING TO DO WHAT WAS RIGHT FOR EVERYONE.
I DID MY BEST...
OKAY, LET'S GO...EVERYONE THROUGH THE BRIDGE. IF WE CAN'T CLOSE IT, WE'LL TRY TO DESTROY IT FROM THE OTHER SIDE.
I AM STAYING AS WELL.
WHAT?
YOU HEARD ME, CHILD.
THAT MAN IS A POOR SHADOW OF YOUR FATHER, AND EVEN HE WOULD NOT BE ABLE TO DO THIS HIMSELF.
MY PEOPLE LIVE WITHIN REACH OF THAT GATE...WHO BUT DOOM COULD BE TRUSTED WITH THIS BURDEN?
I DON'T WANT ANYTHING TO HAPPEN TO YOU.
YOU ARE WORRIED? YOU THINK THIS COULD BE THE END OF ME?
YES.
DO NOT WORRY, VALERIA, I WILL NOT DIE-- I KNOW IT.
HOW DO YOU KNOW?
HOW CAN YOU BE SURE?

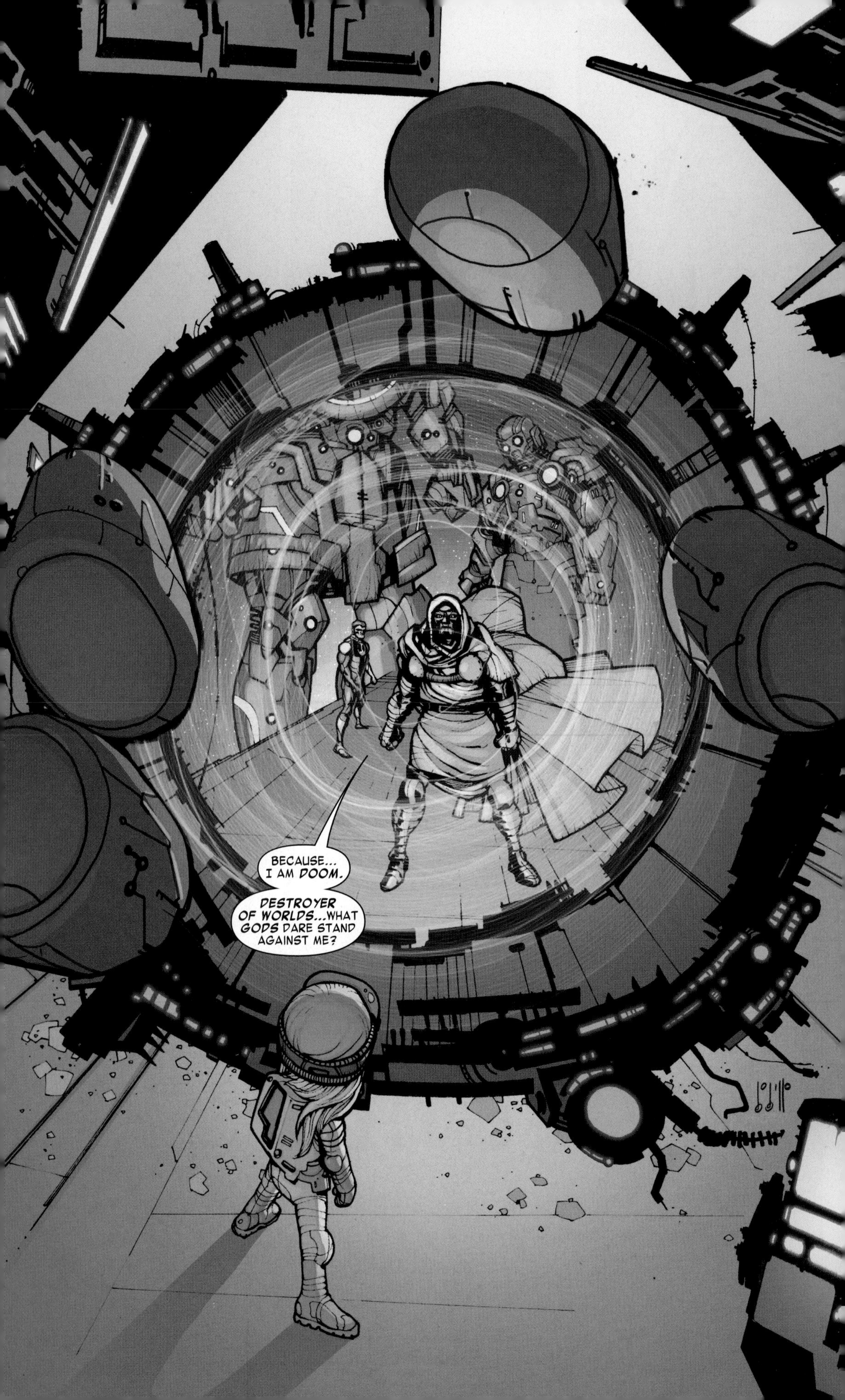
BECAUSE... I AM DOOM.
DESTROYER OF WORLDS...WHAT GODS DARE STAND AGAINST ME?

LIES

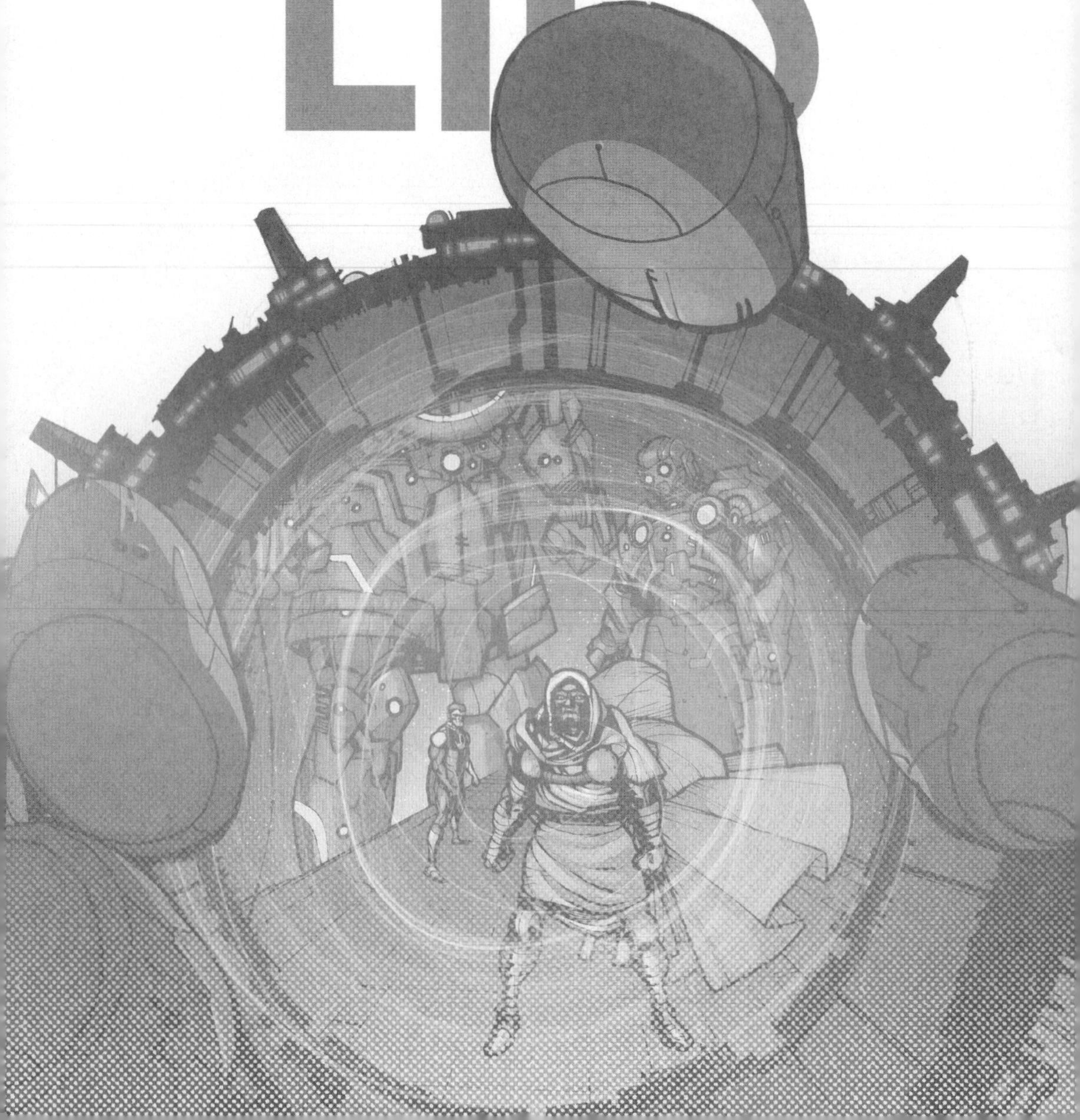

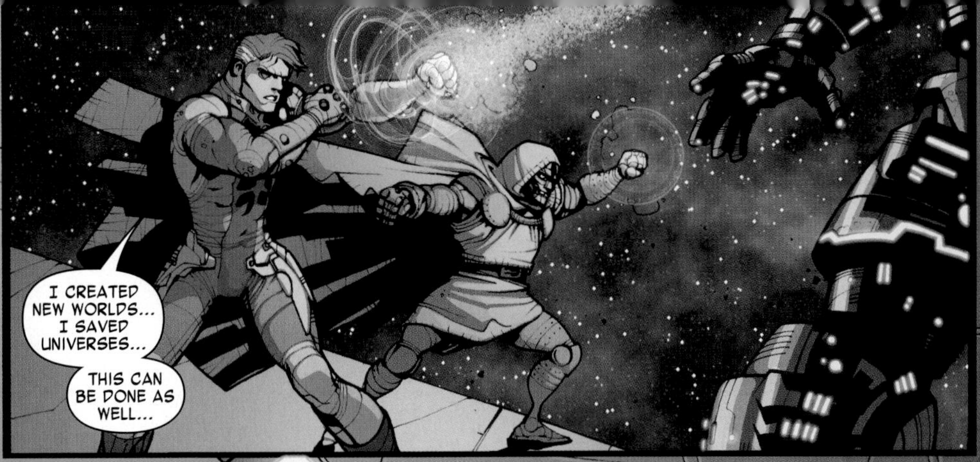
I CREATED NEW WORLDS... I SAVED UNIVERSES...
THIS CAN BE DONE AS WELL...

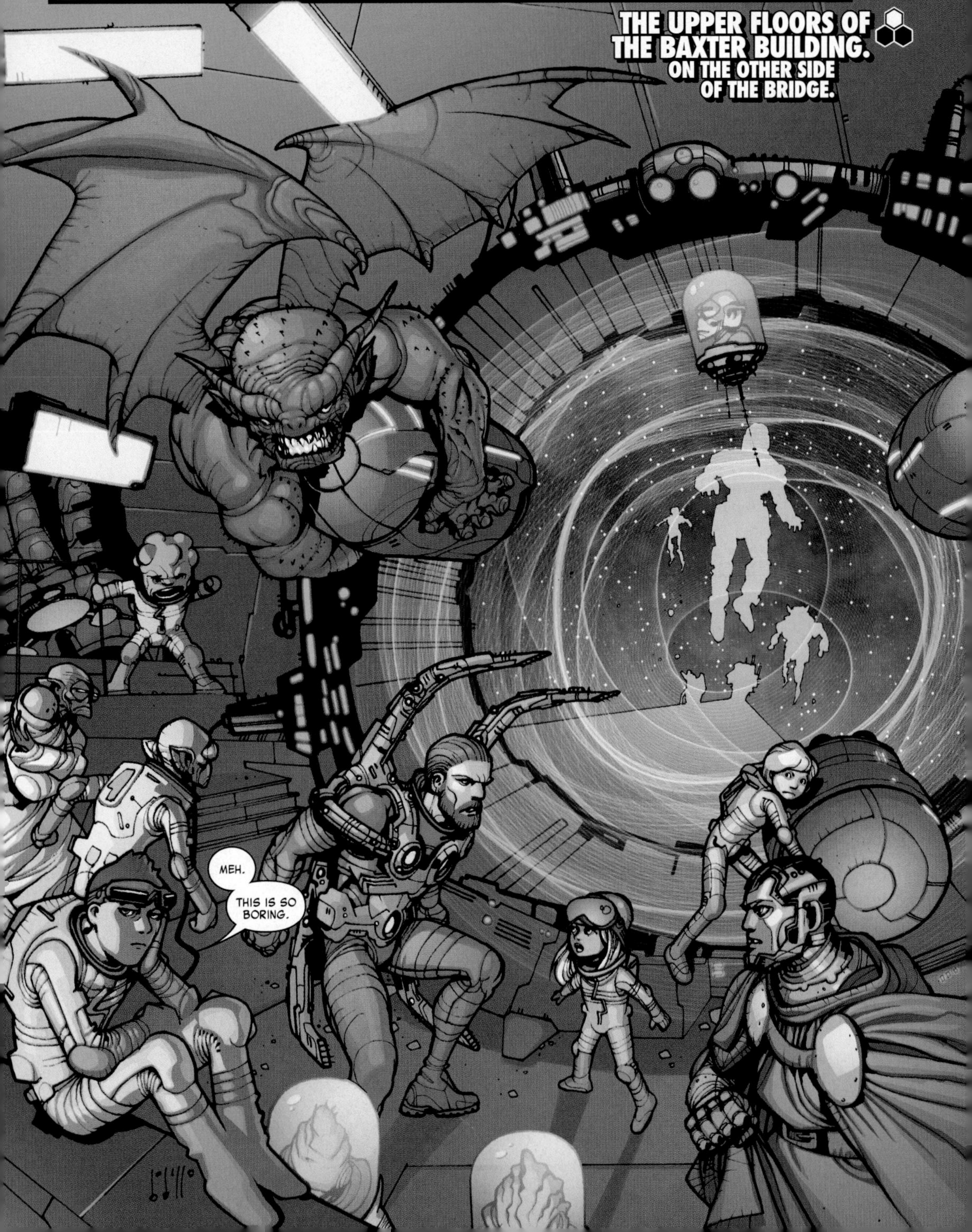
THE UPPER FLOORS OF THE BAXTER BUILDING.
ON THE OTHER SIDE OF THE BRIDGE.
MEH.
THIS IS SO BORING.

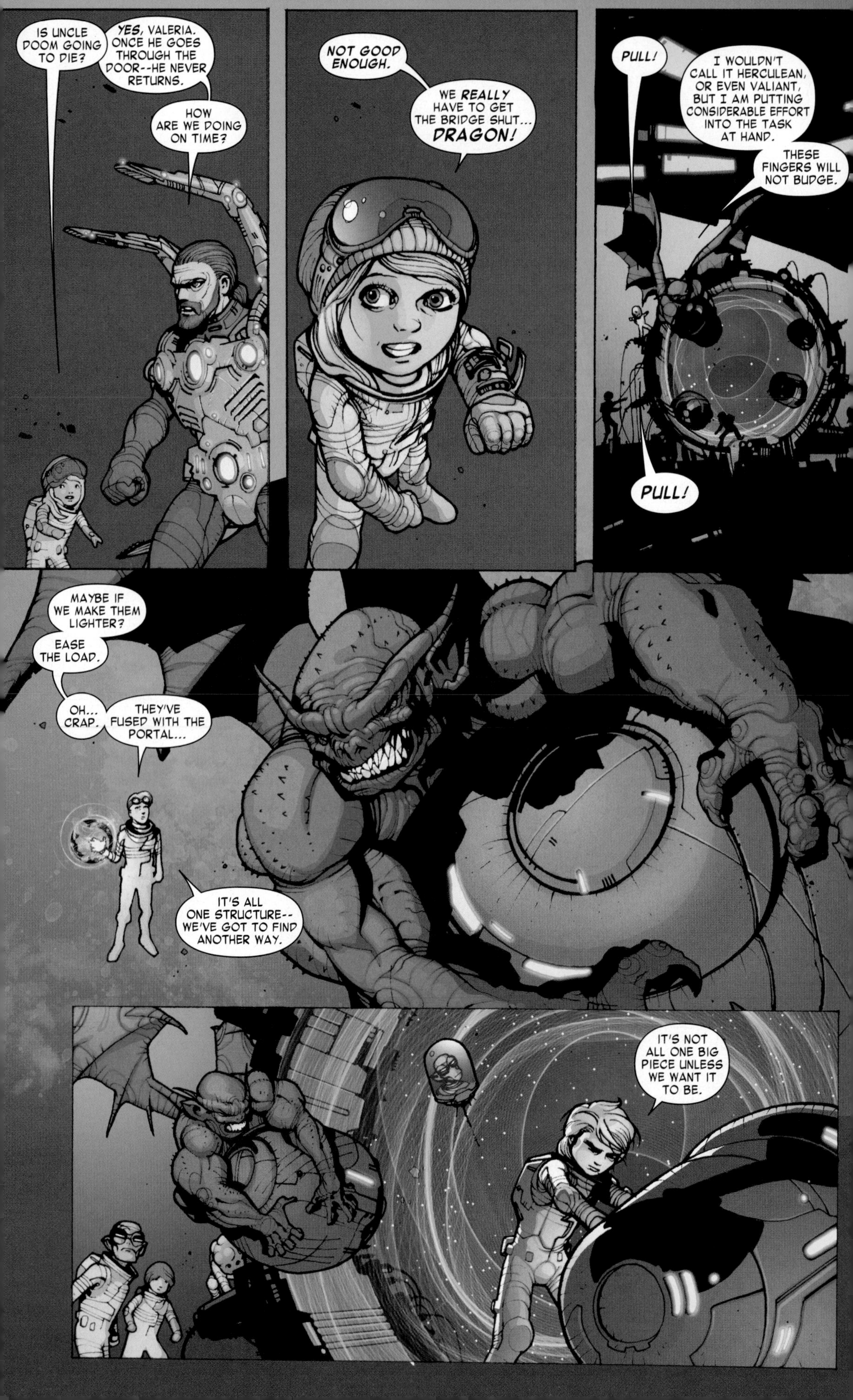
IS UNCLE DOOM GOING TO DIE?
YES, VALERIA. ONCE HE GOES THROUGH THE DOOR--HE NEVER RETURNS.
HOW ARE WE DOING ON TIME?
NOT GOOD ENOUGH.
WE REALLY HAVE TO GET THE BRIDGE SHUT... DRAGON!
PULL!
I WOULDN'T CALL IT HERCULEAN, OR EVEN VALIANT, BUT I AM PUTTING CONSIDERABLE EFFORT INTO THE TASK AT HAND.
THESE FINGERS WILL NOT BUDGE.
PULL!
MAYBE IF WE MAKE THEM LIGHTER?
EASE THE LOAD.
OH... CRAP.
THEY'VE FUSED WITH THE PORTAL...
IT'S ALL ONE STRUCTURE-- WE'VE GOT TO FIND ANOTHER WAY.
IT'S NOT ALL ONE BIG PIECE UNLESS WE WANT IT TO BE.

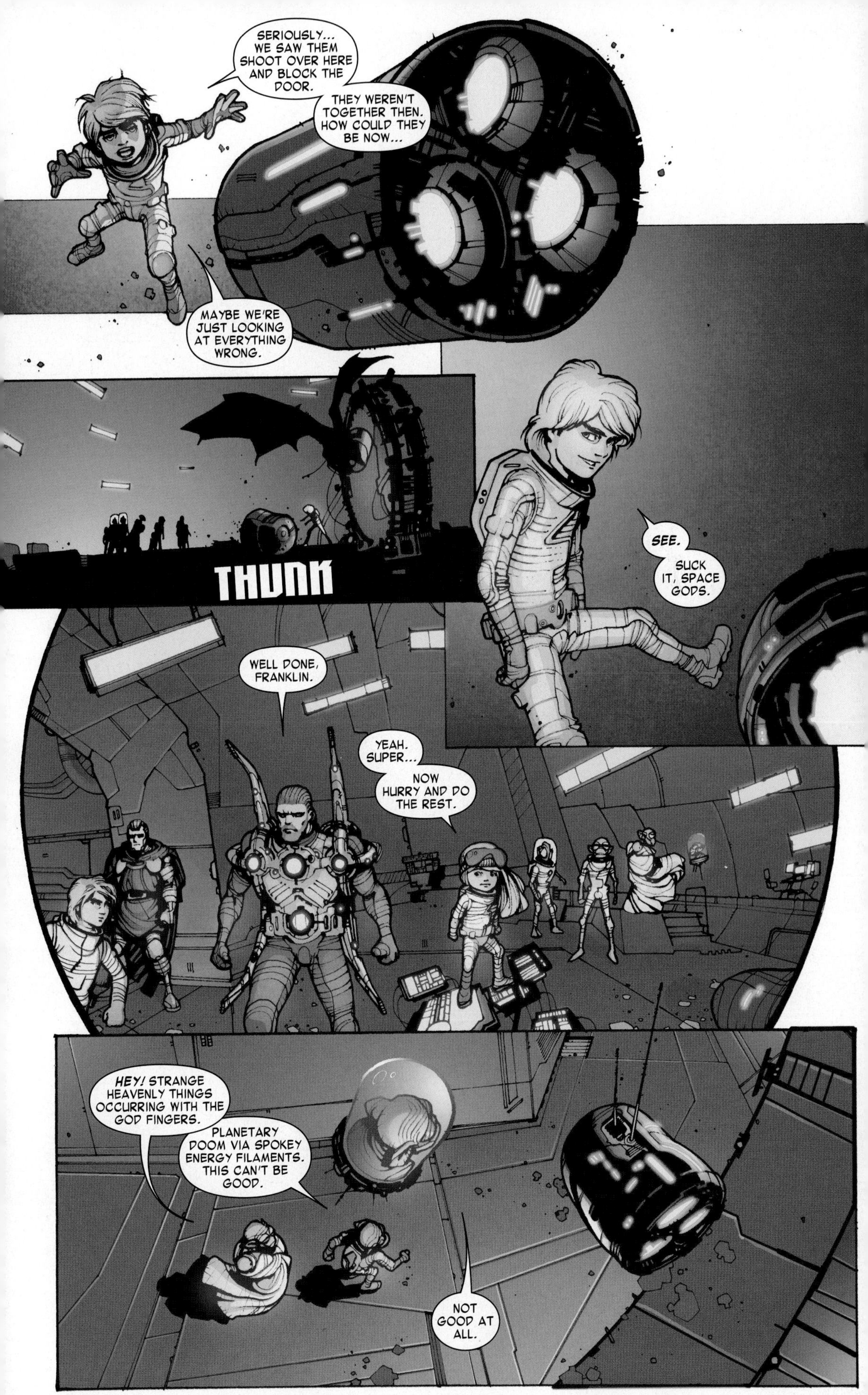
SERIOUSLY... WE SAW THEM SHOOT OVER HERE AND BLOCK THE DOOR.
THEY WEREN'T TOGETHER THEN. HOW COULD THEY BE NOW...
MAYBE WE'RE JUST LOOKING AT EVERYTHING WRONG.
THUNK
SEE.
SUCK IT, SPACE GODS.
WELL DONE, FRANKLIN.
YEAH. SUPER...
NOW HURRY AND DO THE REST.
HEY! STRANGE HEAVENLY THINGS OCCURRING WITH THE GOD FINGERS.
PLANETARY DOOM VIA SPOKEY ENERGY FILAMENTS. THIS CAN'T BE GOOD.
NOT GOOD AT ALL.

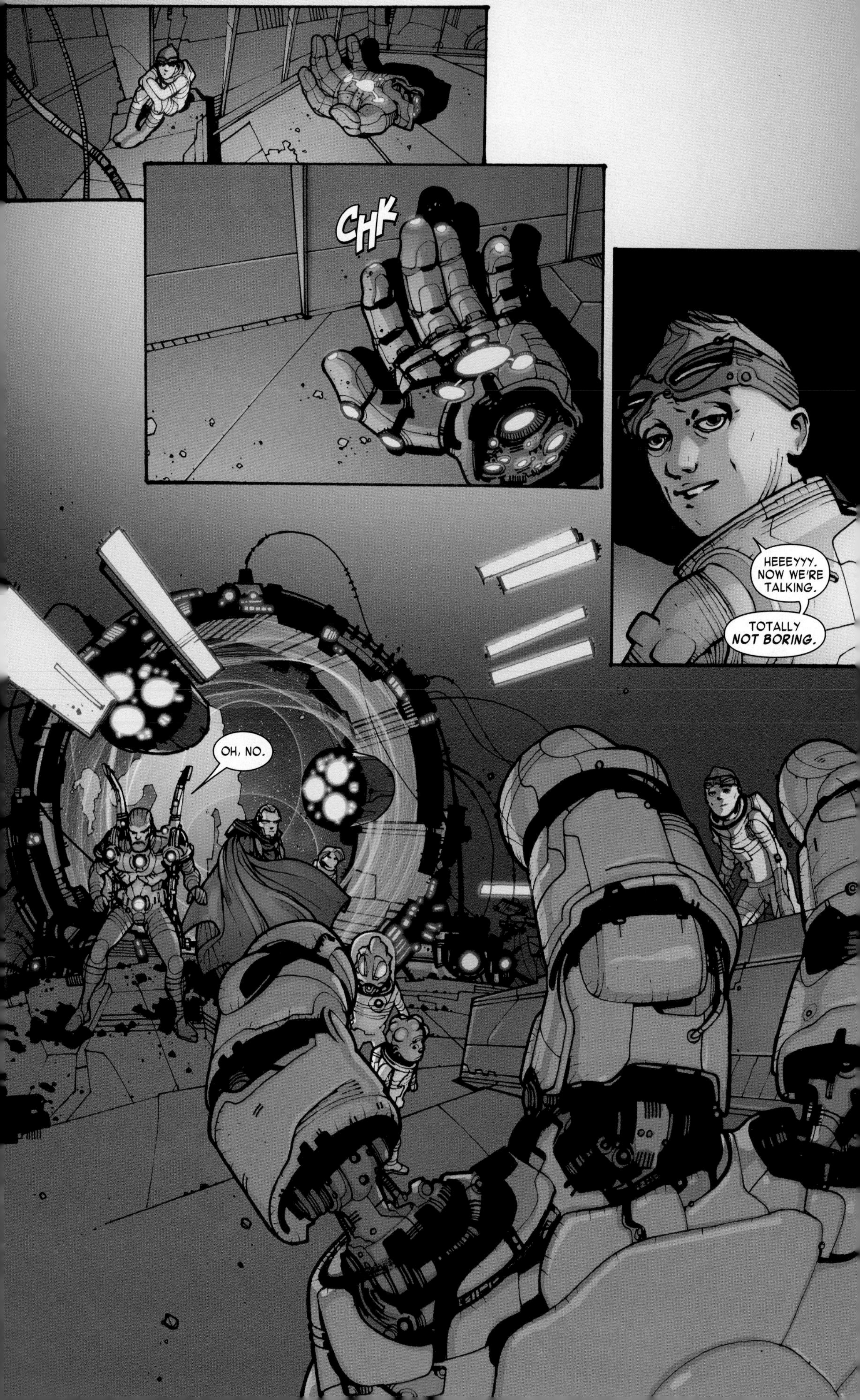

CHK
HEEEYYY. NOW WE'RE TALKING.
TOTALLY NOT BORING.
OH, NO.

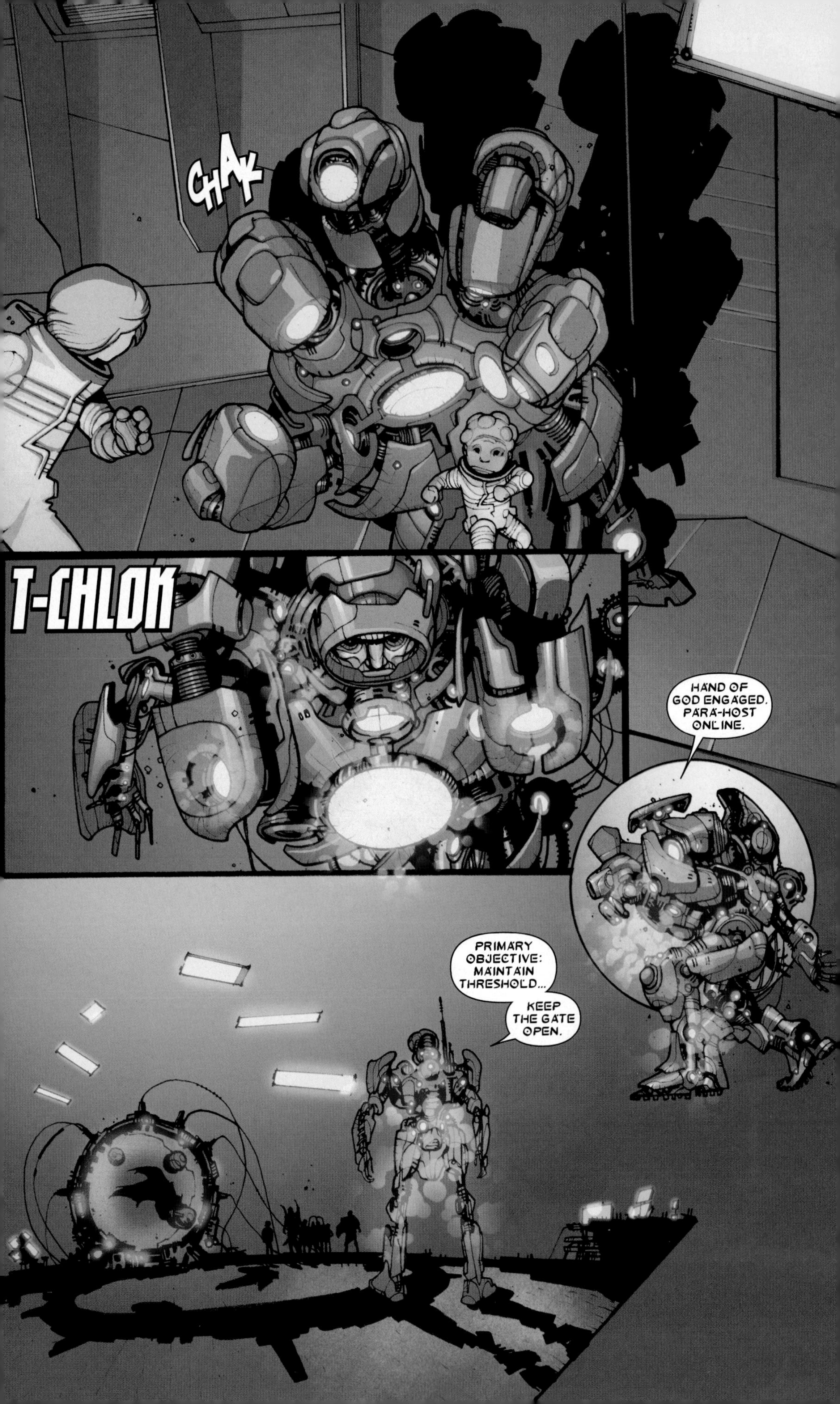
CHAK
T-CHLOK
HAND OF GOD ENGAGED. PARA-HOST ONLINE.
PRIMARY OBJECTIVE: MAINTAIN THRESHOLD...
KEEP THE GATE OPEN.

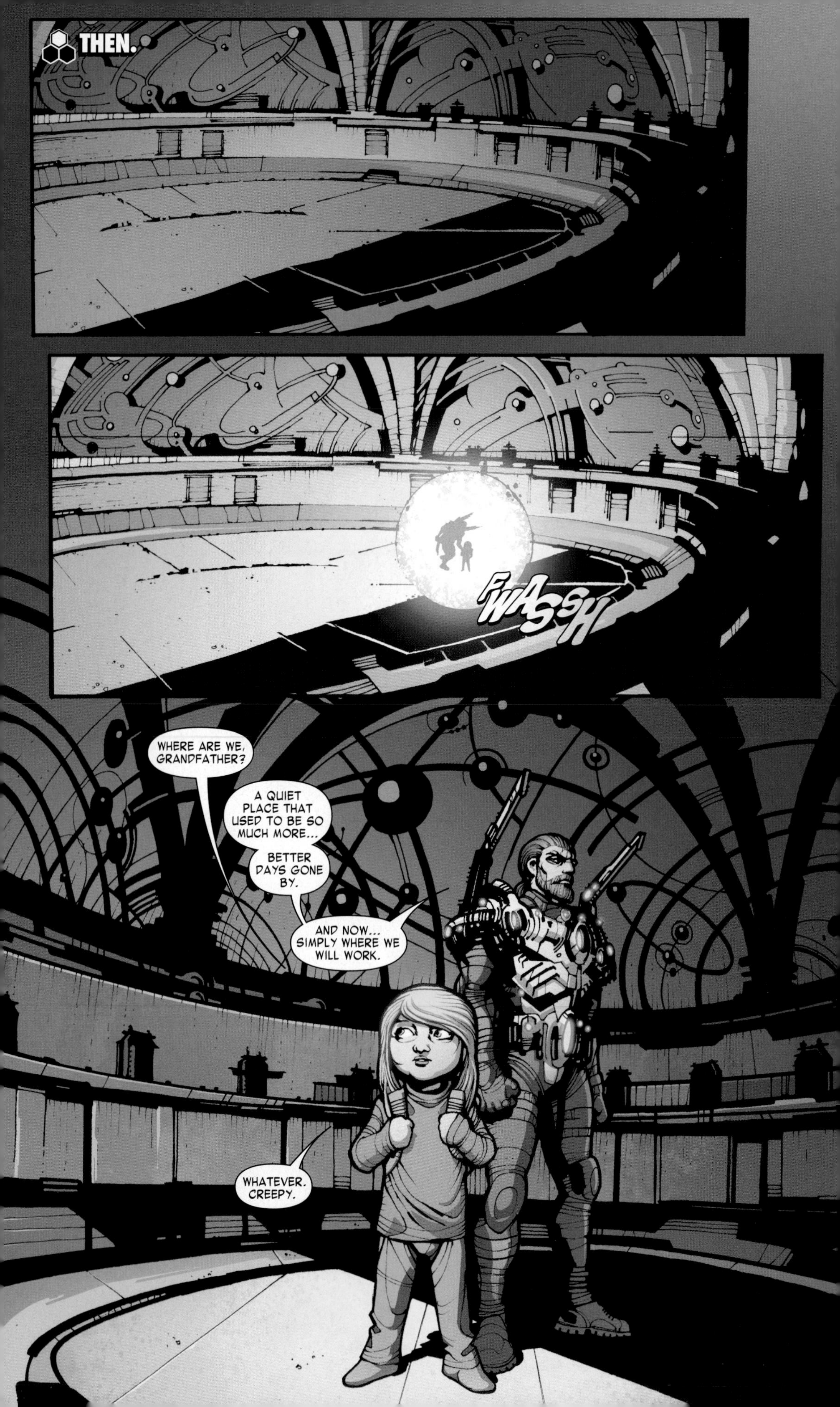
THEN.
FWASSH
WHERE ARE WE, GRANDFATHER?
A QUIET PLACE THAT USED TO BE SO MUCH MORE...
BETTER DAYS GONE BY.
AND NOW... SIMPLY WHERE WE WILL WORK.
WHATEVER. CREEPY.

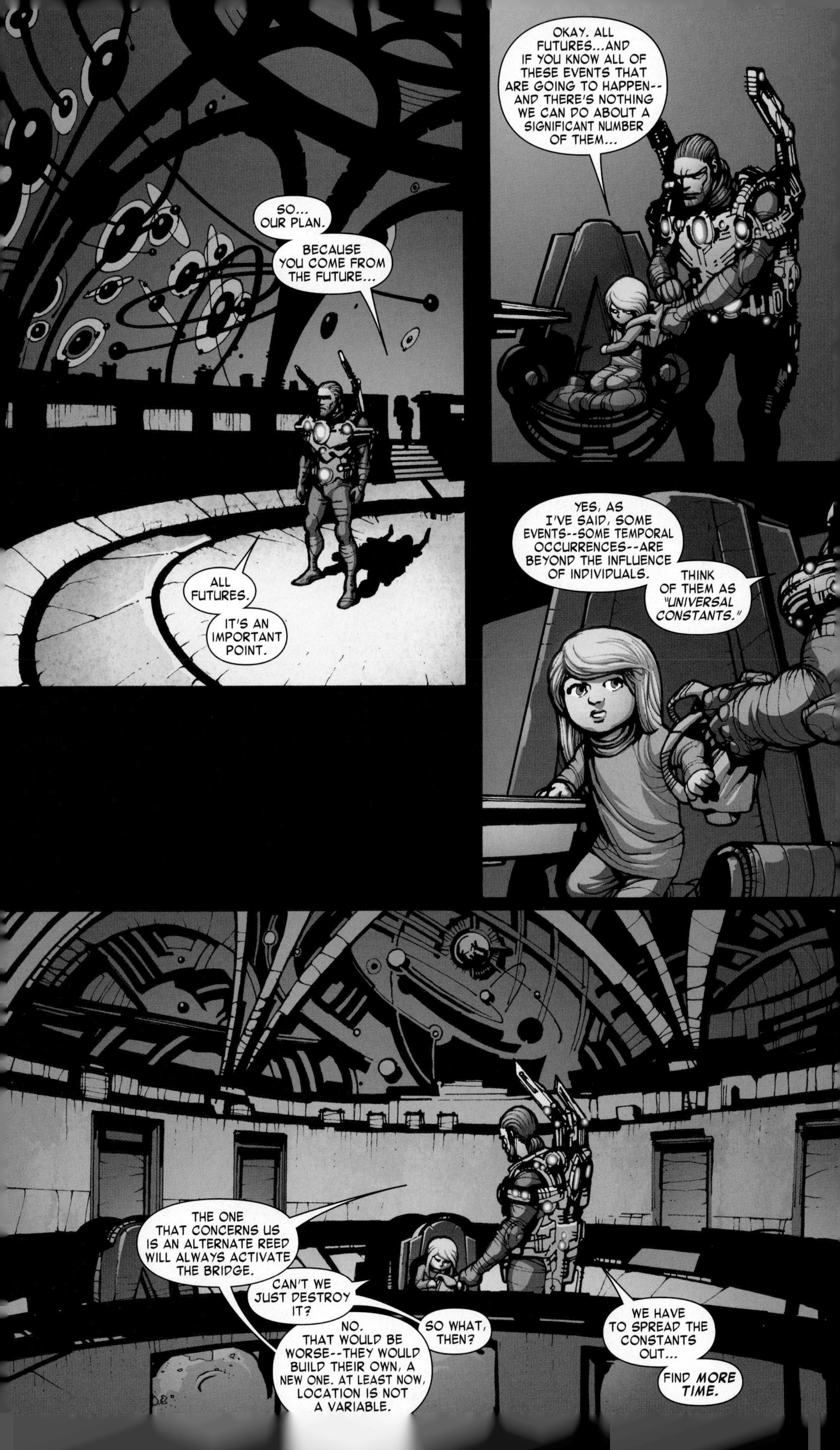
SO... OUR PLAN.
BECAUSE YOU COME FROM THE FUTURE...
ALL FUTURES.
IT'S AN IMPORTANT POINT.
OKAY. ALL FUTURES...AND IF YOU KNOW ALL OF THESE EVENTS THAT ARE GOING TO HAPPEN--AND THERE'S NOTHING WE CAN DO ABOUT A SIGNIFICANT NUMBER OF THEM...
YES, AS I'VE SAID, SOME EVENTS--SOME TEMPORAL OCCURRENCES--ARE BEYOND THE INFLUENCE OF INDIVIDUALS.
THINK OF THEM AS "UNIVERSAL CONSTANTS."
THE ONE THAT CONCERNS US IS AN ALTERNATE REED WILL ALWAYS ACTIVATE THE BRIDGE.
CAN'T WE JUST DESTROY IT?
NO. THAT WOULD BE WORSE--THEY WOULD BUILD THEIR OWN, A NEW ONE. AT LEAST NOW, LOCATION IS NOT A VARIABLE.
SO WHAT, THEN?
WE HAVE TO SPREAD THE CONSTANTS OUT...
FIND MORE TIME.

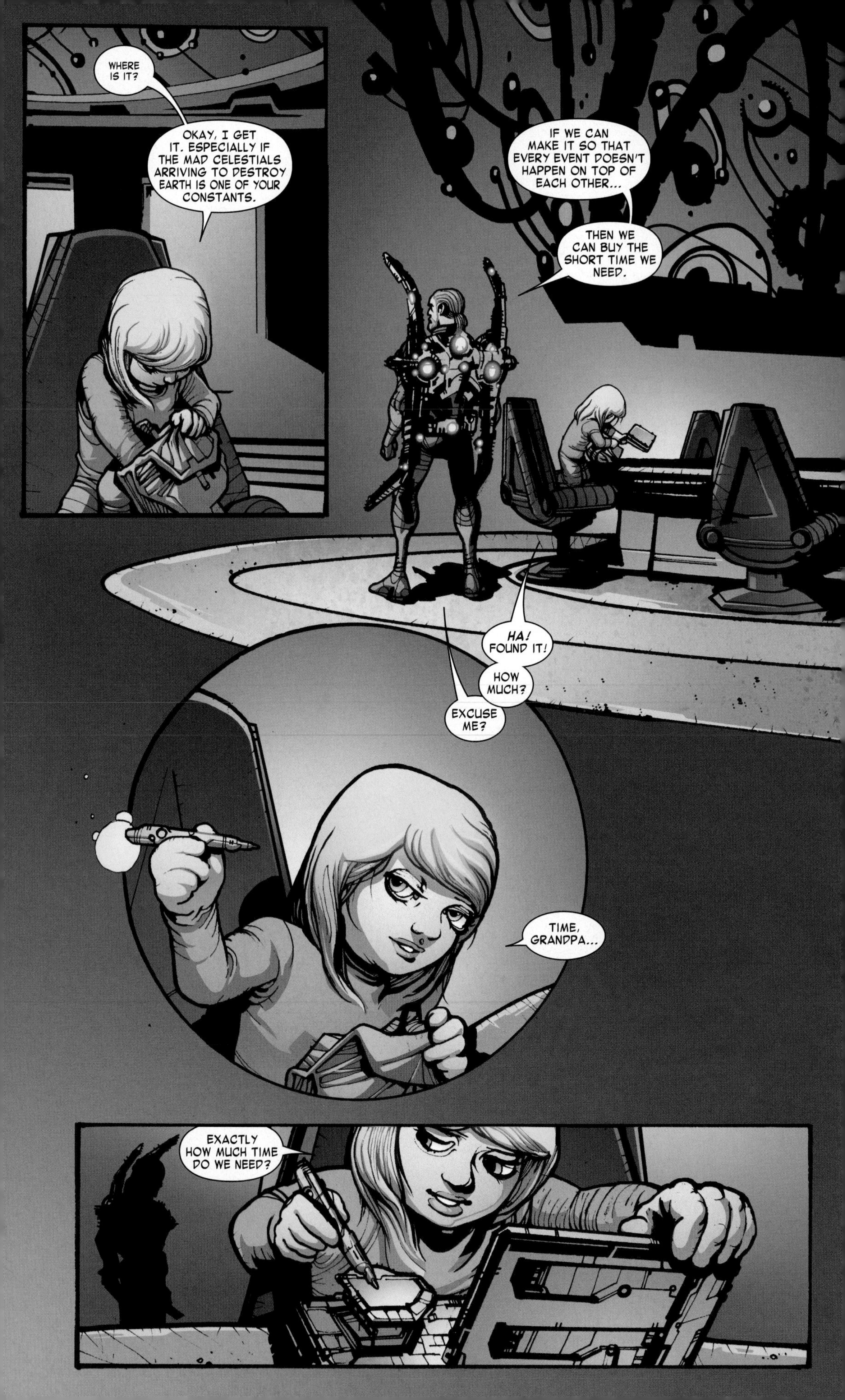
WHERE IS IT?
OKAY, I GET IT. ESPECIALLY IF THE MAD CELESTIALS ARRIVING TO DESTROY EARTH IS ONE OF YOUR CONSTANTS.
IF WE CAN MAKE IT SO THAT EVERY EVENT DOESN'T HAPPEN ON TOP OF EACH OTHER...
THEN WE CAN BUY THE SHORT TIME WE NEED.
HA! FOUND IT!
HOW MUCH?
EXCUSE ME?
TIME, GRANDPA...
EXACTLY HOW MUCH TIME DO WE NEED?

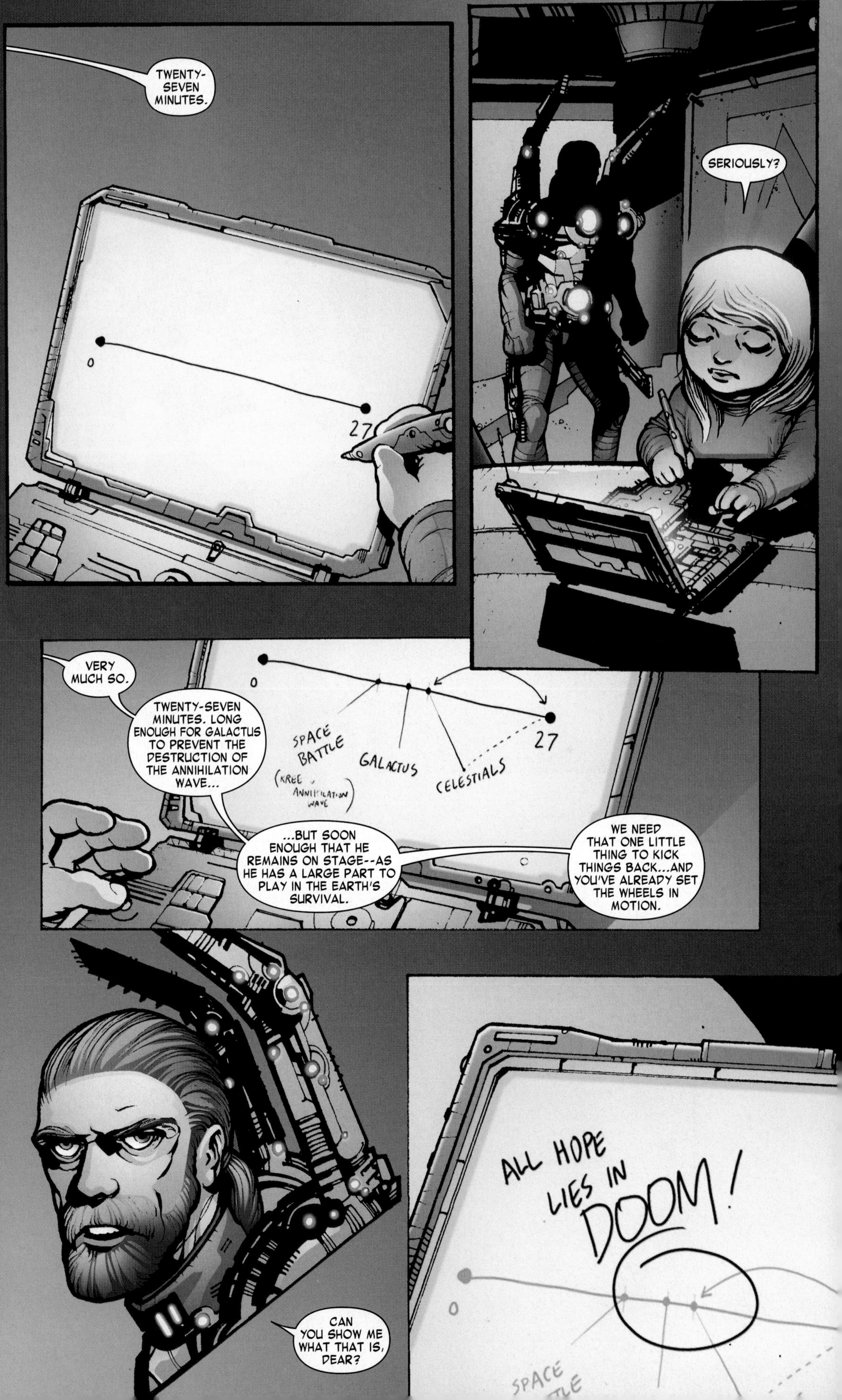
TWENTY-SEVEN MINUTES.
0
27
SERIOUSLY?
VERY MUCH SO.
TWENTY-SEVEN MINUTES. LONG ENOUGH FOR GALACTUS TO PREVENT THE DESTRUCTION OF THE ANNIHILATION WAVE...
...BUT SOON ENOUGH THAT HE REMAINS ON STAGE--AS HE HAS A LARGE PART TO PLAY IN THE EARTH'S SURVIVAL.
WE NEED THAT ONE LITTLE THING TO KICK THINGS BACK...AND YOU'VE ALREADY SET THE WHEELS IN MOTION.
0
27
SPACE BATTLE
GALACTUS
CELESTIALS
CAN YOU SHOW ME WHAT THAT IS, DEAR?
ALL HOPE LIES IN DOOM!
0

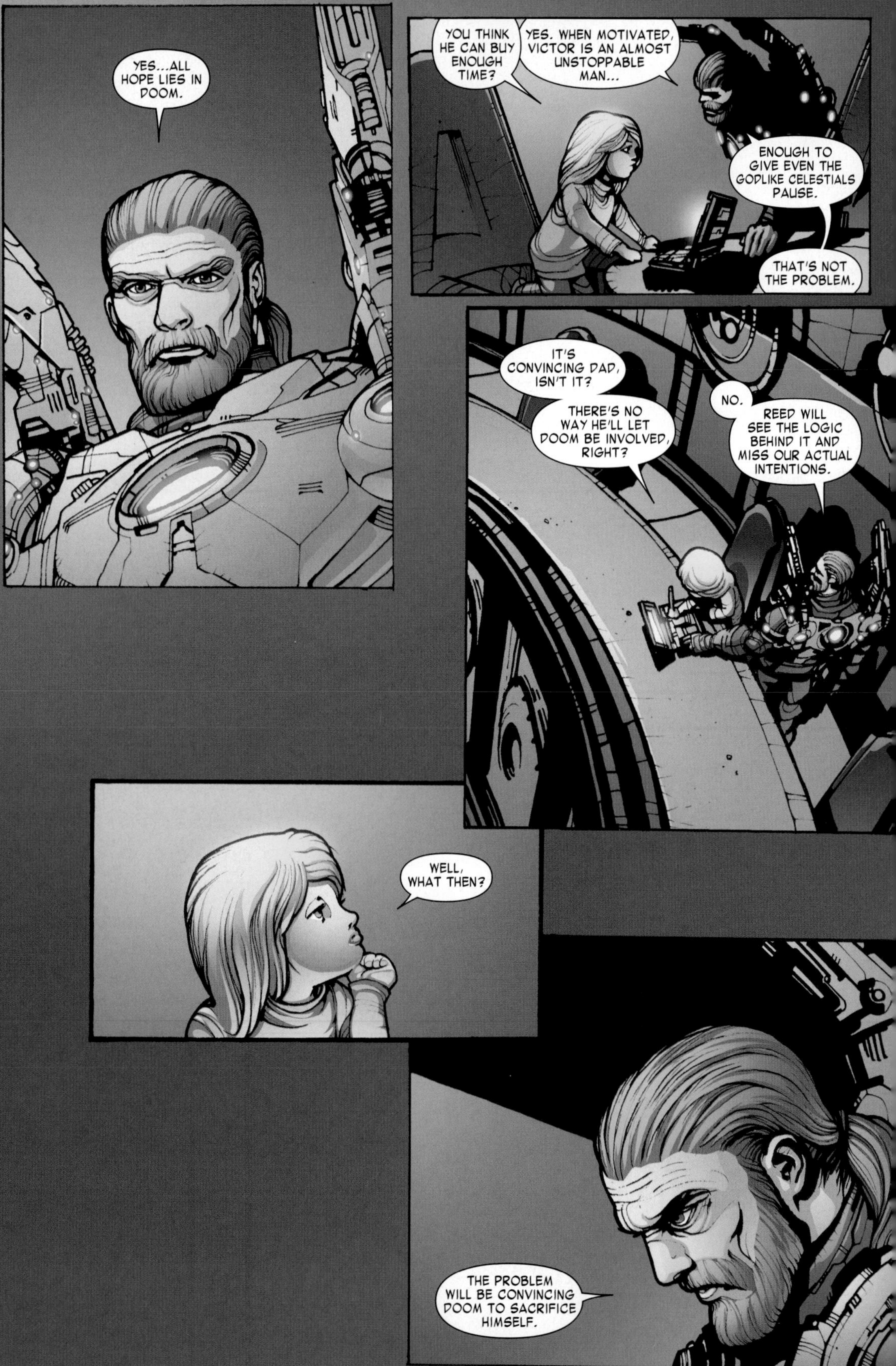
YES...ALL HOPE LIES IN DOOM.
YOU THINK HE CAN BUY ENOUGH TIME?
YES. WHEN MOTIVATED, VICTOR IS AN ALMOST UNSTOPPABLE MAN...
ENOUGH TO GIVE EVEN THE GODLIKE CELESTIALS PAUSE.
THAT'S NOT THE PROBLEM.
IT'S CONVINCING DAD, ISN'T IT?
THERE'S NO WAY HE'LL LET DOOM BE INVOLVED, RIGHT?
NO.
REED WILL SEE THE LOGIC BEHIND IT AND MISS OUR ACTUAL INTENTIONS.
WELL, WHAT THEN?
THE PROBLEM WILL BE CONVINCING DOOM TO SACRIFICE HIMSELF.

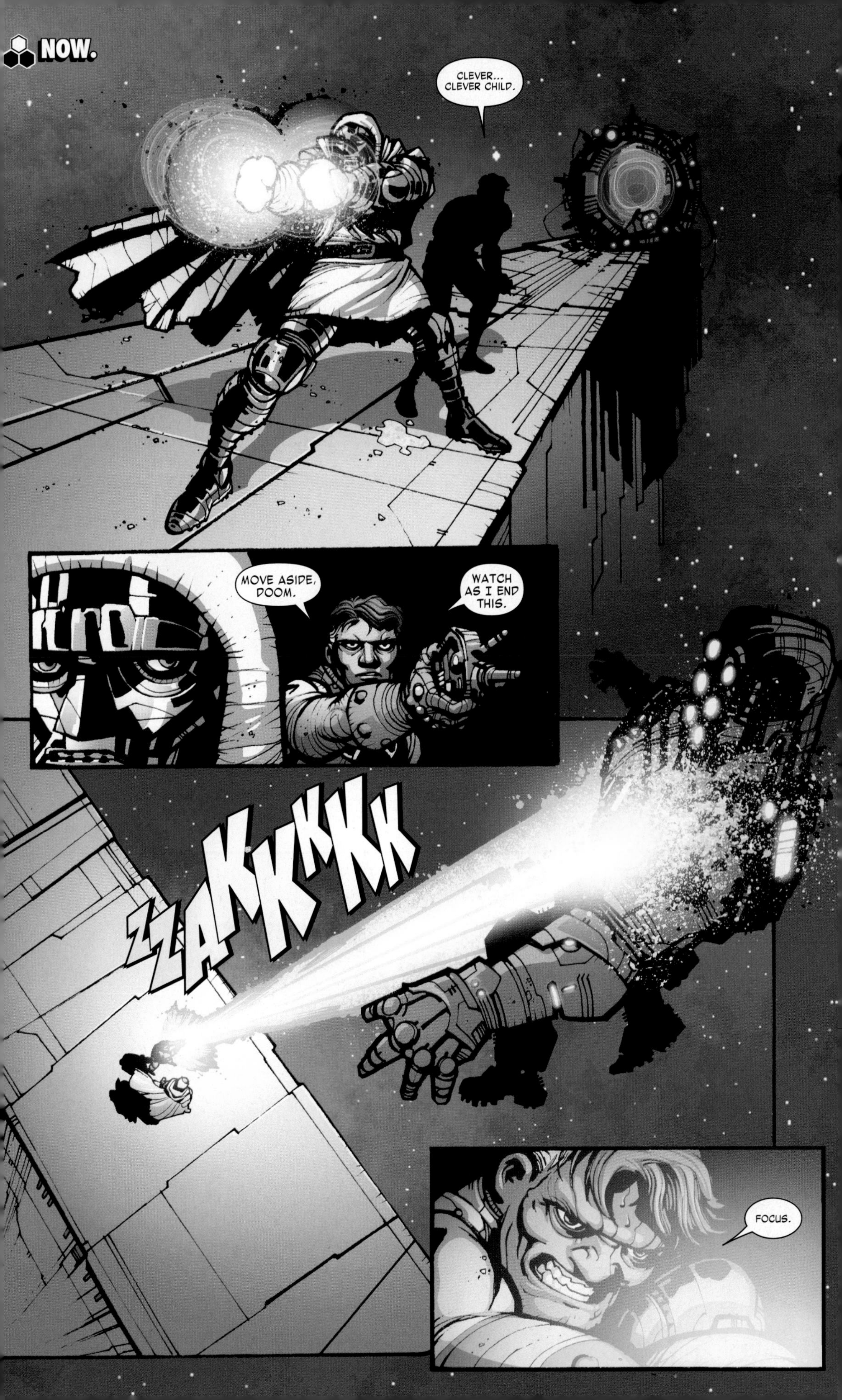
NOW.
CLEVER... CLEVER CHILD.
MOVE ASIDE, DOOM.
WATCH AS I END THIS.
ZZAKKKKK
FOCUS.

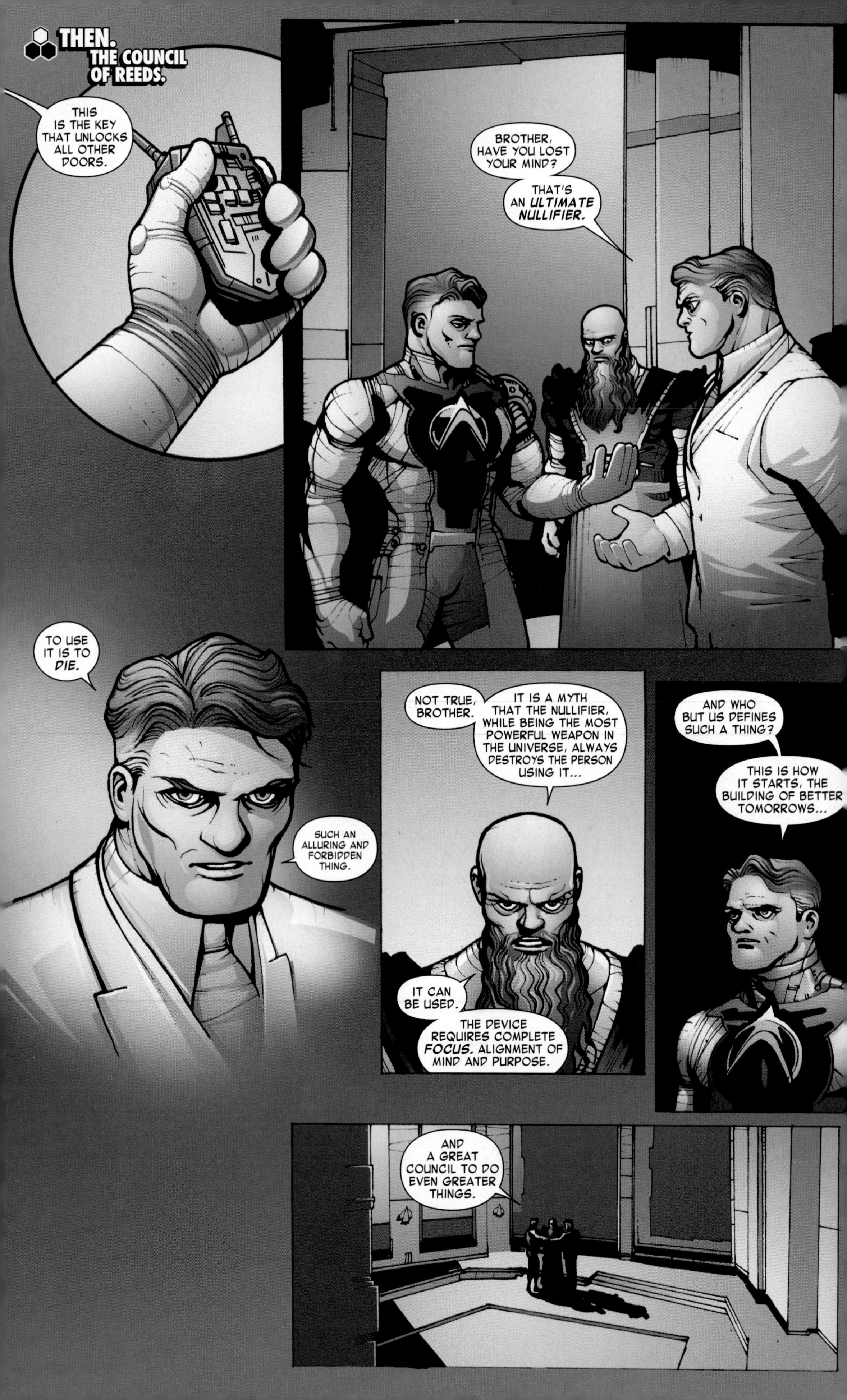
THEN. THE COUNCIL OF REEDS.
THIS IS THE KEY THAT UNLOCKS ALL OTHER DOORS.
BROTHER, HAVE YOU LOST YOUR MIND?
THAT'S AN *ULTIMATE NULLIFIER.*
TO USE IT IS TO *DIE.*
SUCH AN ALLURING AND FORBIDDEN THING.
NOT TRUE, BROTHER.
IT IS A MYTH THAT THE NULLIFIER, WHILE BEING THE MOST POWERFUL WEAPON IN THE UNIVERSE, ALWAYS DESTROYS THE PERSON USING IT...
IT CAN BE USED.
THE DEVICE REQUIRES COMPLETE *FOCUS.* ALIGNMENT OF MIND AND PURPOSE.
AND WHO BUT US DEFINES SUCH A THING?
THIS IS HOW IT STARTS, THE BUILDING OF BETTER TOMORROWS...
AND A GREAT COUNCIL TO DO EVEN GREATER THINGS.

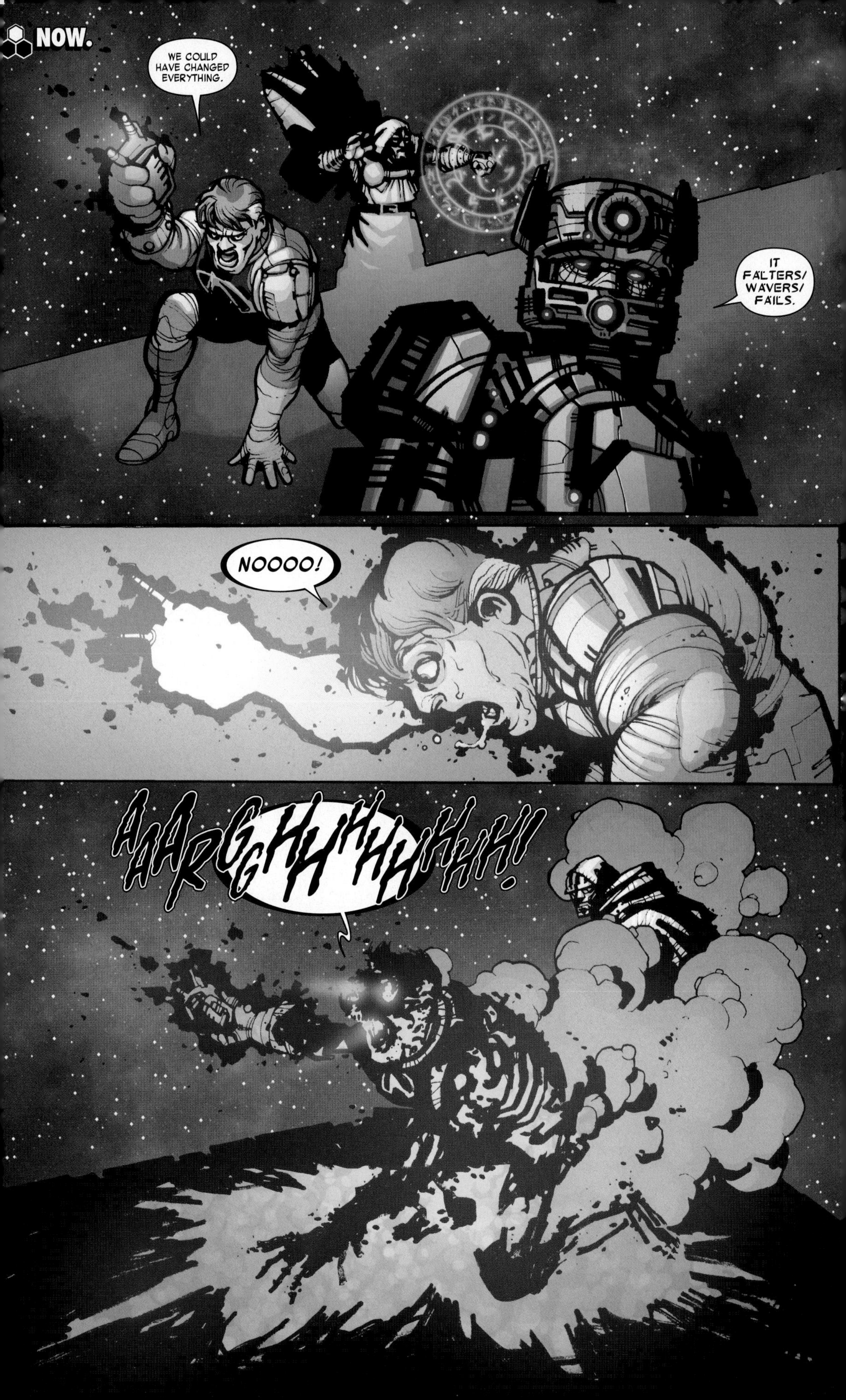
NOW.
WE COULD HAVE CHANGED EVERYTHING.
IT FALTERS/ WAVERS/ FAILS.
NOOOO!
AAARGHHHHHHHHHH!

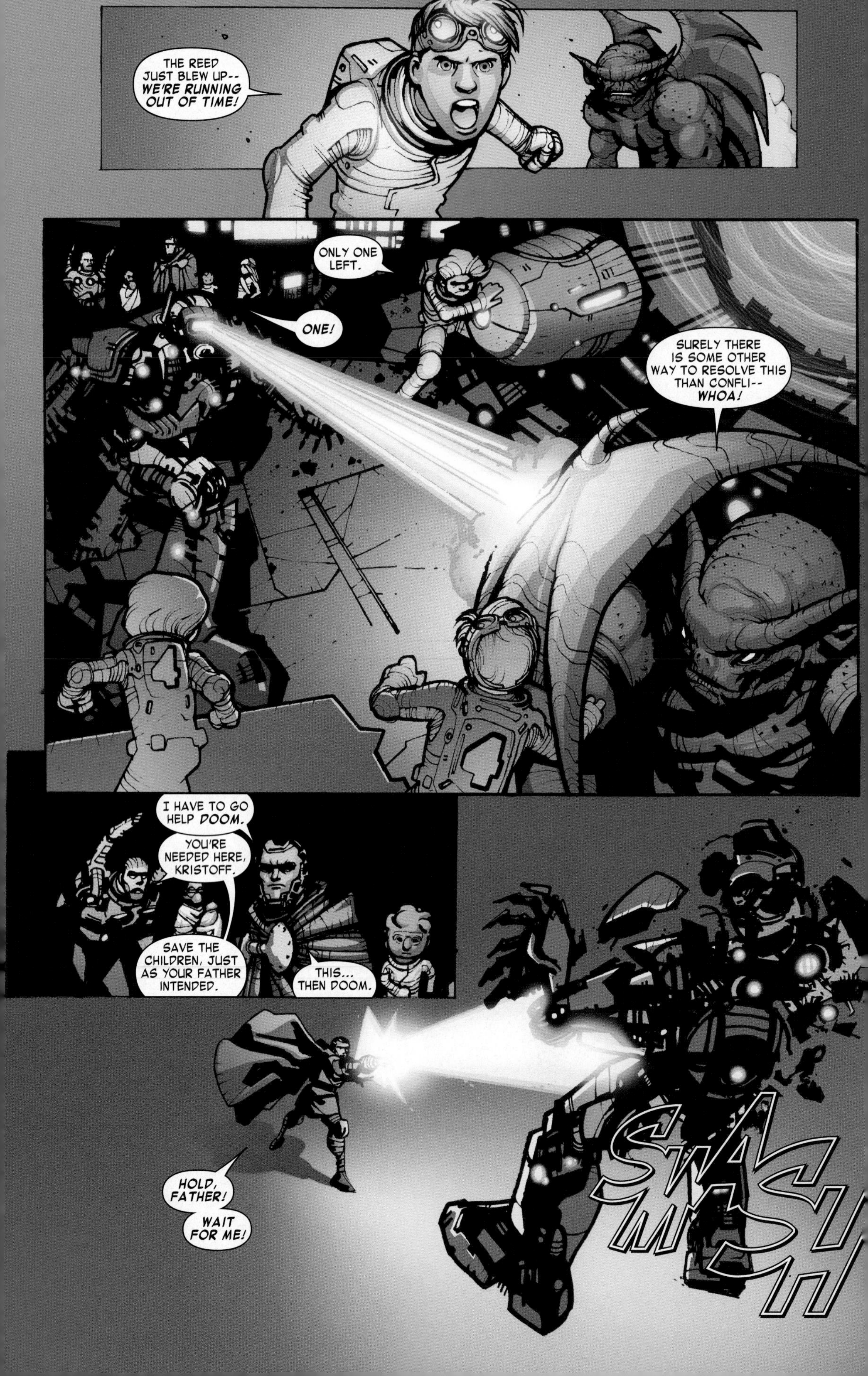
THE REED JUST BLEW UP-- WE'RE RUNNING OUT OF TIME!
ONLY ONE LEFT.
ONE!
SURELY THERE IS SOME OTHER WAY TO RESOLVE THIS THAN CONFLI-- WHOA!
I HAVE TO GO HELP DOOM.
YOU'RE NEEDED HERE, KRISTOFF.
SAVE THE CHILDREN, JUST AS YOUR FATHER INTENDED.
THIS... THEN DOOM.
HOLD, FATHER!
WAIT FOR ME!
SWASH
MASH

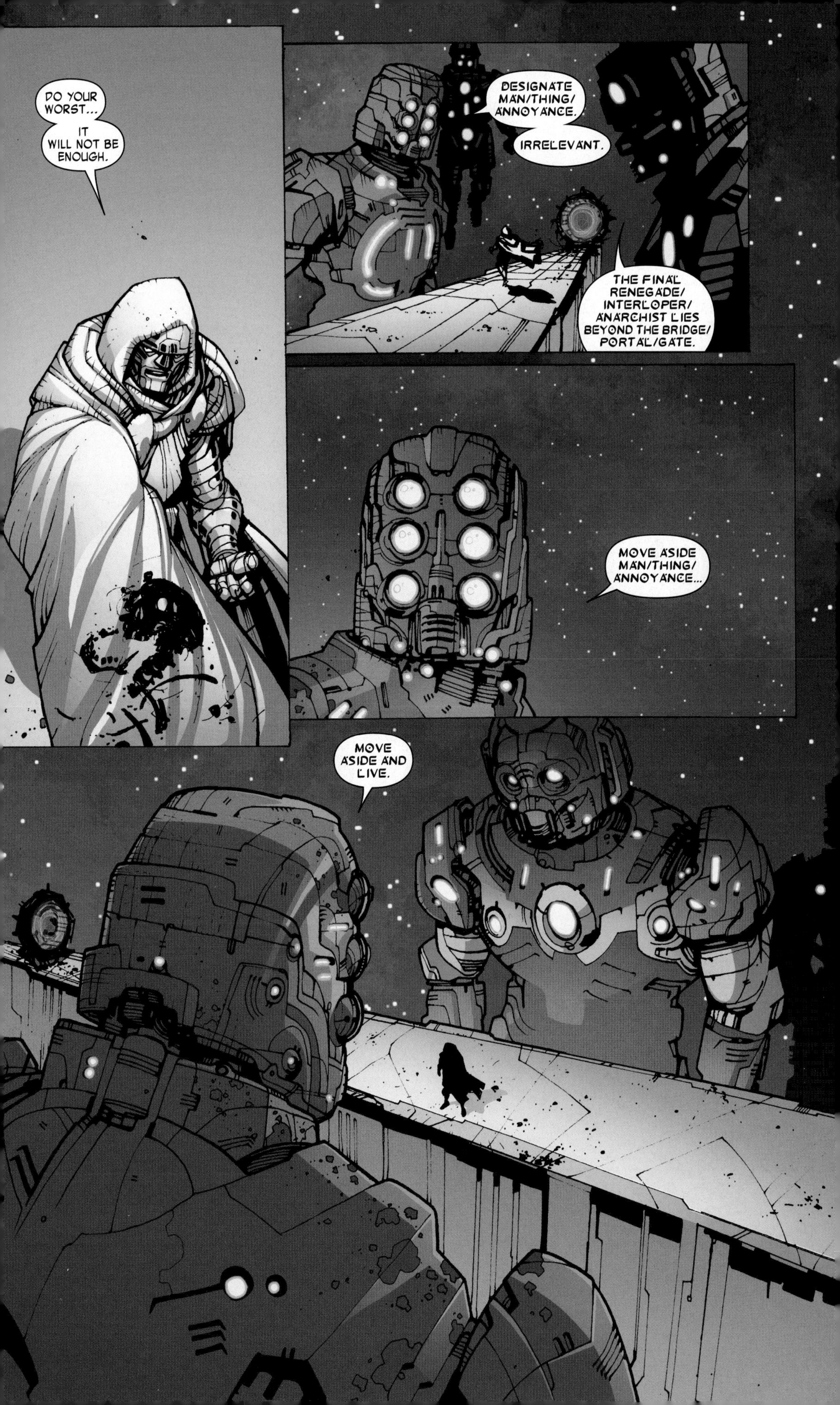
DO YOUR WORST... IT WILL NOT BE ENOUGH.
DESIGNATE MAN/THING/ ANNOYANCE.
IRRELEVANT.
THE FINAL RENEGADE/ INTERLOPER/ ANARCHIST LIES BEYOND THE BRIDGE/ PORTAL/GATE.
MOVE ASIDE MAN/THING/ ANNOYANCE...
MOVE ASIDE AND LIVE.

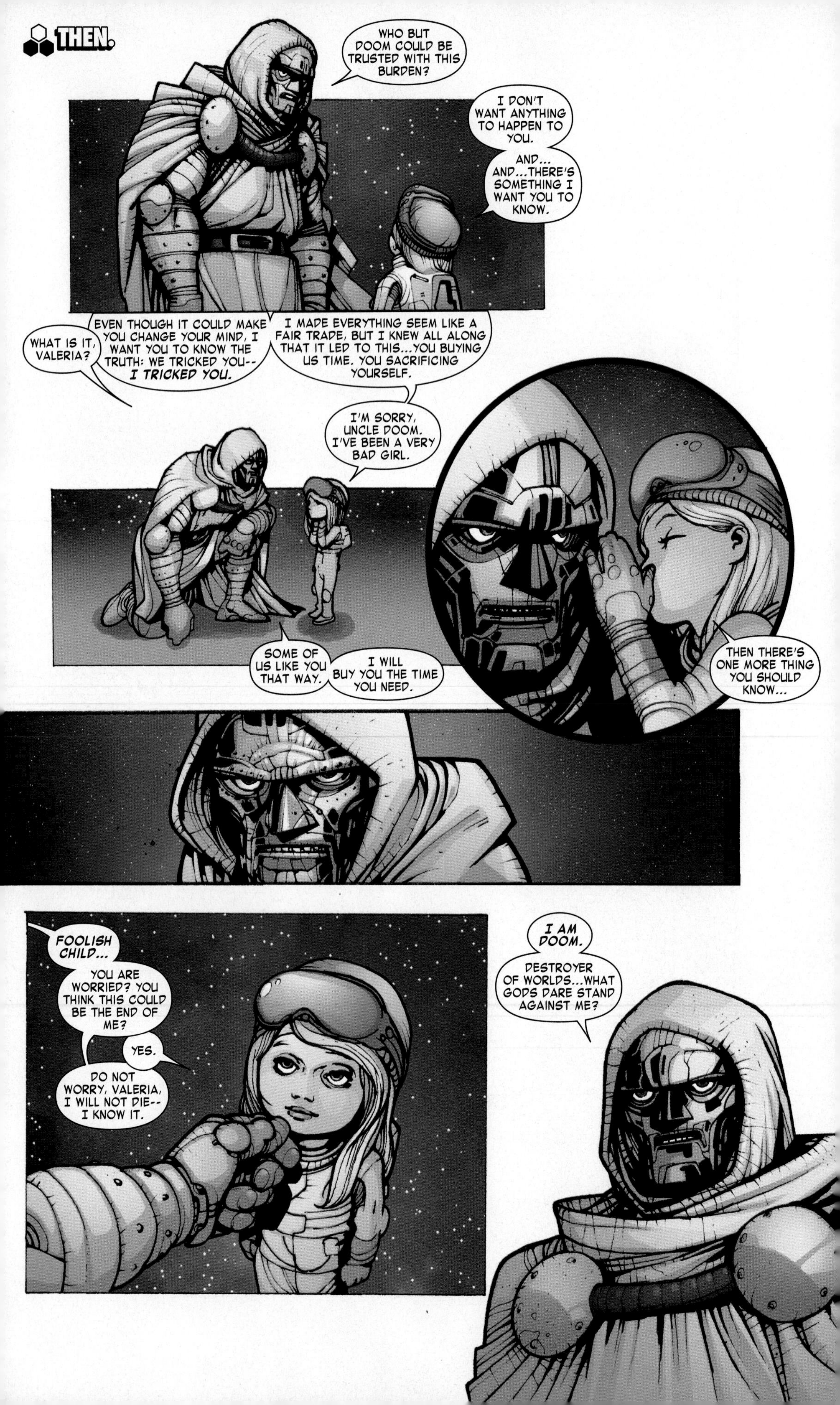
THEN.
WHO BUT DOOM COULD BE TRUSTED WITH THIS BURDEN?
I DON'T WANT ANYTHING TO HAPPEN TO YOU.
AND... AND...THERE'S SOMETHING I WANT YOU TO KNOW.
WHAT IS IT, VALERIA?
EVEN THOUGH IT COULD MAKE YOU CHANGE YOUR MIND, I WANT YOU TO KNOW THE TRUTH: WE TRICKED YOU-- I TRICKED YOU.
I MADE EVERYTHING SEEM LIKE A FAIR TRADE, BUT I KNEW ALL ALONG THAT IT LED TO THIS...YOU BUYING US TIME. YOU SACRIFICING YOURSELF.
I'M SORRY, UNCLE DOOM. I'VE BEEN A VERY BAD GIRL.
SOME OF US LIKE YOU THAT WAY.
I WILL BUY YOU THE TIME YOU NEED.
THEN THERE'S ONE MORE THING YOU SHOULD KNOW...
FOOLISH CHILD...
YOU ARE WORRIED? YOU THINK THIS COULD BE THE END OF ME?
YES.
DO NOT WORRY, VALERIA, I WILL NOT DIE-- I KNOW IT.
I AM DOOM.
DESTROYER OF WORLDS...WHAT GODS DARE STAND AGAINST ME?

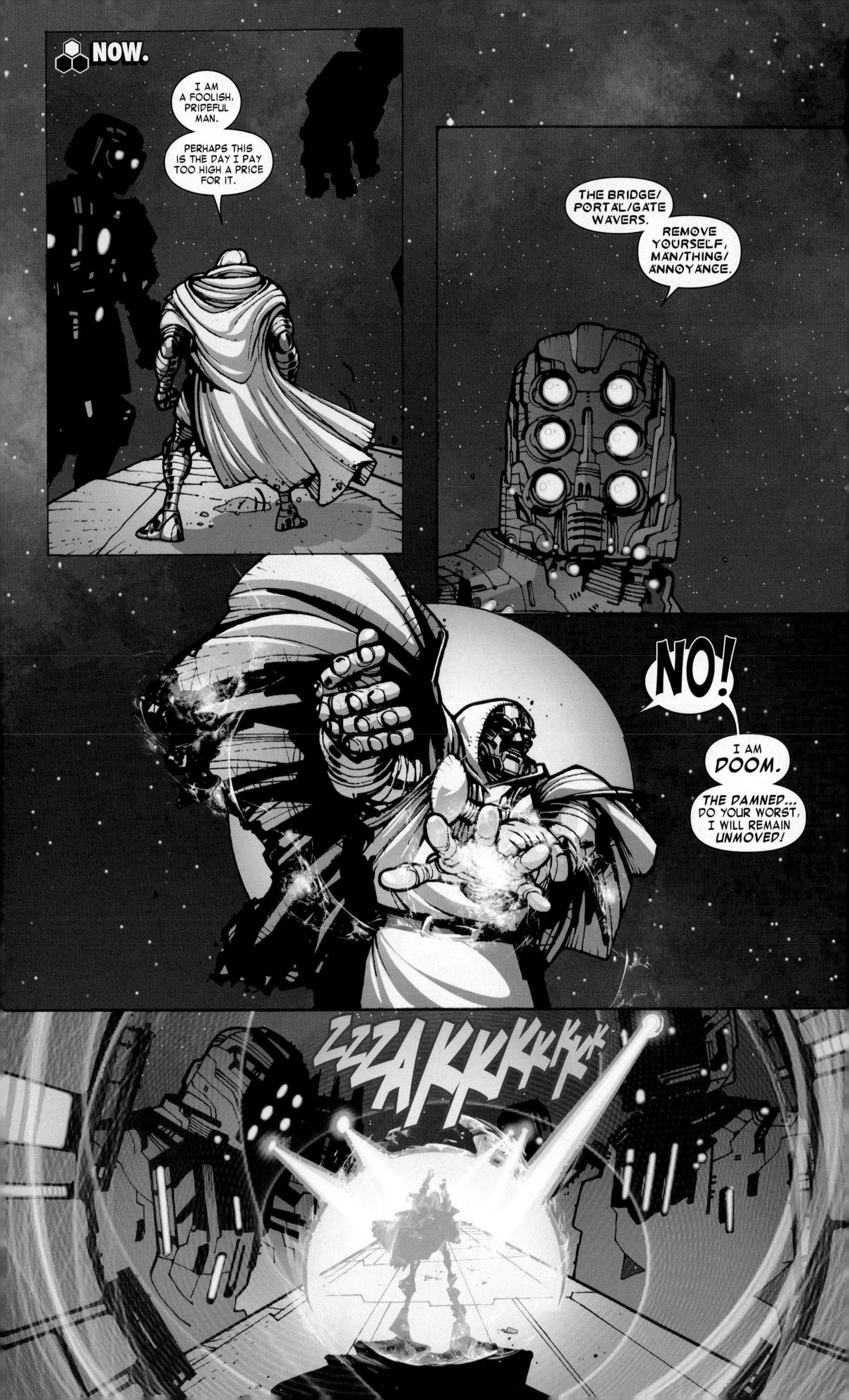
NOW.
I AM A FOOLISH, PRIDEFUL MAN.
PERHAPS THIS IS THE DAY I PAY TOO HIGH A PRICE FOR IT.
THE BRIDGE/ PORTAL/GATE WAVERS.
REMOVE YOURSELF, MAN/THING/ ANNOYANCE.
NO!
I AM DOOM.
THE DAMNED... DO YOUR WORST, I WILL REMAIN UNMOVED!
ZZZAKKKKKK

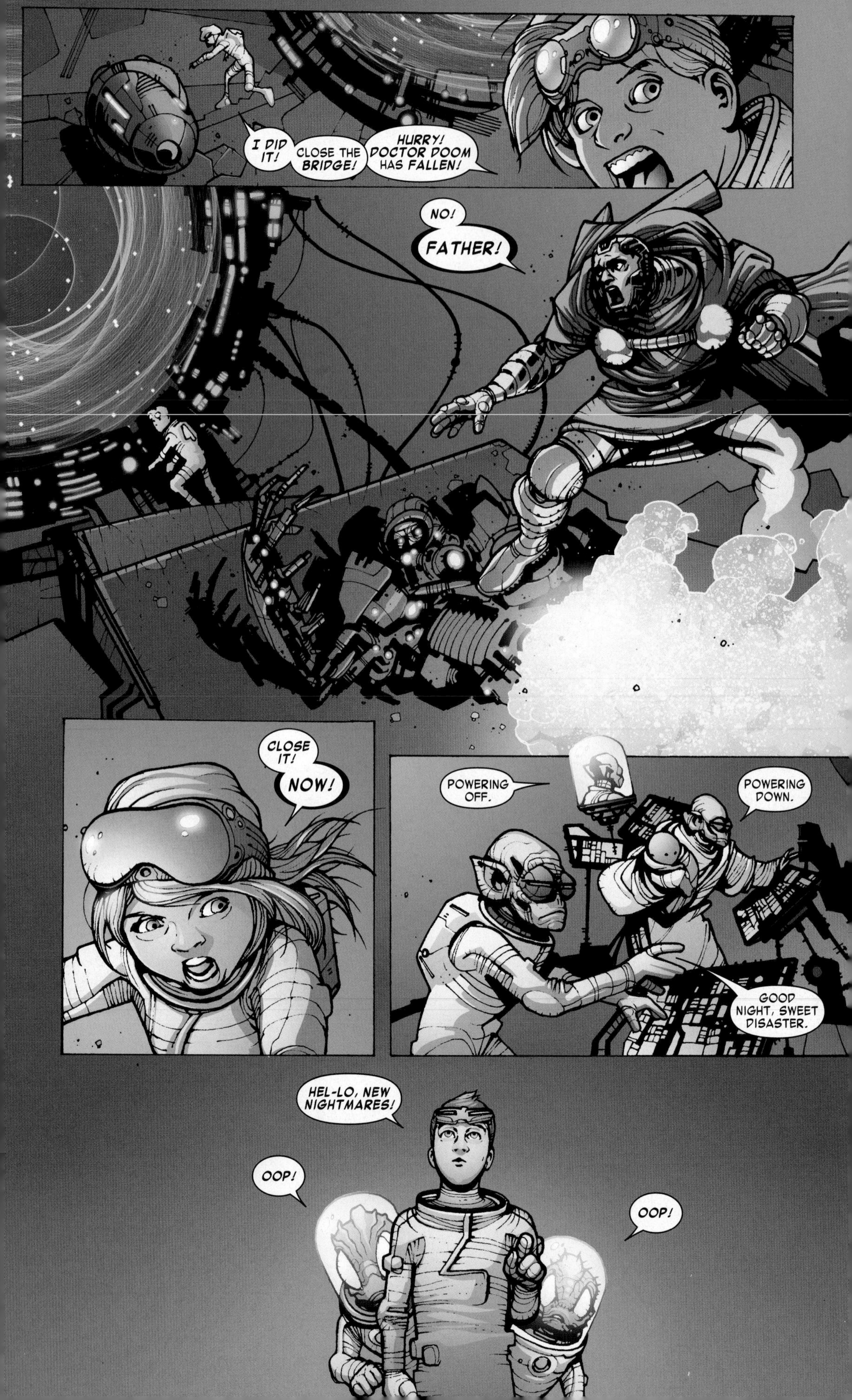
I DID IT!
CLOSE THE BRIDGE!
HURRY! DOCTOR DOOM HAS FALLEN!
NO!
FATHER!
CLOSE IT!
NOW!
POWERING OFF.
POWERING DOWN.
GOOD NIGHT, SWEET DISASTER.
HEL-LO, NEW NIGHTMARES!
OOP!
OOP!

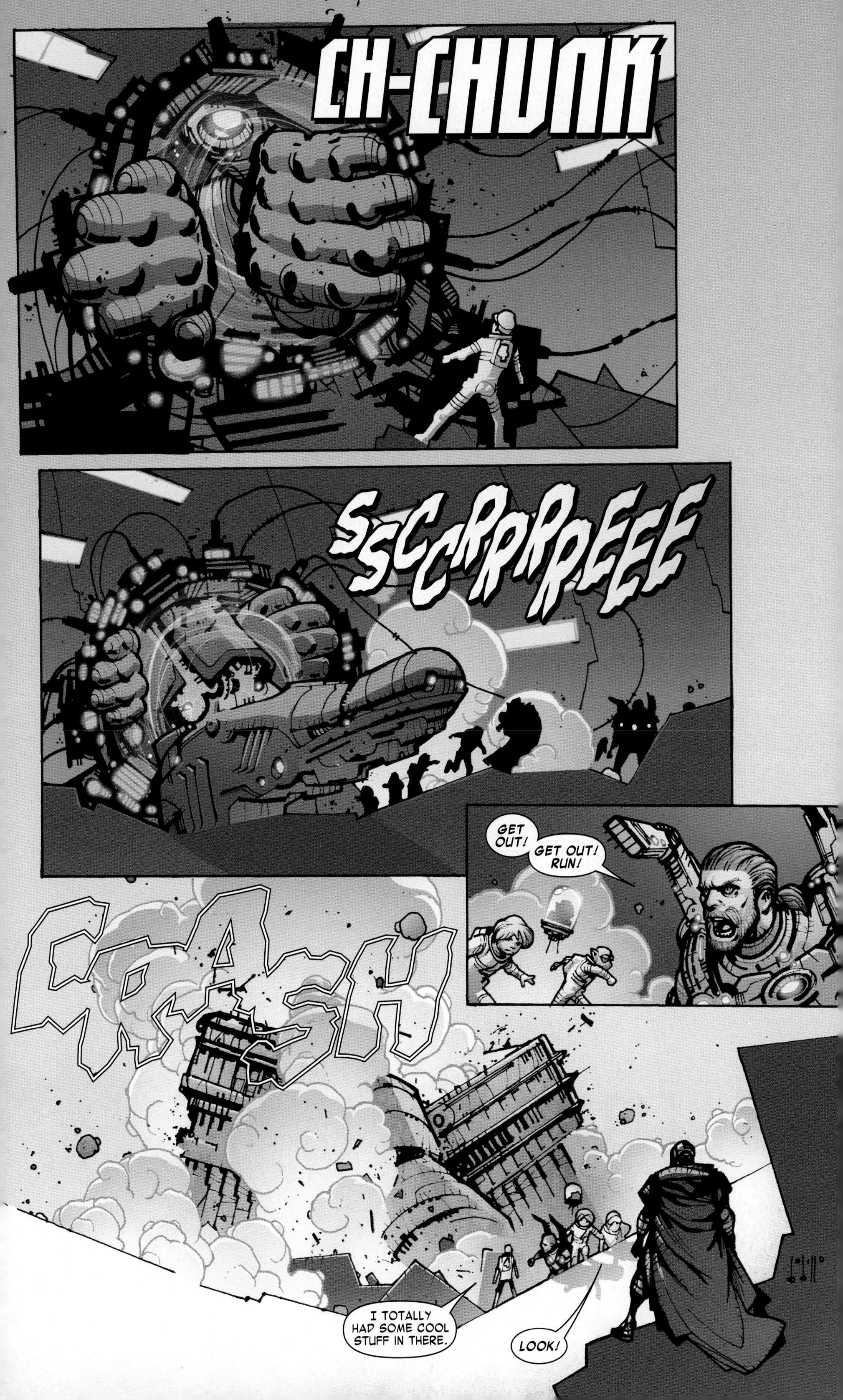
CH-CHUNK
SSCRRRREEE
GET OUT!
GET OUT! RUN!
CRASH
I TOTALLY HAD SOME COOL STUFF IN THERE.
LOOK!

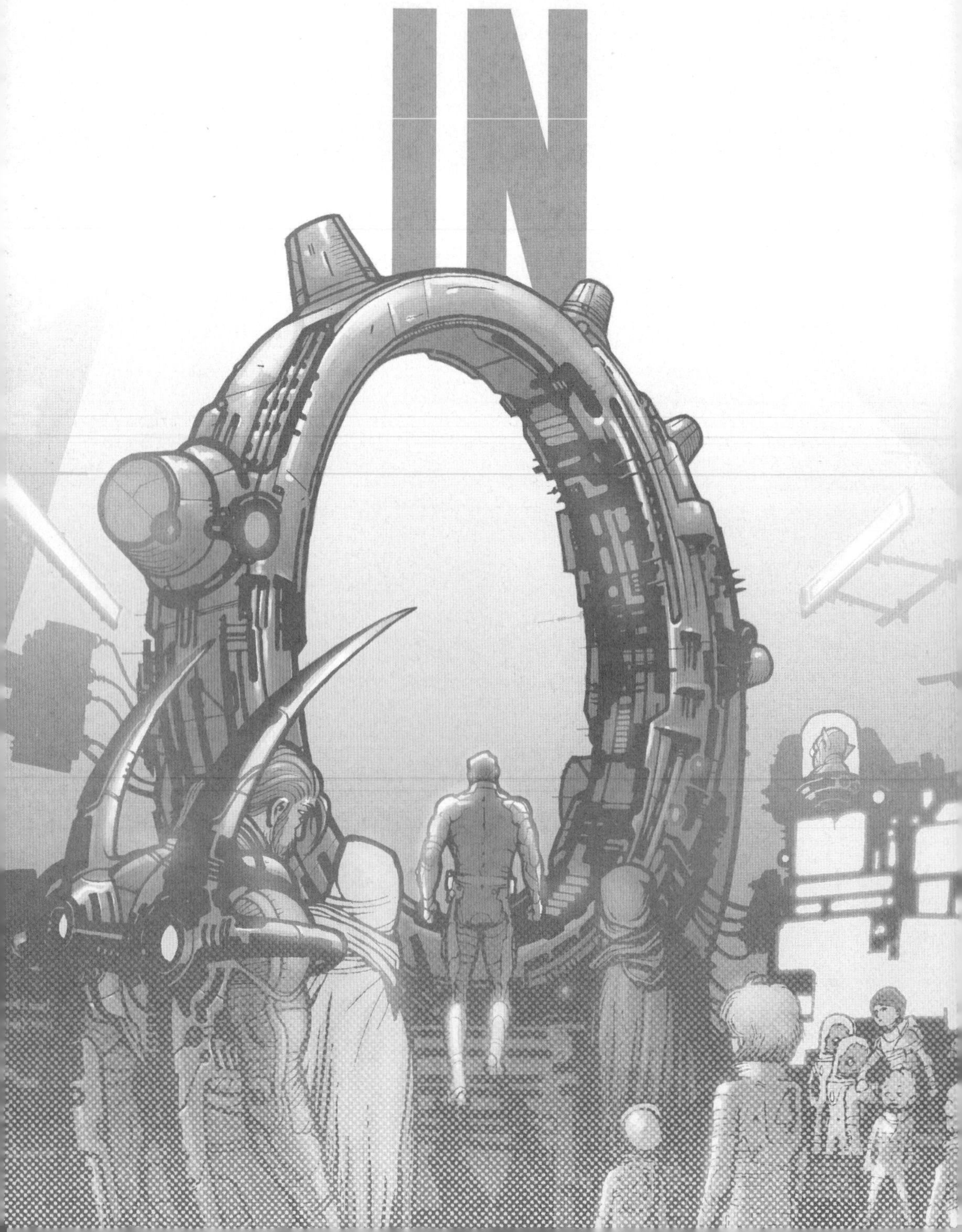
IN

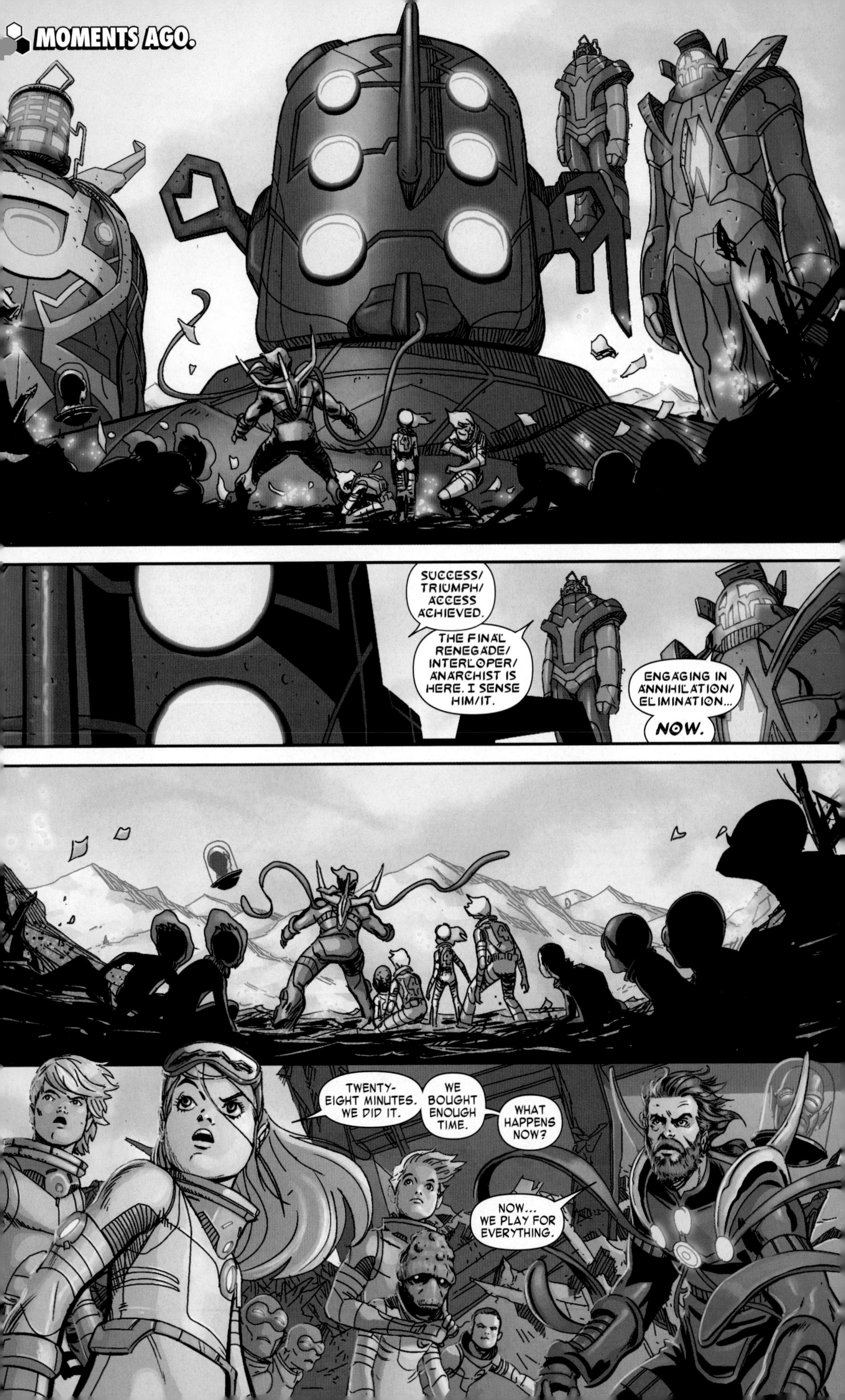
MOMENTS AGO.
SUCCESS/ TRIUMPH/ ACCESS ACHIEVED.
THE FINAL RENEGADE/ INTERLOPER/ ANARCHIST IS HERE. I SENSE HIM/IT.
ENGAGING IN ANNIHILATION/ ELIMINATION...
NOW.
TWENTY-EIGHT MINUTES. WE DID IT.
WE BOUGHT ENOUGH TIME.
WHAT HAPPENS NOW?
NOW... WE PLAY FOR EVERYTHING.

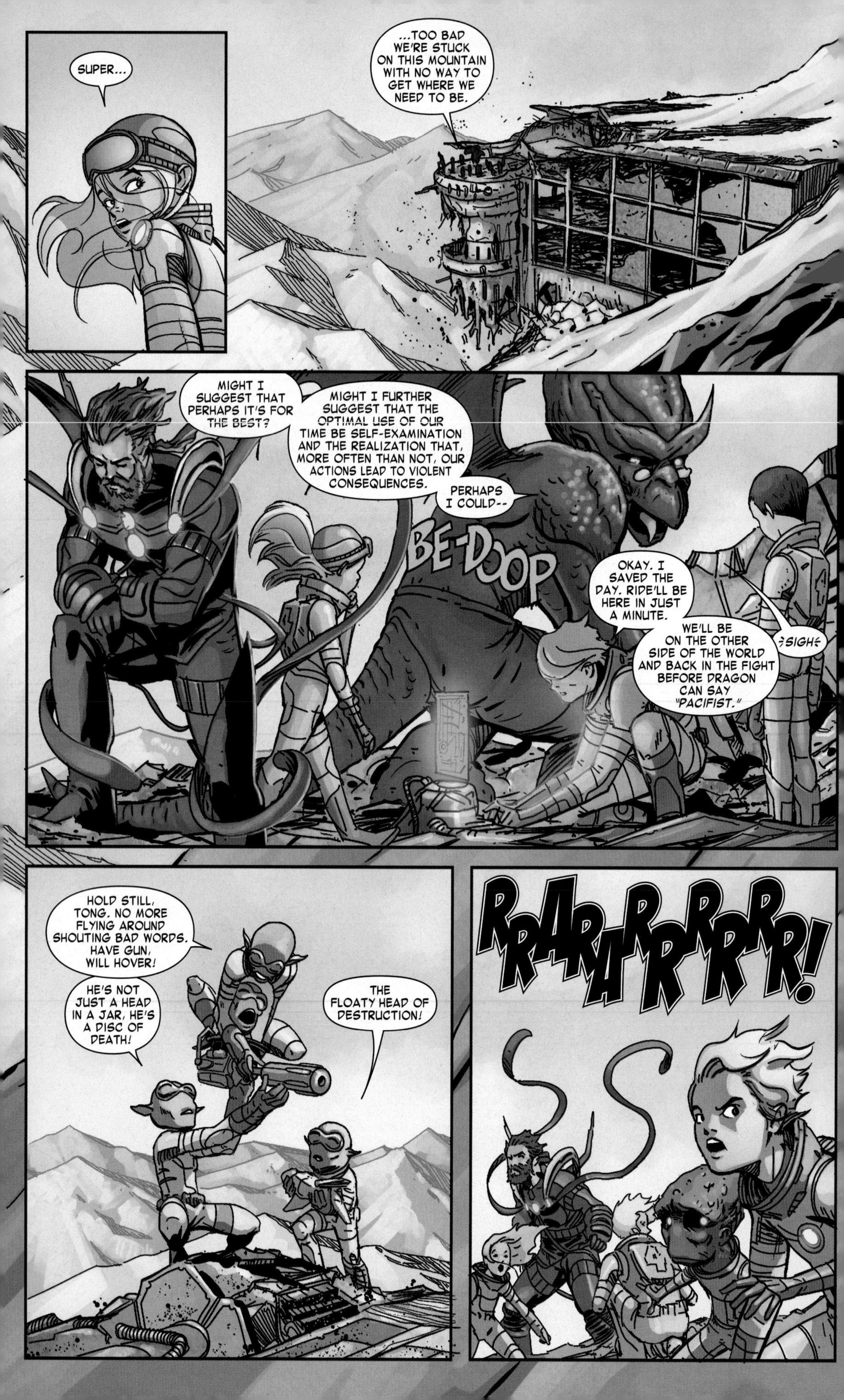
SUPER...
...TOO BAD WE'RE STUCK ON THIS MOUNTAIN WITH NO WAY TO GET WHERE WE NEED TO BE.
MIGHT I SUGGEST THAT PERHAPS IT'S FOR THE BEST?
MIGHT I FURTHER SUGGEST THAT THE OPTIMAL USE OF OUR TIME BE SELF-EXAMINATION AND THE REALIZATION THAT, MORE OFTEN THAN NOT, OUR ACTIONS LEAD TO VIOLENT CONSEQUENCES.
PERHAPS I COULD--
BE-DOOP
OKAY. I SAVED THE DAY. RIDE'LL BE HERE IN JUST A MINUTE.
WE'LL BE ON THE OTHER SIDE OF THE WORLD AND BACK IN THE FIGHT BEFORE DRAGON CAN SAY "PACIFIST."
SIGH
HOLD STILL, TONG. NO MORE FLYING AROUND SHOUTING BAD WORDS. HAVE GUN, WILL HOVER!
HE'S NOT JUST A HEAD IN A JAR, HE'S A DISC OF DEATH!
THE FLOATY HEAD OF DESTRUCTION!
RRARARRRRR!

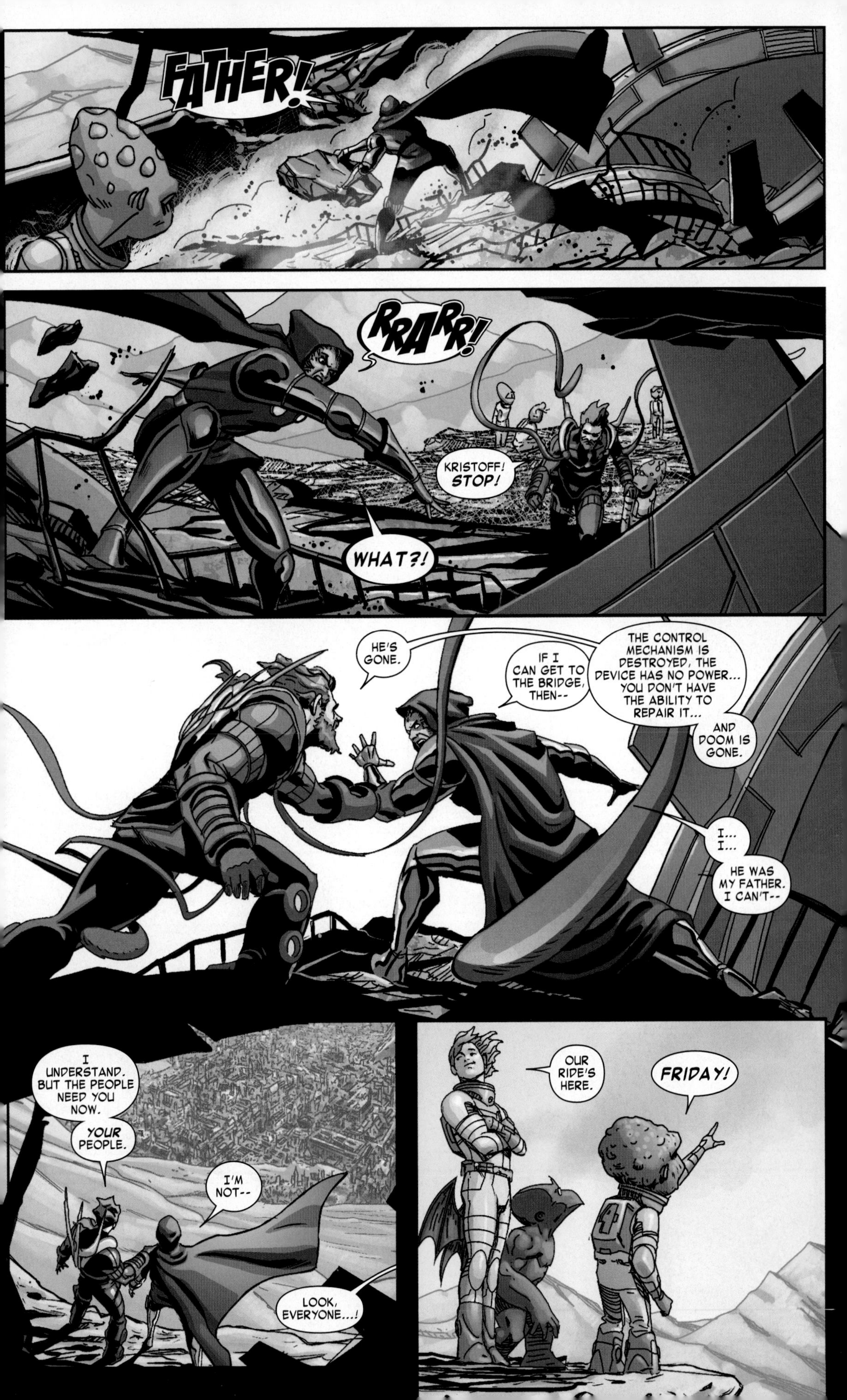
FATHER!
RRARR!
KRISTOFF! STOP!
WHAT?!
HE'S GONE.
IF I CAN GET TO THE BRIDGE, THEN--
THE CONTROL MECHANISM IS DESTROYED, THE DEVICE HAS NO POWER... YOU DON'T HAVE THE ABILITY TO REPAIR IT...
AND DOOM IS GONE.
I... I...
HE WAS MY FATHER. I CAN'T--
I UNDERSTAND. BUT THE PEOPLE NEED YOU NOW.
YOUR PEOPLE.
I'M NOT--
LOOK, EVERYONE...!
OUR RIDE'S HERE.
FRIDAY!

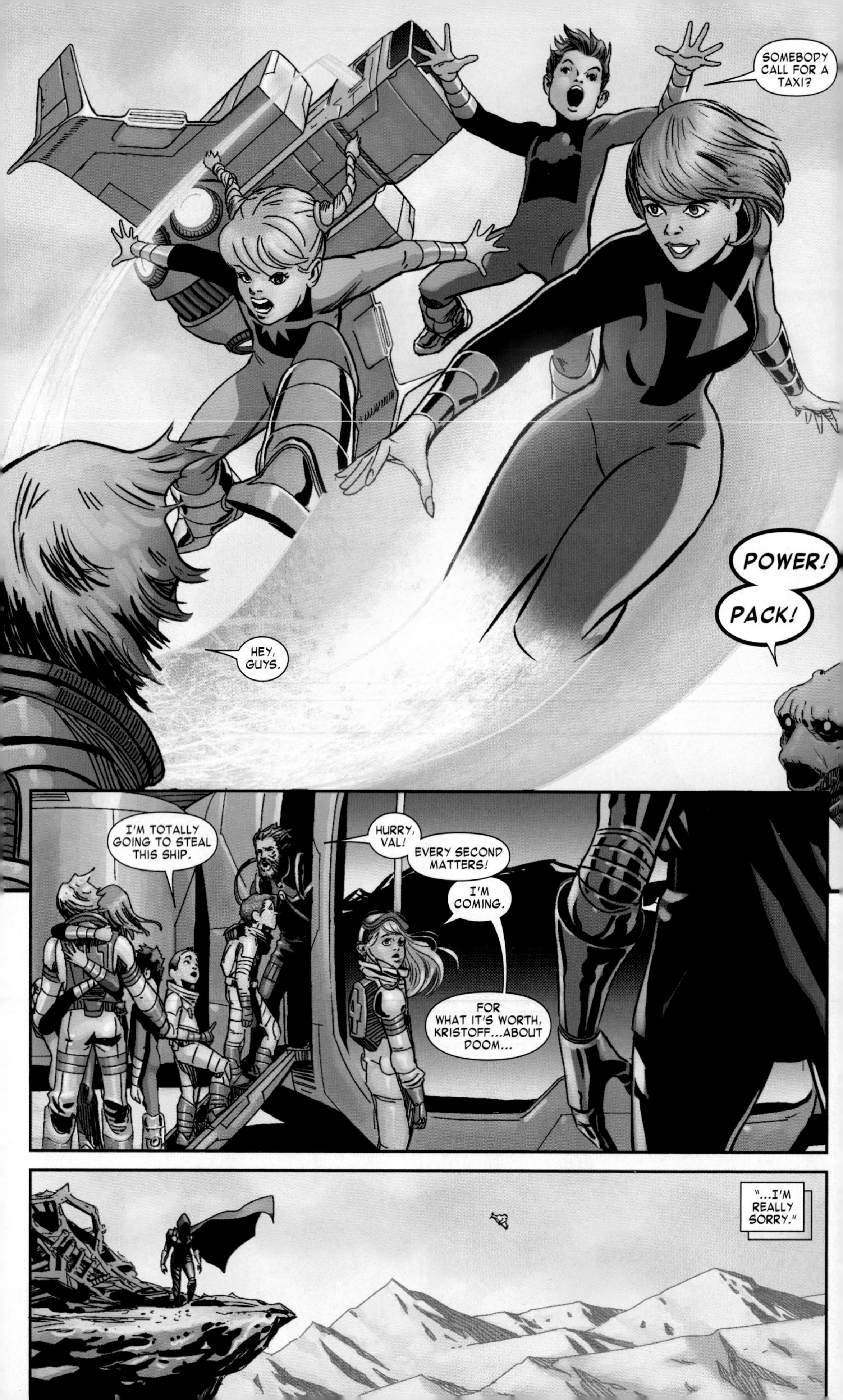
SOMEBODY CALL FOR A TAXI?
HEY, GUYS.
POWER!
PACK!
I'M TOTALLY GOING TO STEAL THIS SHIP.
HURRY, VAL!
EVERY SECOND MATTERS!
I'M COMING.
FOR WHAT IT'S WORTH, KRISTOFF...ABOUT DOOM...
"...I'M REALLY SORRY."

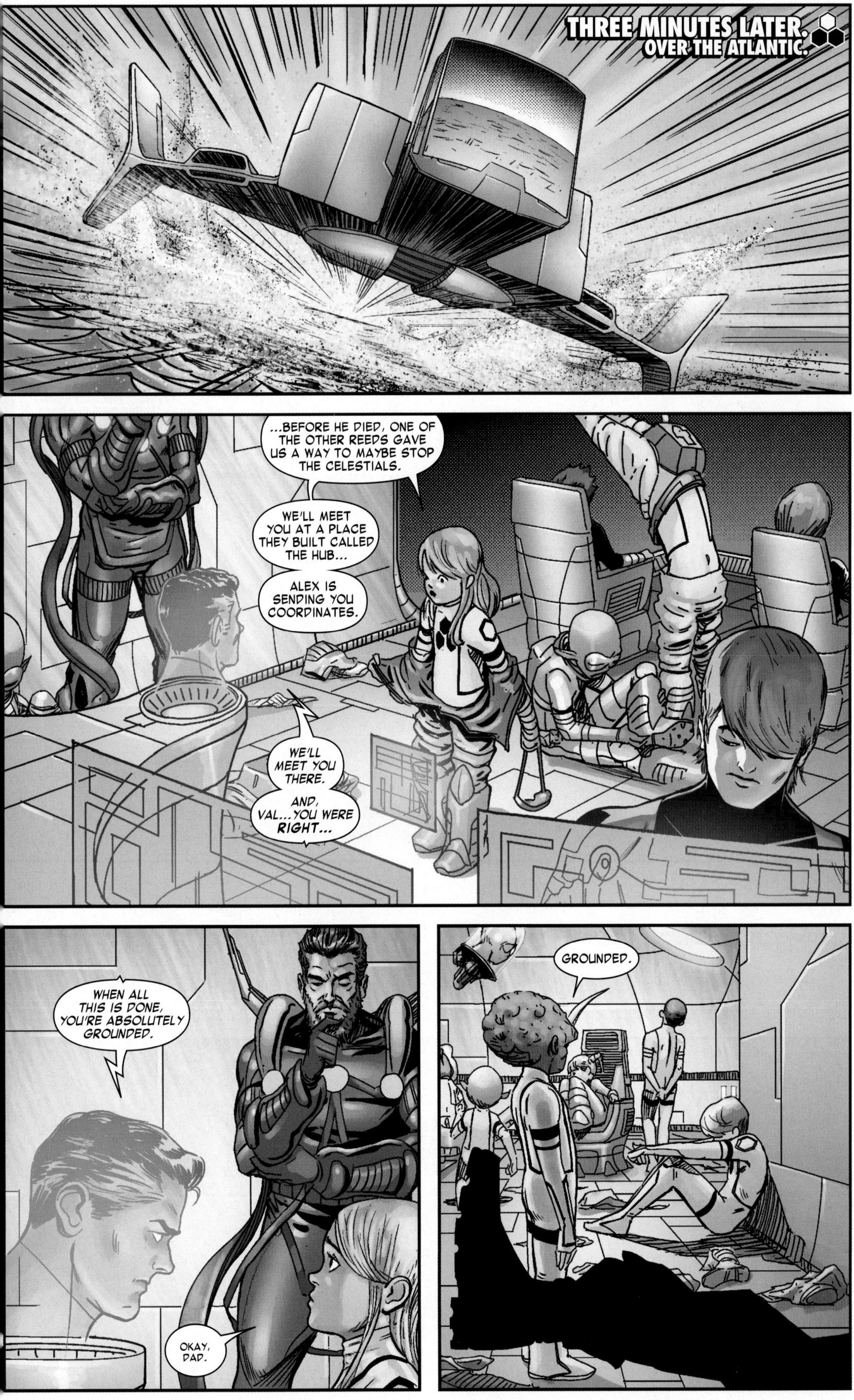
THREE MINUTES LATER. OVER THE ATLANTIC.
...BEFORE HE DIED, ONE OF THE OTHER REEDS GAVE US A WAY TO MAYBE STOP THE CELESTIALS.
WE'LL MEET YOU AT A PLACE THEY BUILT CALLED THE HUB...
ALEX IS SENDING YOU COORDINATES.
WE'LL MEET YOU THERE.
AND, VAL...YOU WERE RIGHT...
WHEN ALL THIS IS DONE, YOU'RE ABSOLUTELY GROUNDED.
OKAY, DAD.
GROUNDED.

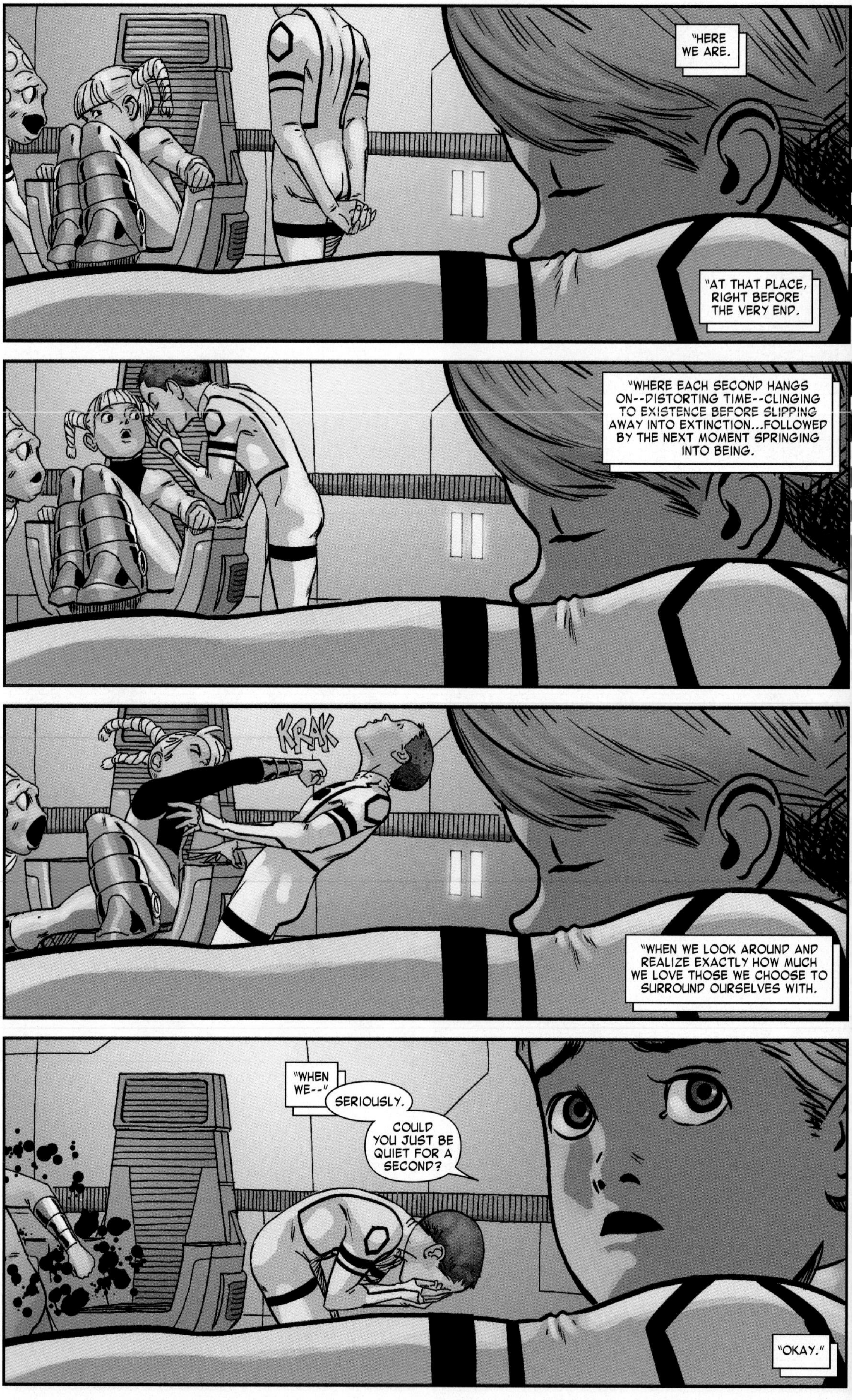
"HERE WE ARE.
"AT THAT PLACE, RIGHT BEFORE THE VERY END.
"WHERE EACH SECOND HANGS ON--DISTORTING TIME--CLINGING TO EXISTENCE BEFORE SLIPPING AWAY INTO EXTINCTION...FOLLOWED BY THE NEXT MOMENT SPRINGING INTO BEING.
KRAK
"WHEN WE LOOK AROUND AND REALIZE EXACTLY HOW MUCH WE LOVE THOSE WE CHOOSE TO SURROUND OURSELVES WITH.
"WHEN WE--"
SERIOUSLY.
COULD YOU JUST BE QUIET FOR A SECOND?
"OKAY."

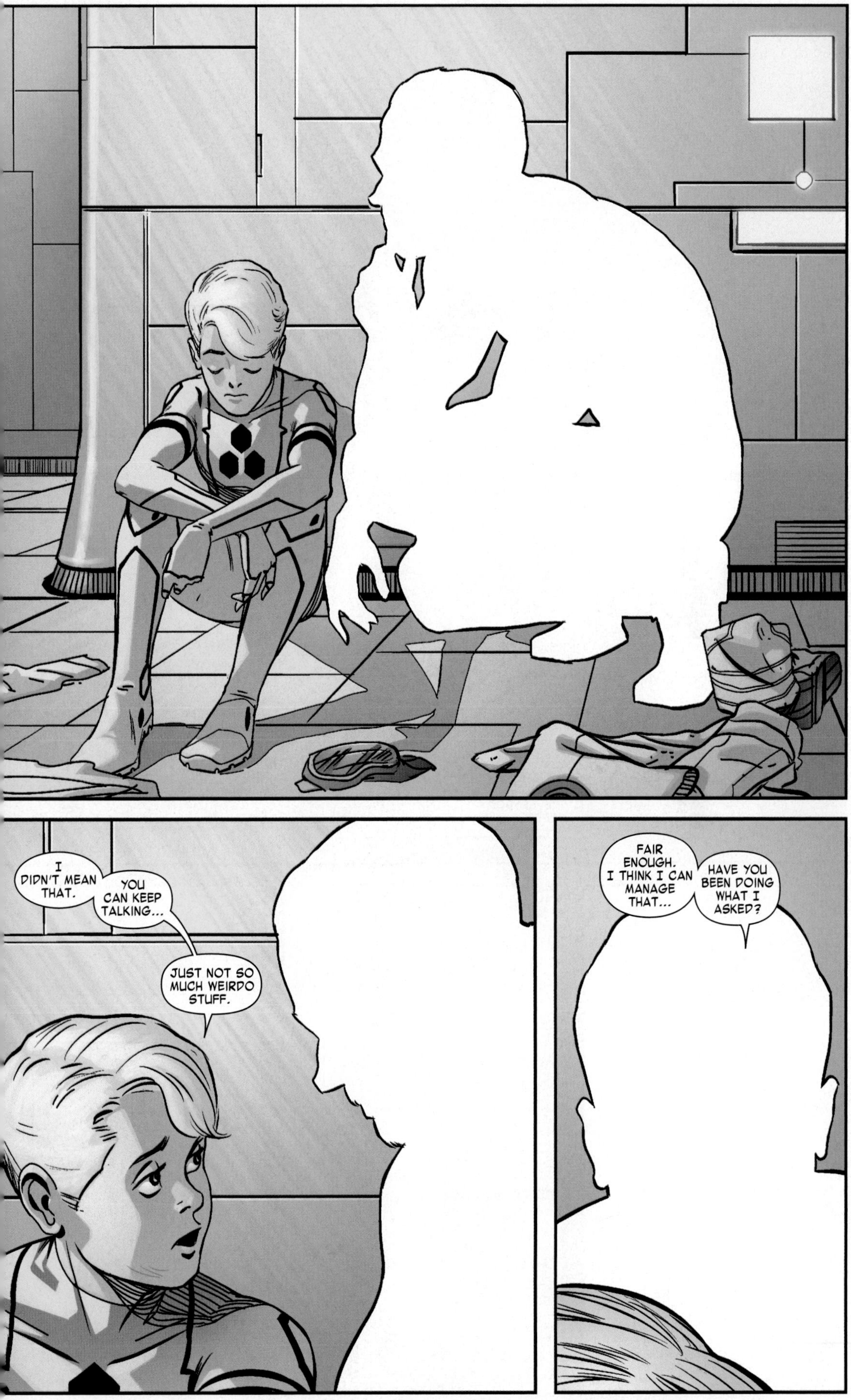
I DIDN'T MEAN THAT.
YOU CAN KEEP TALKING...
JUST NOT SO MUCH WEIRDO STUFF.
FAIR ENOUGH. I THINK I CAN MANAGE THAT...
HAVE YOU BEEN DOING WHAT I ASKED?

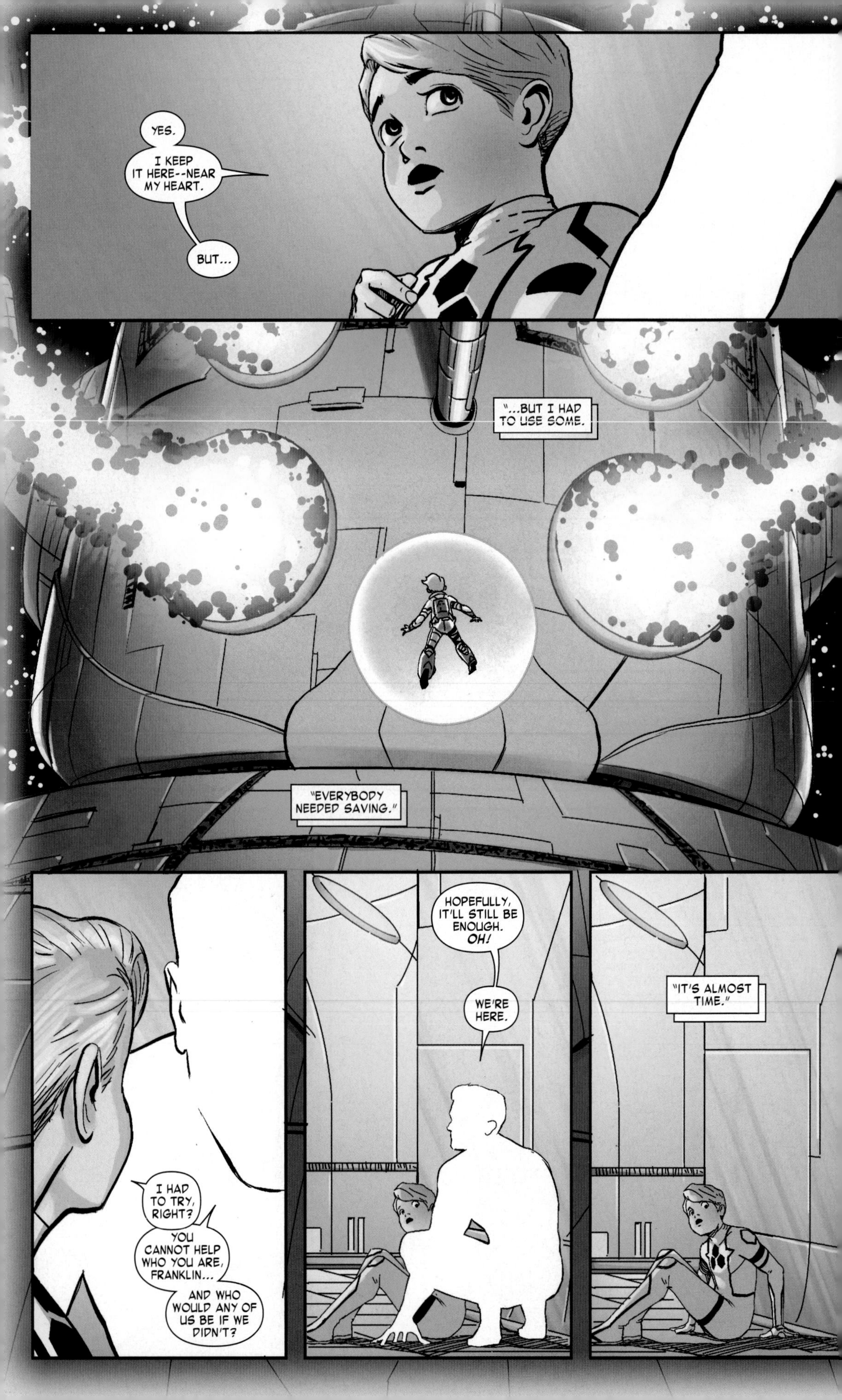
YES.
I KEEP IT HERE--NEAR MY HEART.
BUT...
"...BUT I HAD TO USE SOME.
"EVERYBODY NEEDED SAVING."
I HAD TO TRY, RIGHT?
YOU CANNOT HELP WHO YOU ARE, FRANKLIN...
AND WHO WOULD ANY OF US BE IF WE DIDN'T?
HOPEFULLY, IT'LL STILL BE ENOUGH. *OH!*
WE'RE HERE.
"IT'S ALMOST TIME."

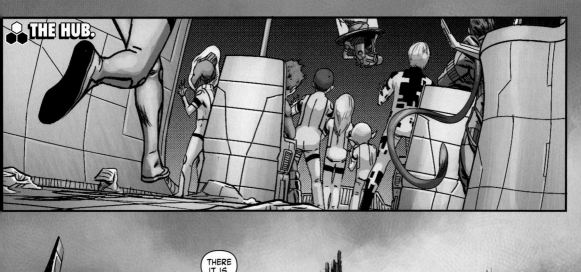

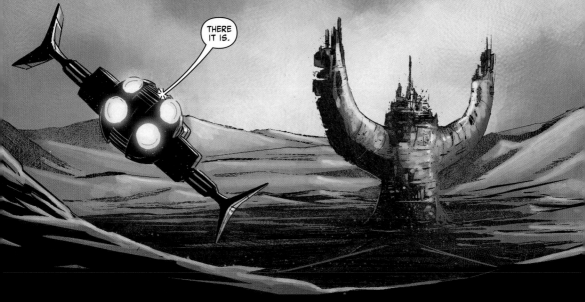

THERE IT IS.

LOOK AT THE SIZE OF THAT THING.

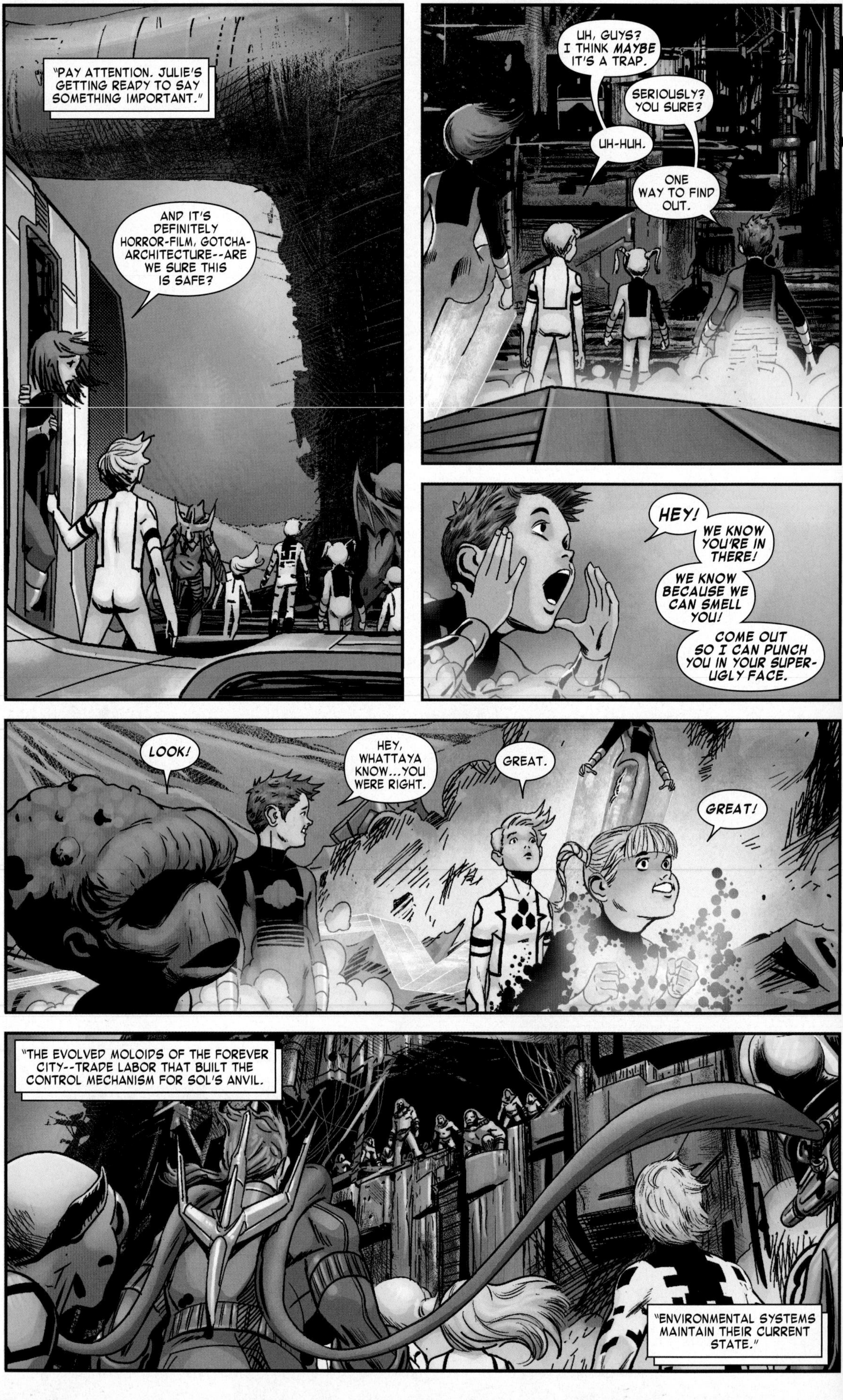

"PAY ATTENTION. JULIE'S GETTING READY TO SAY SOMETHING IMPORTANT."
AND IT'S DEFINITELY HORROR-FILM, GOTCHA-ARCHITECTURE--ARE WE SURE THIS IS SAFE?
UH, GUYS? I THINK MAYBE IT'S A TRAP.
SERIOUSLY? YOU SURE?
UH-HUH.
ONE WAY TO FIND OUT.
HEY!
WE KNOW YOU'RE IN THERE!
WE KNOW BECAUSE WE CAN SMELL YOU!
COME OUT SO I CAN PUNCH YOU IN YOUR SUPER-UGLY FACE.
LOOK!
HEY, WHATTAYA KNOW...YOU WERE RIGHT.
GREAT.
GREAT!
"THE EVOLVED MOLOIDS OF THE FOREVER CITY--TRADE LABOR THAT BUILT THE CONTROL MECHANISM FOR SOL'S ANVIL.
"ENVIRONMENTAL SYSTEMS MAINTAIN THEIR CURRENT STATE."

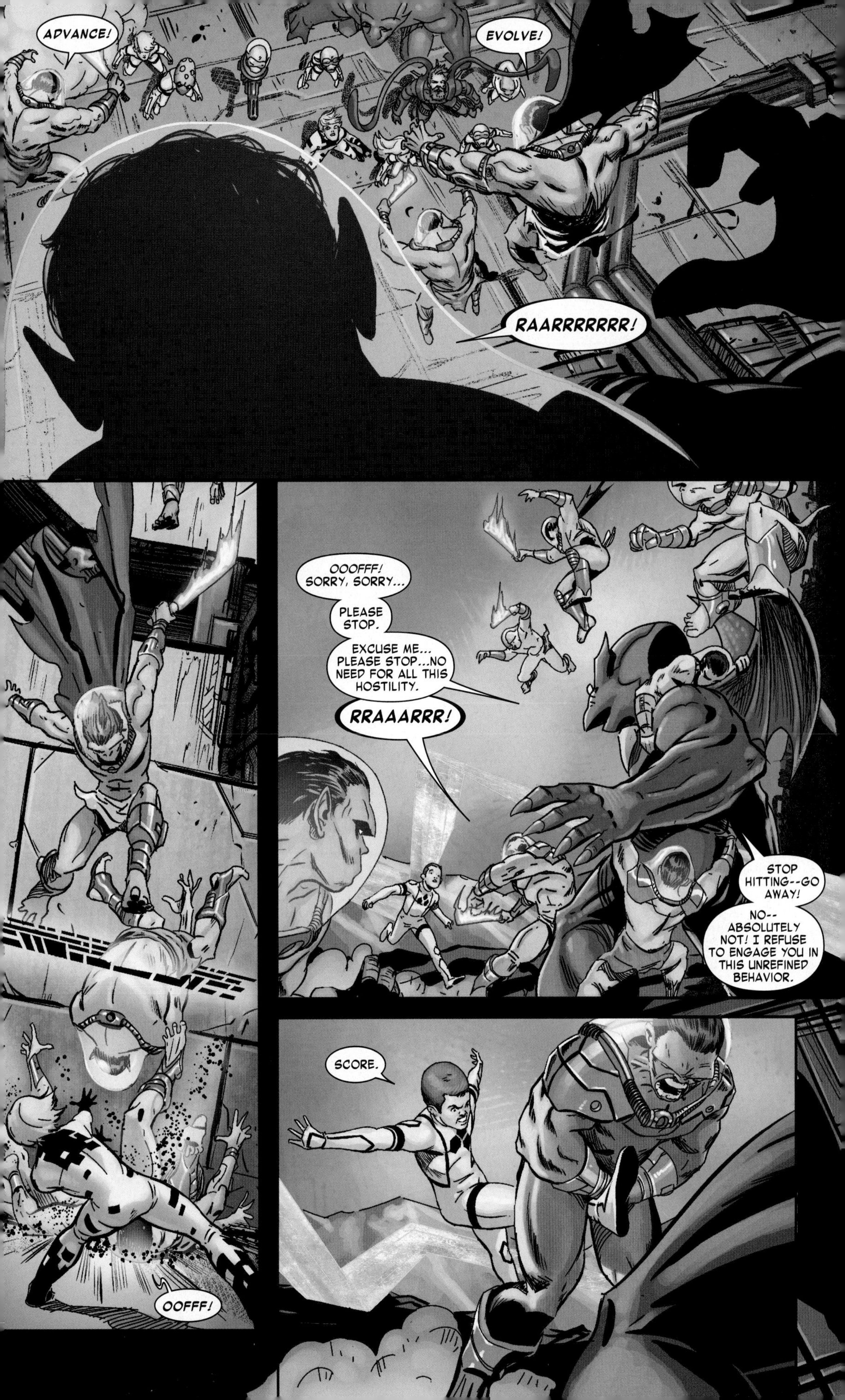
ADVANCE!
EVOLVE!
RAARRRRRRR!
OOOFFF! SORRY, SORRY...
PLEASE STOP.
EXCUSE ME... PLEASE STOP...NO NEED FOR ALL THIS HOSTILITY.
RRAAARRR!
STOP HITTING--GO AWAY!
NO--ABSOLUTELY NOT! I REFUSE TO ENGAGE YOU IN THIS UNREFINED BEHAVIOR.
OOFFF!
SCORE.

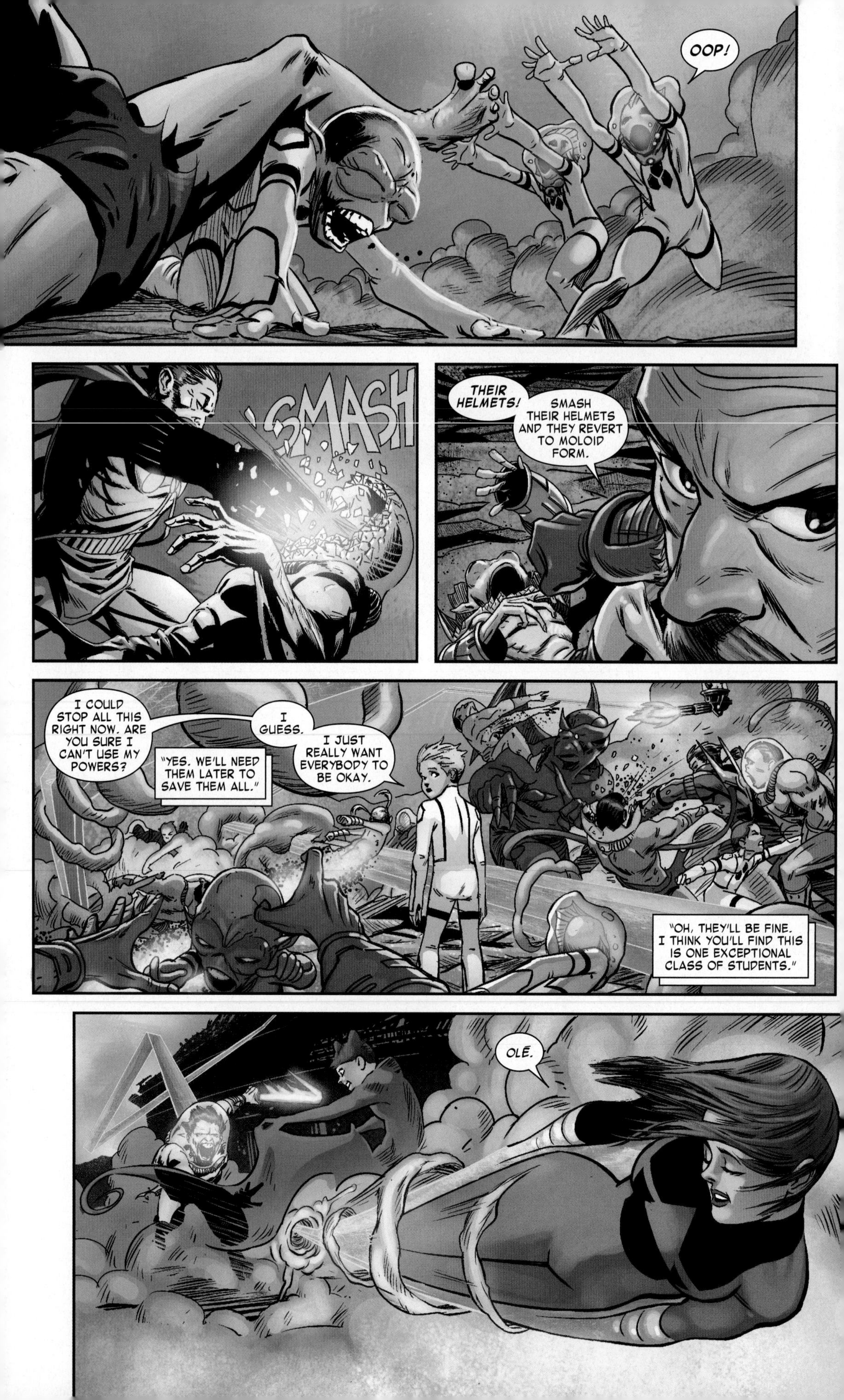
OOP!
SMASH
THEIR HELMETS!
SMASH THEIR HELMETS AND THEY REVERT TO MOLOID FORM.
I COULD STOP ALL THIS RIGHT NOW. ARE YOU SURE I CAN'T USE MY POWERS?
"YES. WE'LL NEED THEM LATER TO SAVE THEM ALL."
I GUESS.
I JUST REALLY WANT EVERYBODY TO BE OKAY.
"OH, THEY'LL BE FINE. I THINK YOU'LL FIND THIS IS ONE EXCEPTIONAL CLASS OF STUDENTS."
OLÉ.

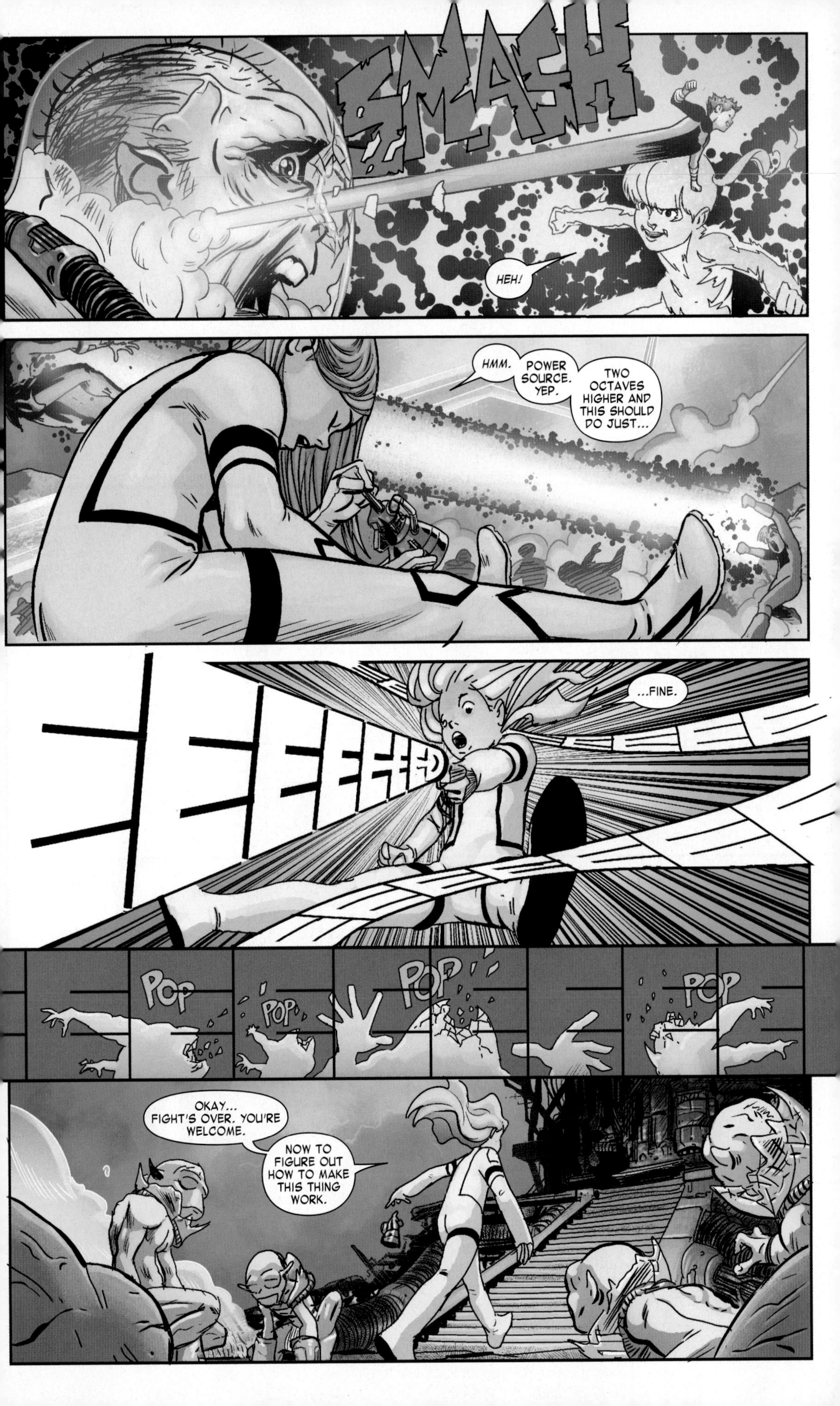
SMASH
HEH!
HMM.
POWER SOURCE. YEP.
TWO OCTAVES HIGHER AND THIS SHOULD DO JUST...
...FINE.
POP
POP
POP
POP
OKAY... FIGHT'S OVER. YOU'RE WELCOME.
NOW TO FIGURE OUT HOW TO MAKE THIS THING WORK.

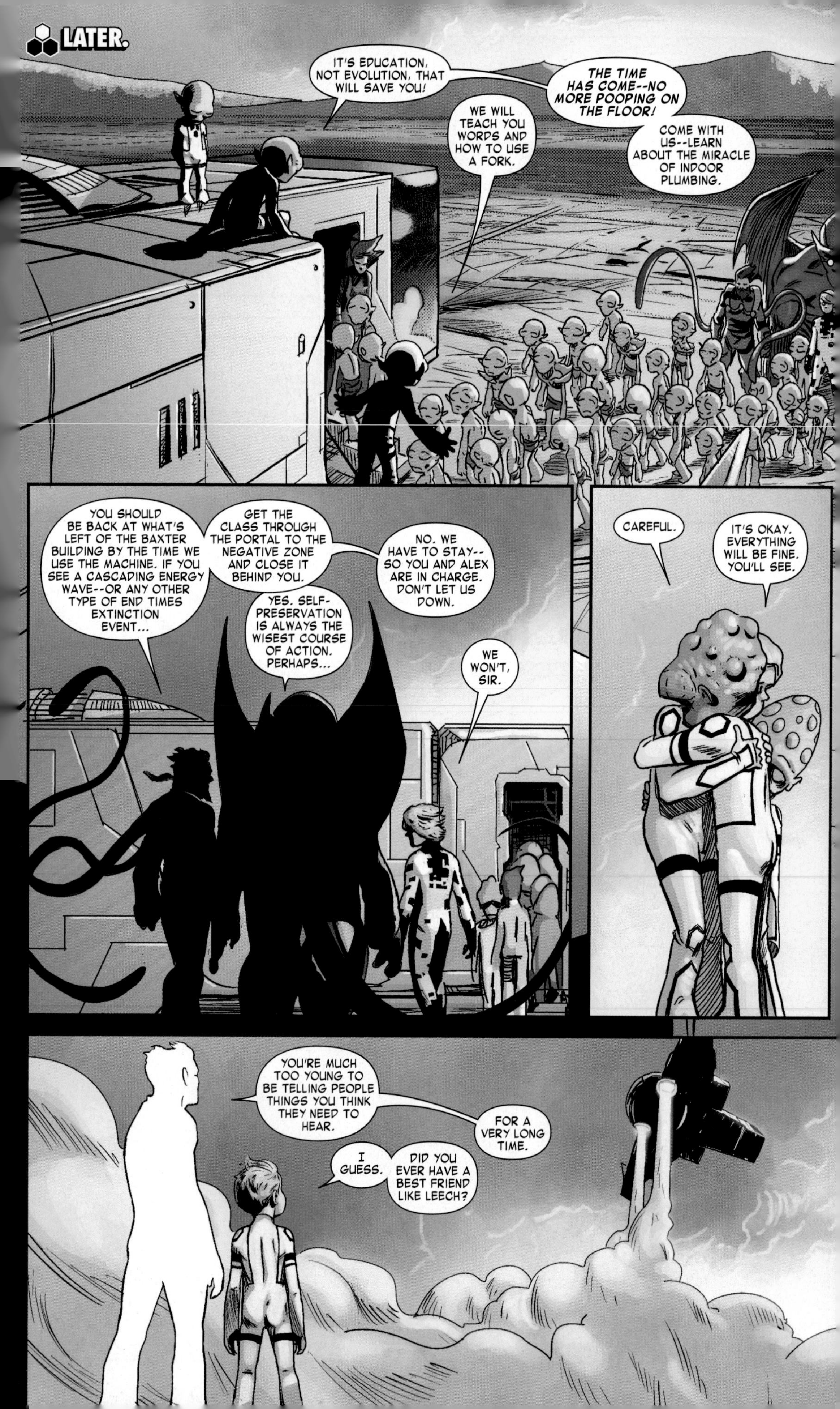
LATER.
IT'S EDUCATION, NOT EVOLUTION, THAT WILL SAVE YOU!
THE TIME HAS COME--NO MORE POOPING ON THE FLOOR!
COME WITH US--LEARN ABOUT THE MIRACLE OF INDOOR PLUMBING.
WE WILL TEACH YOU WORDS AND HOW TO USE A FORK.
YOU SHOULD BE BACK AT WHAT'S LEFT OF THE BAXTER BUILDING BY THE TIME WE USE THE MACHINE. IF YOU SEE A CASCADING ENERGY WAVE--OR ANY OTHER TYPE OF END TIMES EXTINCTION EVENT...
GET THE CLASS THROUGH THE PORTAL TO THE NEGATIVE ZONE AND CLOSE IT BEHIND YOU.
YES. SELF-PRESERVATION IS ALWAYS THE WISEST COURSE OF ACTION. PERHAPS...
NO. WE HAVE TO STAY--SO YOU AND ALEX ARE IN CHARGE. DON'T LET US DOWN.
WE WON'T, SIR.
CAREFUL.
IT'S OKAY. EVERYTHING WILL BE FINE. YOU'LL SEE.
YOU'RE MUCH TOO YOUNG TO BE TELLING PEOPLE THINGS YOU THINK THEY NEED TO HEAR.
FOR A VERY LONG TIME.
I GUESS.
DID YOU EVER HAVE A BEST FRIEND LIKE LEECH?

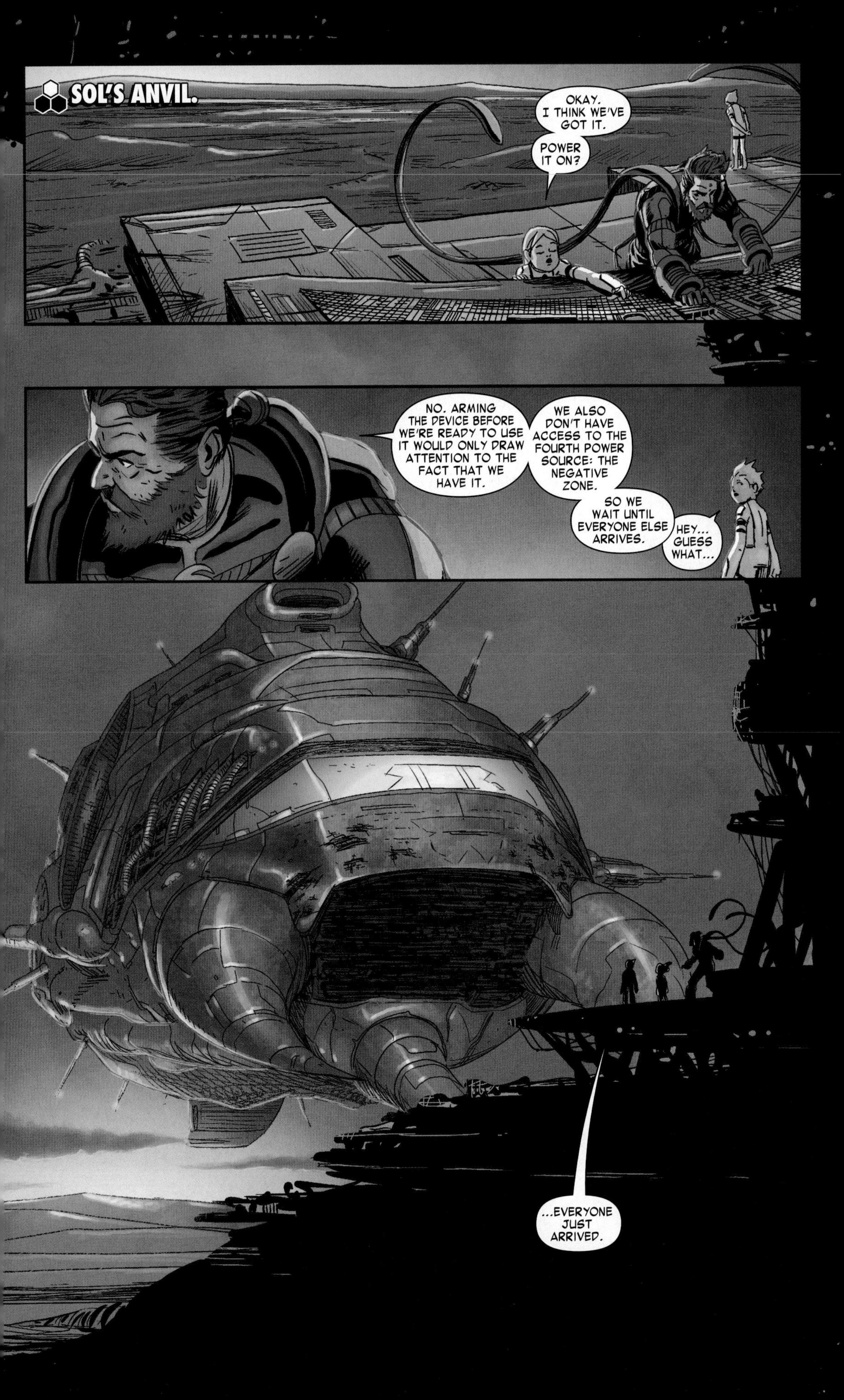
SOL'S ANVIL.
OKAY. I THINK WE'VE GOT IT.
POWER IT ON?
NO. ARMING THE DEVICE BEFORE WE'RE READY TO USE IT WOULD ONLY DRAW ATTENTION TO THE FACT THAT WE HAVE IT.
WE ALSO DON'T HAVE ACCESS TO THE FOURTH POWER SOURCE: THE NEGATIVE ZONE.
SO WE WAIT UNTIL EVERYONE ELSE ARRIVES.
HEY... GUESS WHAT...
...EVERYONE JUST ARRIVED.

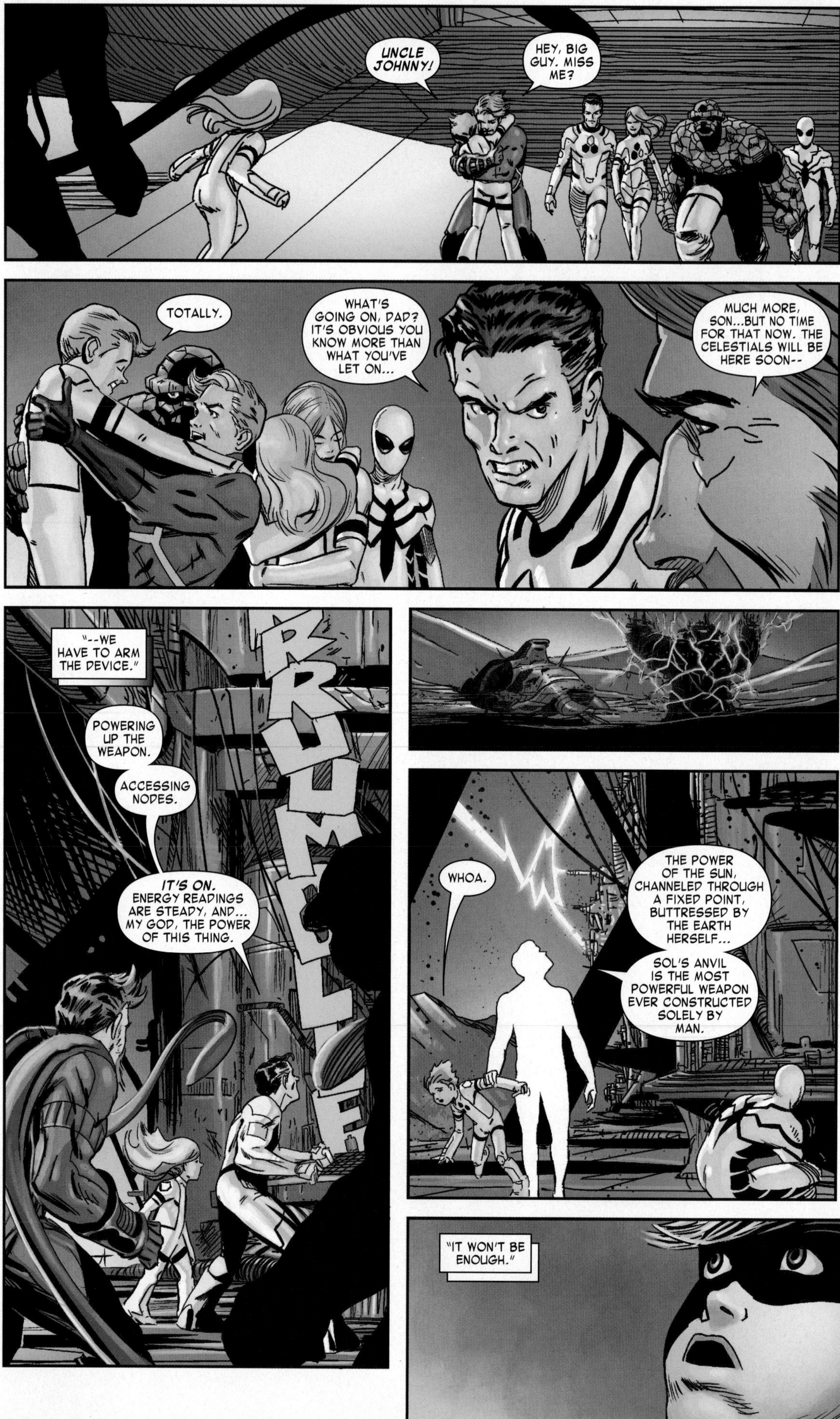
UNCLE JOHNNY!
HEY, BIG GUY. MISS ME?
TOTALLY.
WHAT'S GOING ON, DAD? IT'S OBVIOUS YOU KNOW MORE THAN WHAT YOU'VE LET ON...
MUCH MORE, SON...BUT NO TIME FOR THAT NOW. THE CELESTIALS WILL BE HERE SOON--
"--WE HAVE TO ARM THE DEVICE."
RRUMMBLE
POWERING UP THE WEAPON.
ACCESSING NODES.
IT'S ON. ENERGY READINGS ARE STEADY, AND... MY GOD, THE POWER OF THIS THING.
WHOA.
THE POWER OF THE SUN, CHANNELED THROUGH A FIXED POINT, BUTTRESSED BY THE EARTH HERSELF...
SOL'S ANVIL IS THE MOST POWERFUL WEAPON EVER CONSTRUCTED SOLELY BY MAN.
"IT WON'T BE ENOUGH."

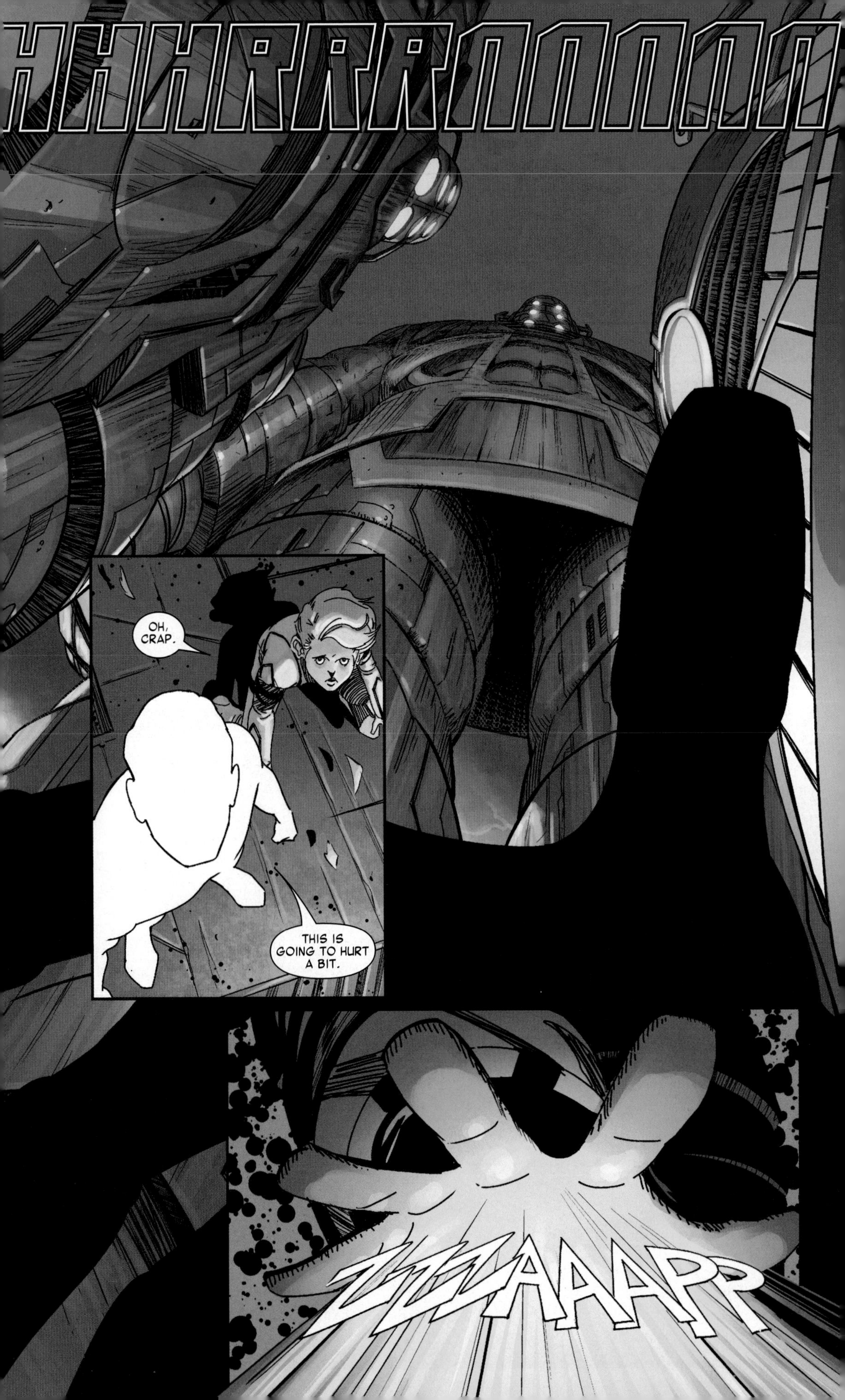
HHHRRRNNNNNN
OH, CRAP.
THIS IS GOING TO HURT A BIT.
ZZZAAAPP

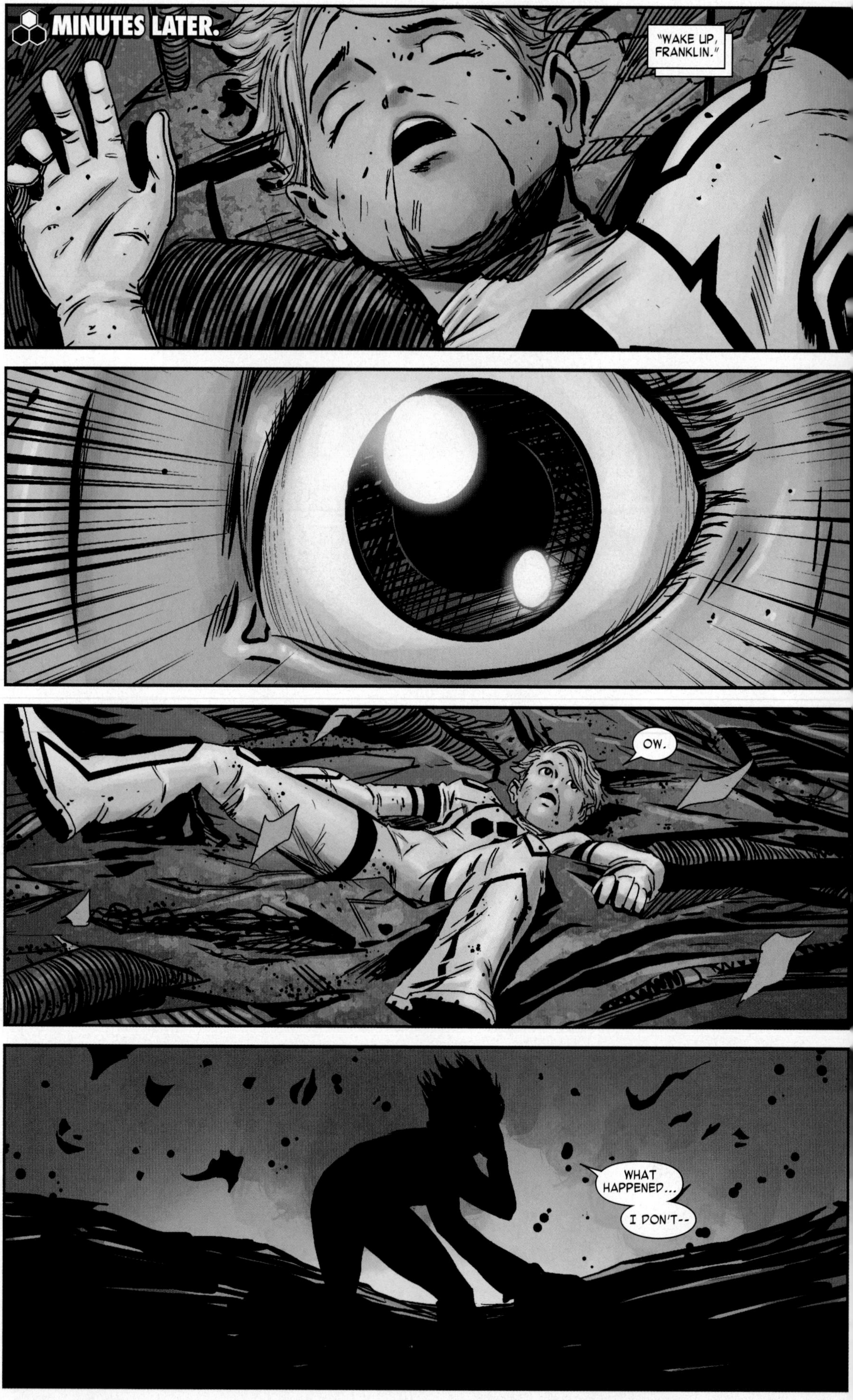
MINUTES LATER.
"WAKE UP, FRANKLIN."
OW.
WHAT HAPPENED...
I DON'T--

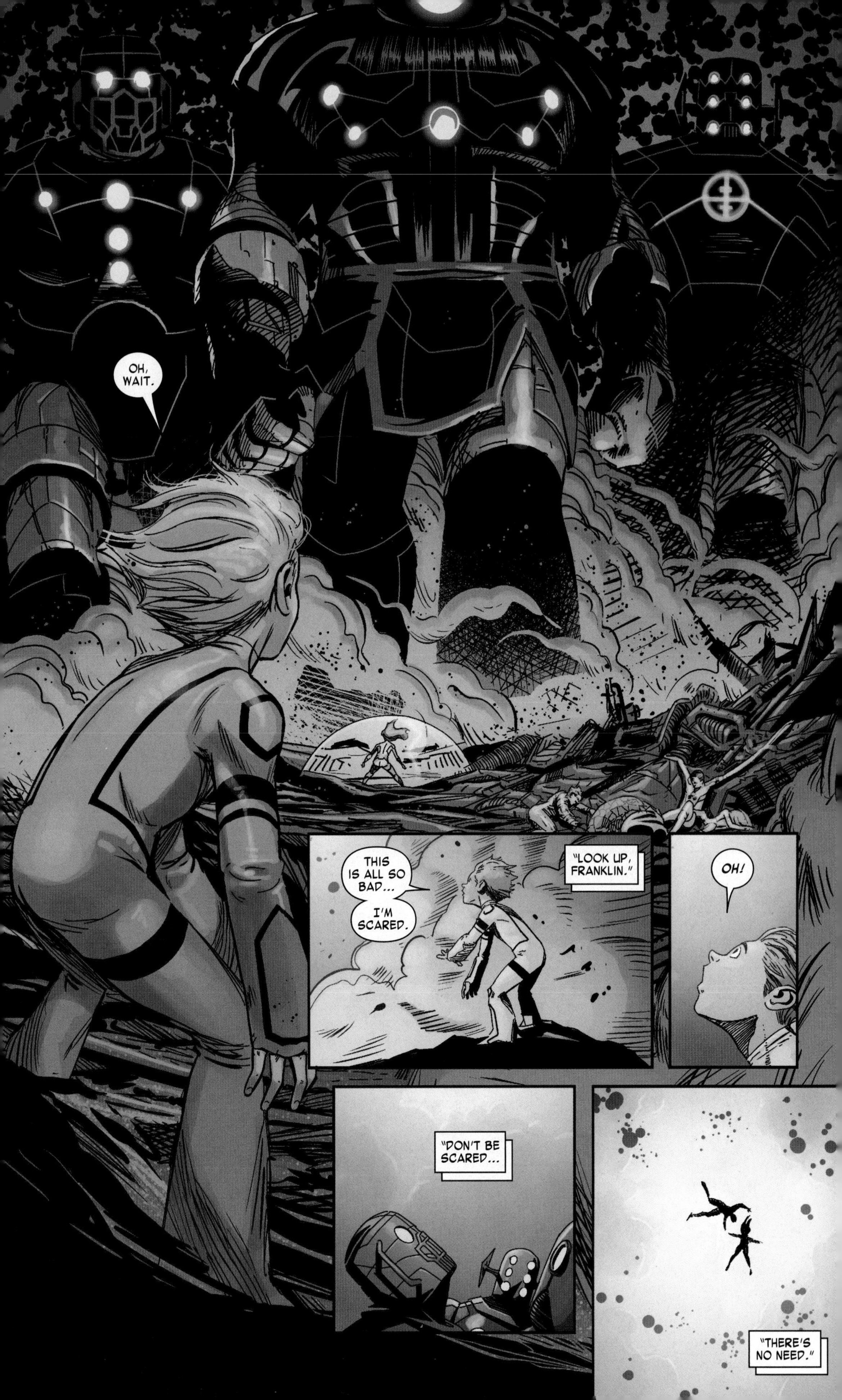
OH, WAIT.
THIS IS ALL SO BAD...
I'M SCARED.
"LOOK UP, FRANKLIN."
OH!
"DON'T BE SCARED...
"THERE'S NO NEED."

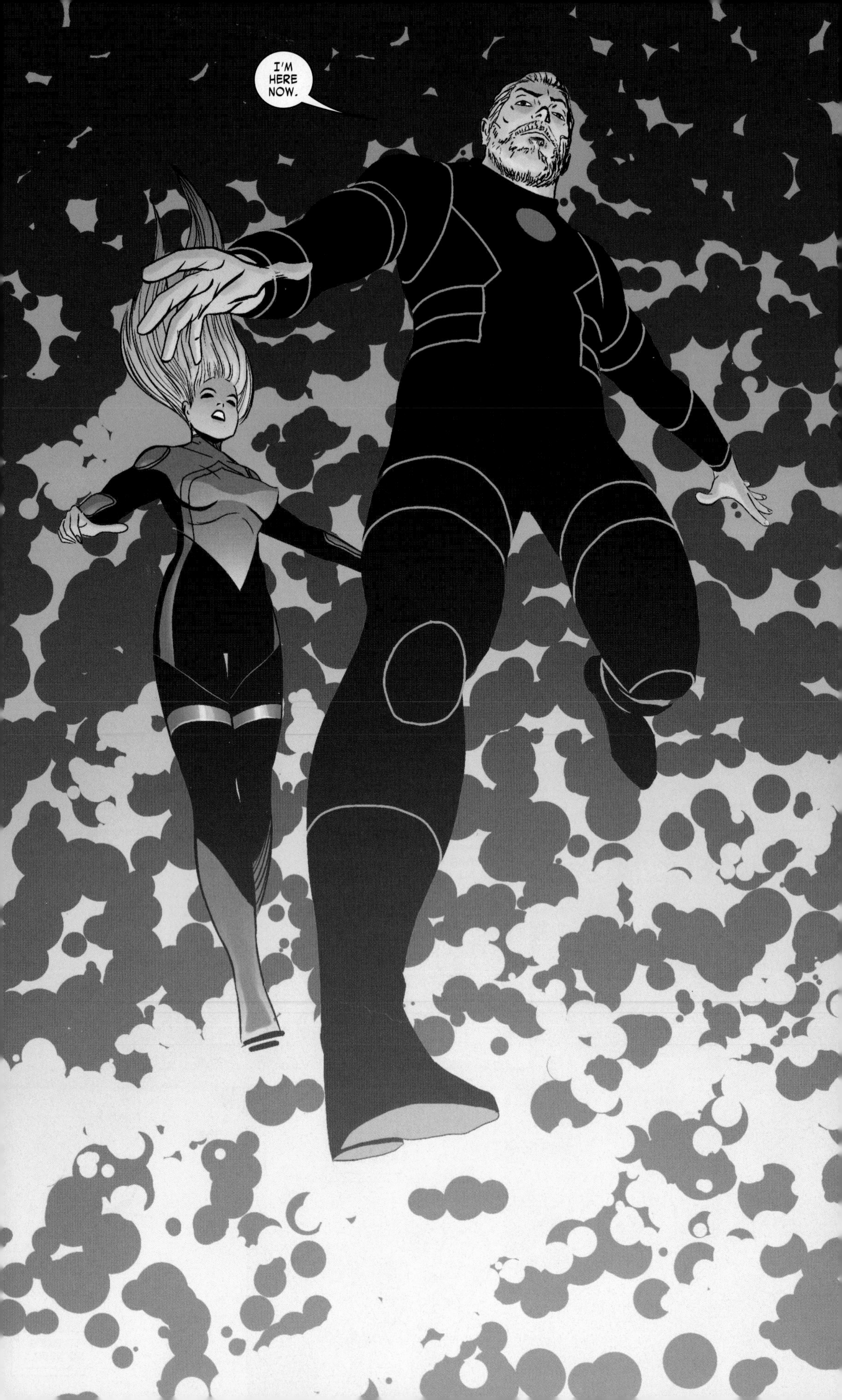
I'M HERE NOW.

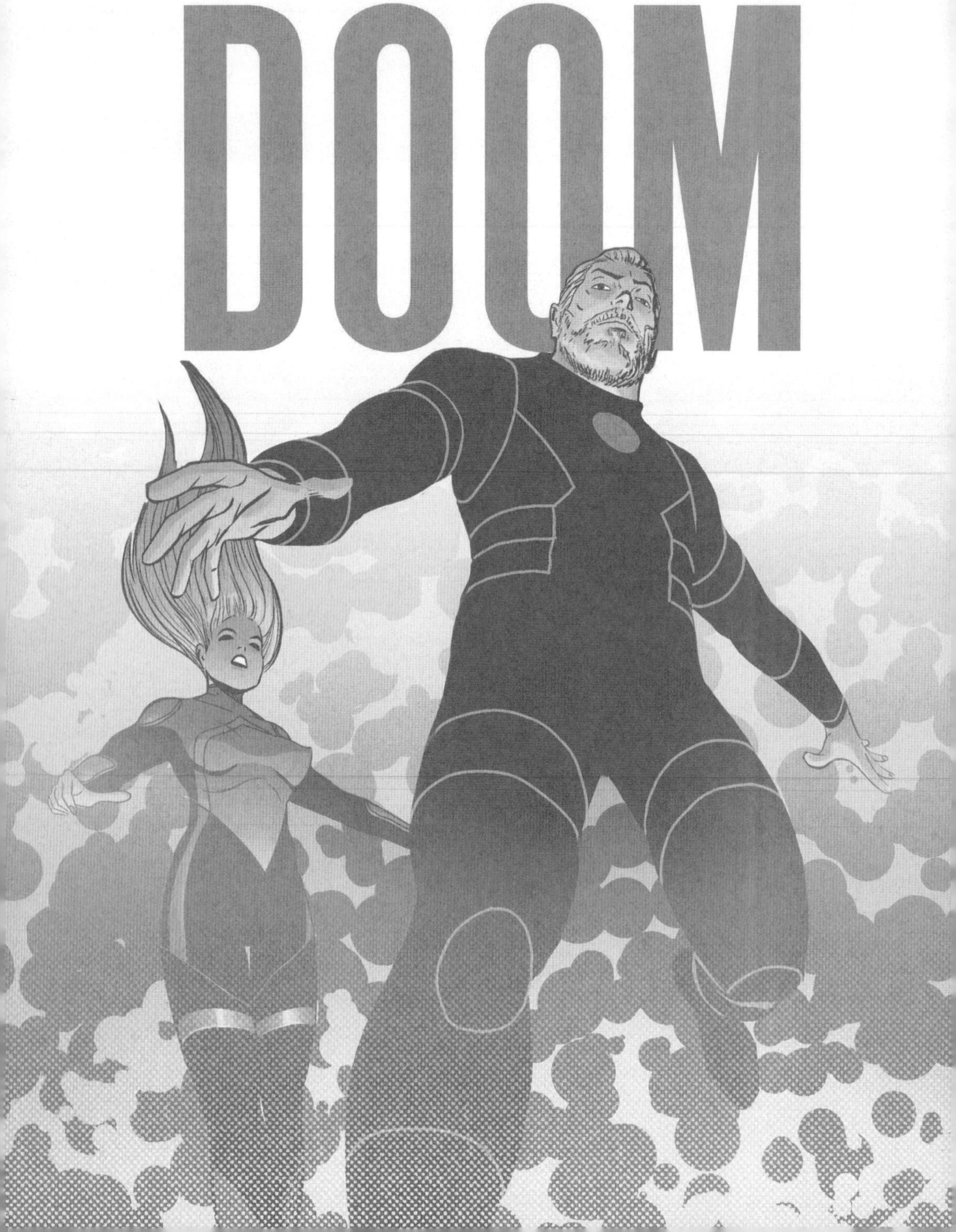
DOOM

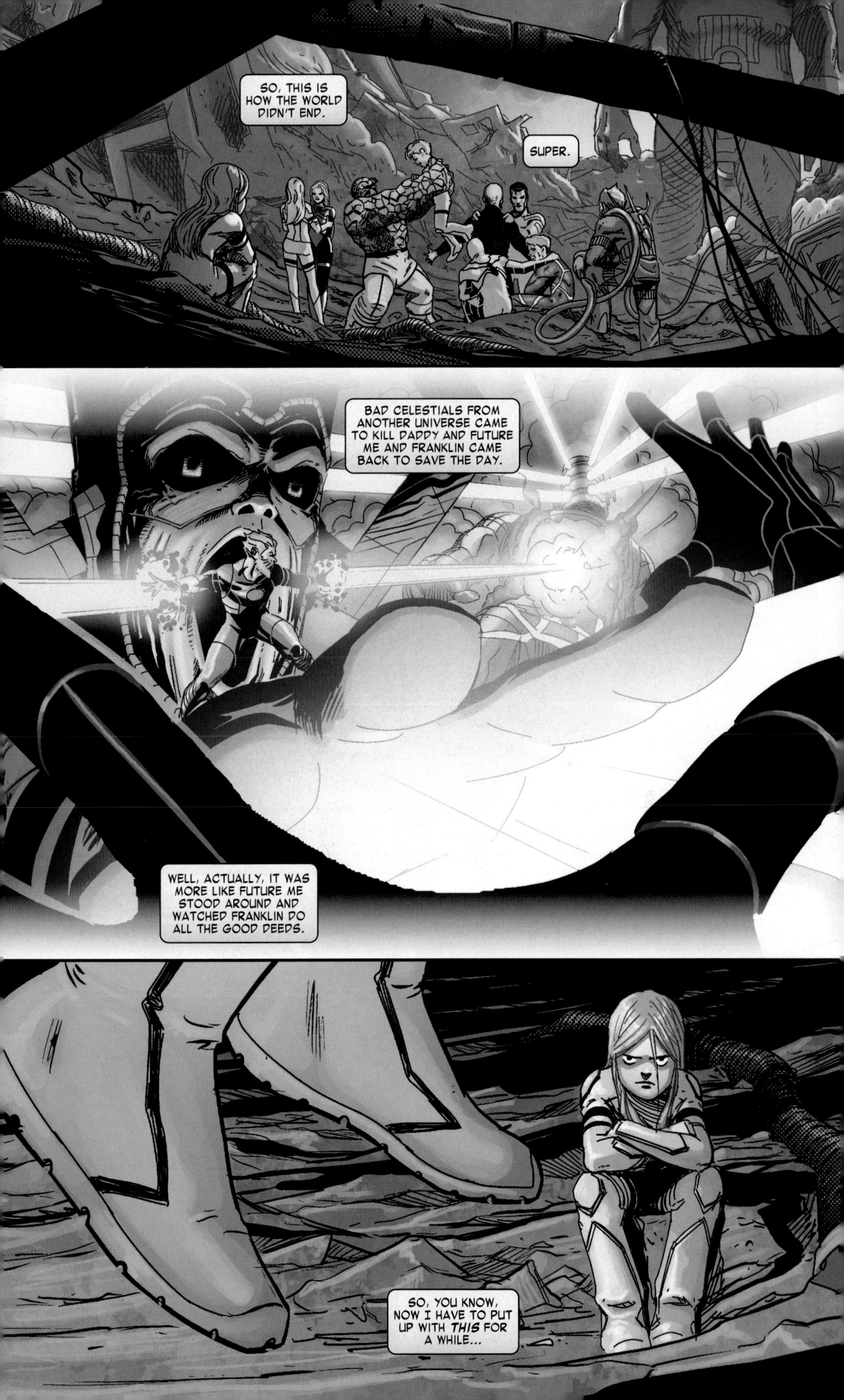
SO, THIS IS HOW THE WORLD DIDN'T END.
SUPER.
BAD CELESTIALS FROM ANOTHER UNIVERSE CAME TO KILL DADDY AND FUTURE ME AND FRANKLIN CAME BACK TO SAVE THE DAY.
WELL, ACTUALLY, IT WAS MORE LIKE FUTURE ME STOOD AROUND AND WATCHED FRANKLIN DO ALL THE GOOD DEEDS.
SO, YOU KNOW, NOW I HAVE TO PUT UP WITH *THIS* FOR A WHILE...

SO...WHO'S AWESOME?

ME!

IT'S ME!

I. AM. AWESOME!

WE TOTALLY CRUSHED THOSE SPACE GODS.

AND I'VE GOT A BEARD. IS IT ITCHY?

NOT REALLY.

OKAY, I'M GOING TO CALL YOU MISTER FRANKLIN.

ONLY IF I CAN CALL YOU KID FRANKLIN.

COOL.

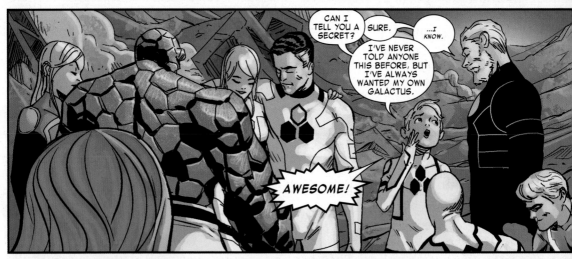

CAN I TELL YOU A SECRET?

SURE.

...I KNOW.

I'VE NEVER TOLD ANYONE THIS BEFORE, BUT I'VE ALWAYS WANTED MY OWN GALACTUS.

AWESOME!

SO THEY'RE HAPPY. AND GROSS. AND A BEARD, REALLY?

CONTRAST THAT WITH MY FUTURE ME-- THERE'S SOMETHING ABOUT THAT LADY I'M NOT SURE OF...

I DON'T THINK I LIKE HER. AT ALL.

RIGHT BACK AT YOU, KID.

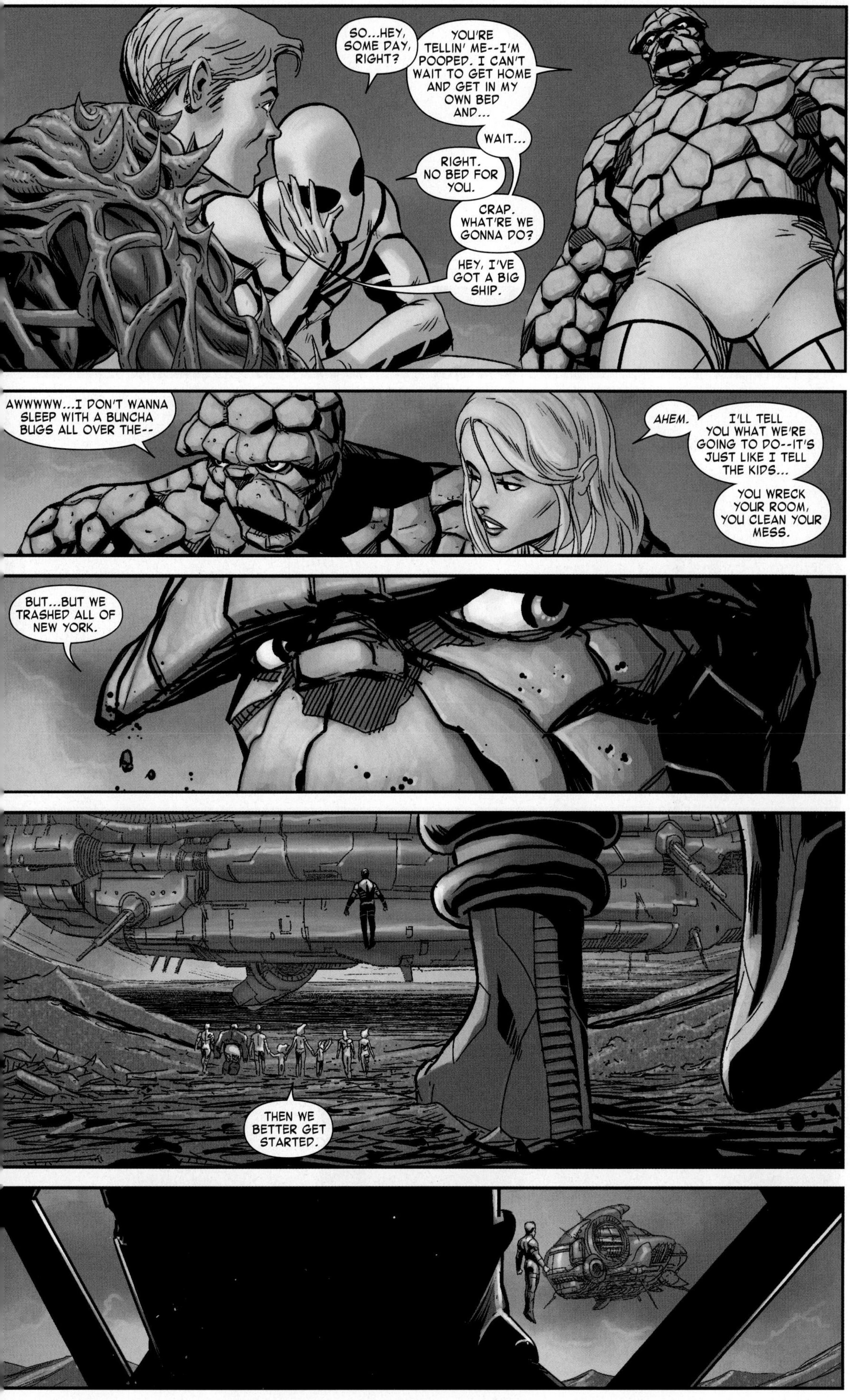
SO...HEY, SOME DAY, RIGHT?
YOU'RE TELLIN' ME--I'M POOPED. I CAN'T WAIT TO GET HOME AND GET IN MY OWN BED AND...
WAIT...
RIGHT. NO BED FOR YOU.
CRAP. WHAT'RE WE GONNA DO?
HEY, I'VE GOT A BIG SHIP.
AWWWWW...I DON'T WANNA SLEEP WITH A BUNCHA BUGS ALL OVER THE--
AHEM.
I'LL TELL YOU WHAT WE'RE GOING TO DO--IT'S JUST LIKE I TELL THE KIDS...
YOU WRECK YOUR ROOM, YOU CLEAN YOUR MESS.
BUT...BUT WE TRASHED ALL OF NEW YORK.
THEN WE BETTER GET STARTED.

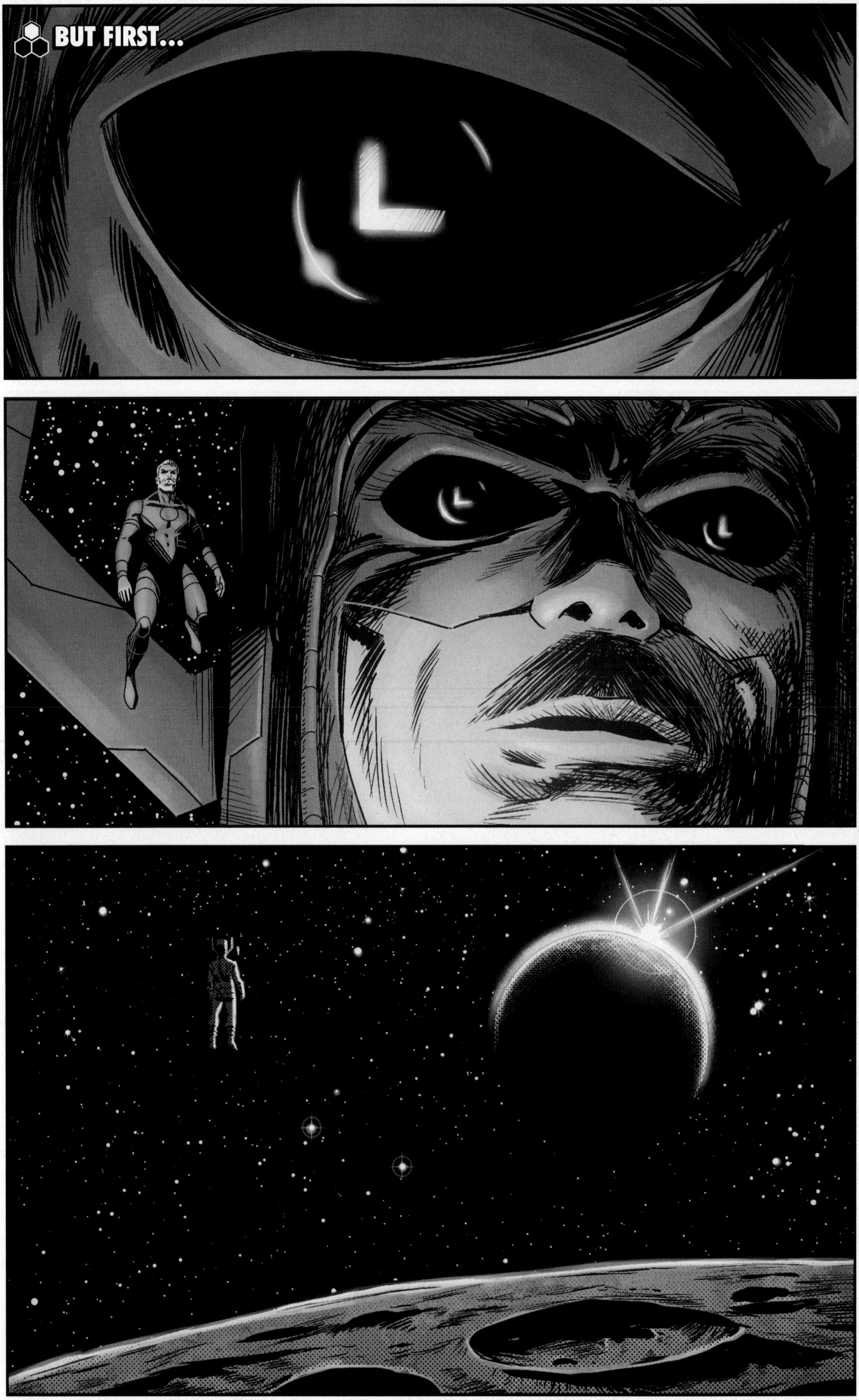
BUT FIRST...

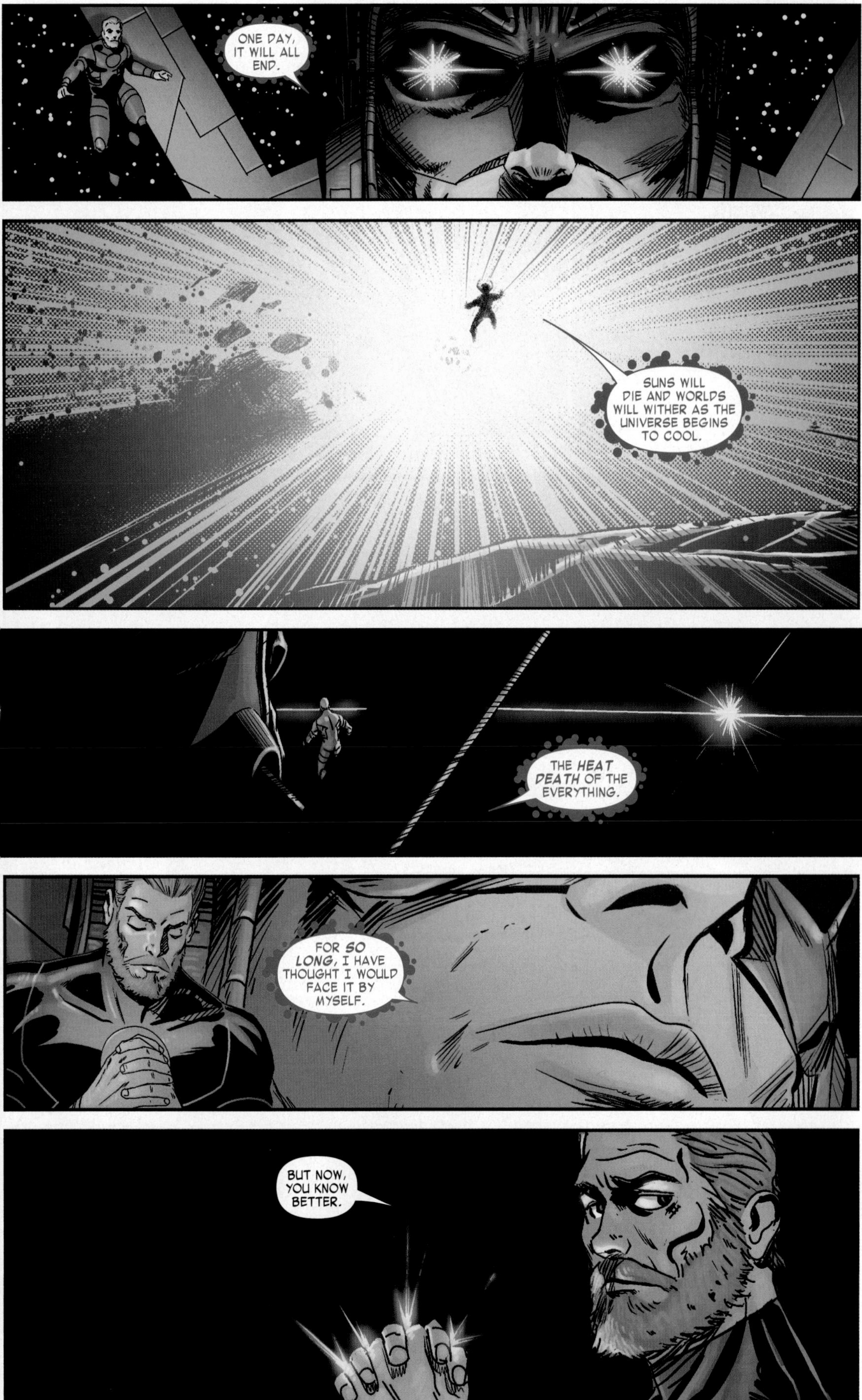
ONE DAY, IT WILL ALL END.
SUNS WILL DIE AND WORLDS WILL WITHER AS THE UNIVERSE BEGINS TO COOL.
THE *HEAT DEATH* OF THE EVERYTHING.
FOR *SO LONG*, I HAVE THOUGHT I WOULD FACE IT BY MYSELF.
BUT NOW, YOU KNOW BETTER.

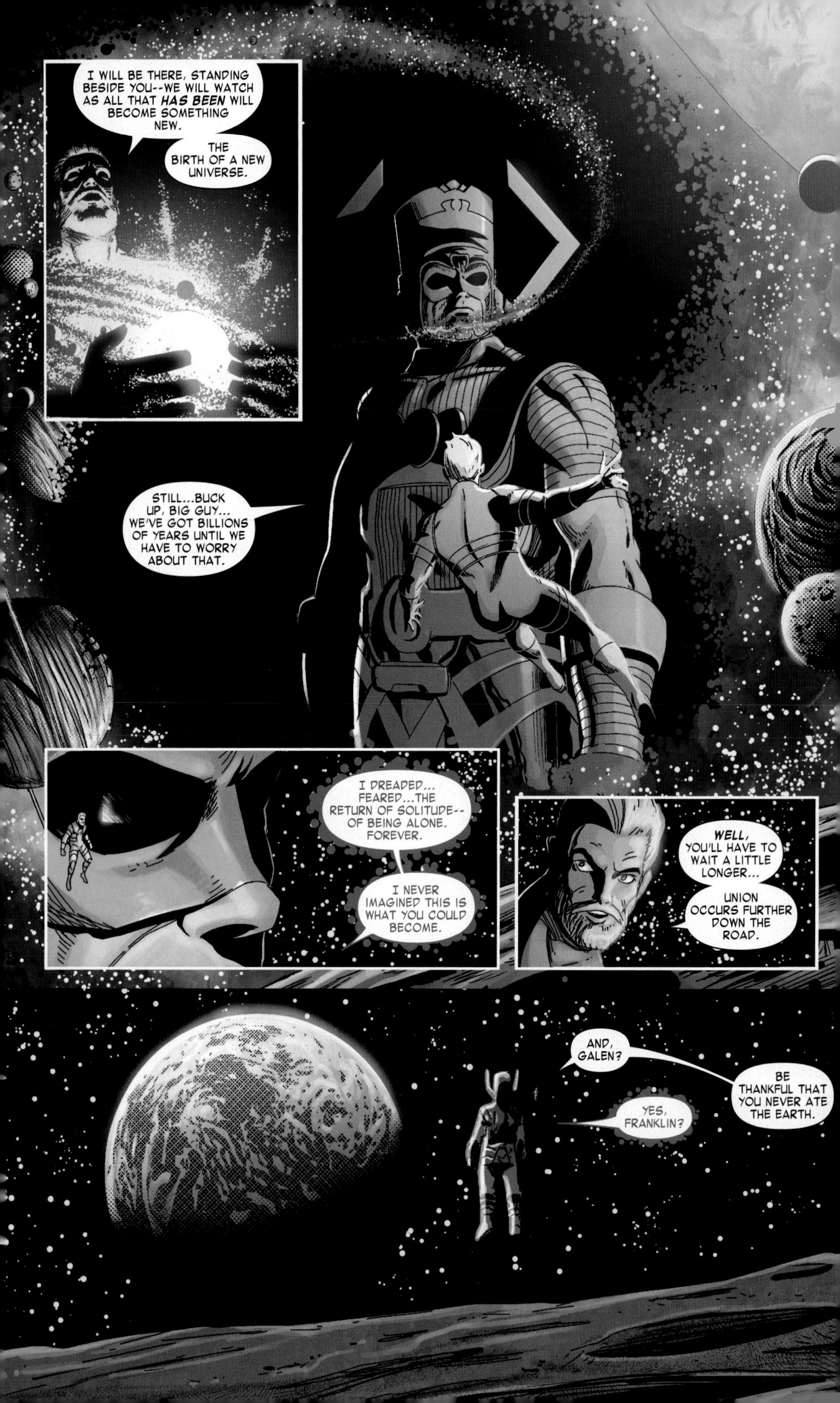

I WILL BE THERE, STANDING BESIDE YOU--WE WILL WATCH AS ALL THAT HAS BEEN WILL BECOME SOMETHING NEW.
THE BIRTH OF A NEW UNIVERSE.
STILL...BUCK UP, BIG GUY... WE'VE GOT BILLIONS OF YEARS UNTIL WE HAVE TO WORRY ABOUT THAT.
I DREADED... FEARED...THE RETURN OF SOLITUDE--OF BEING ALONE. FOREVER.
I NEVER IMAGINED THIS IS WHAT YOU COULD BECOME.
WELL, YOU'LL HAVE TO WAIT A LITTLE LONGER...
UNION OCCURS FURTHER DOWN THE ROAD.
AND, GALEN?
YES, FRANKLIN?
BE THANKFUL THAT YOU NEVER ATE THE EARTH.

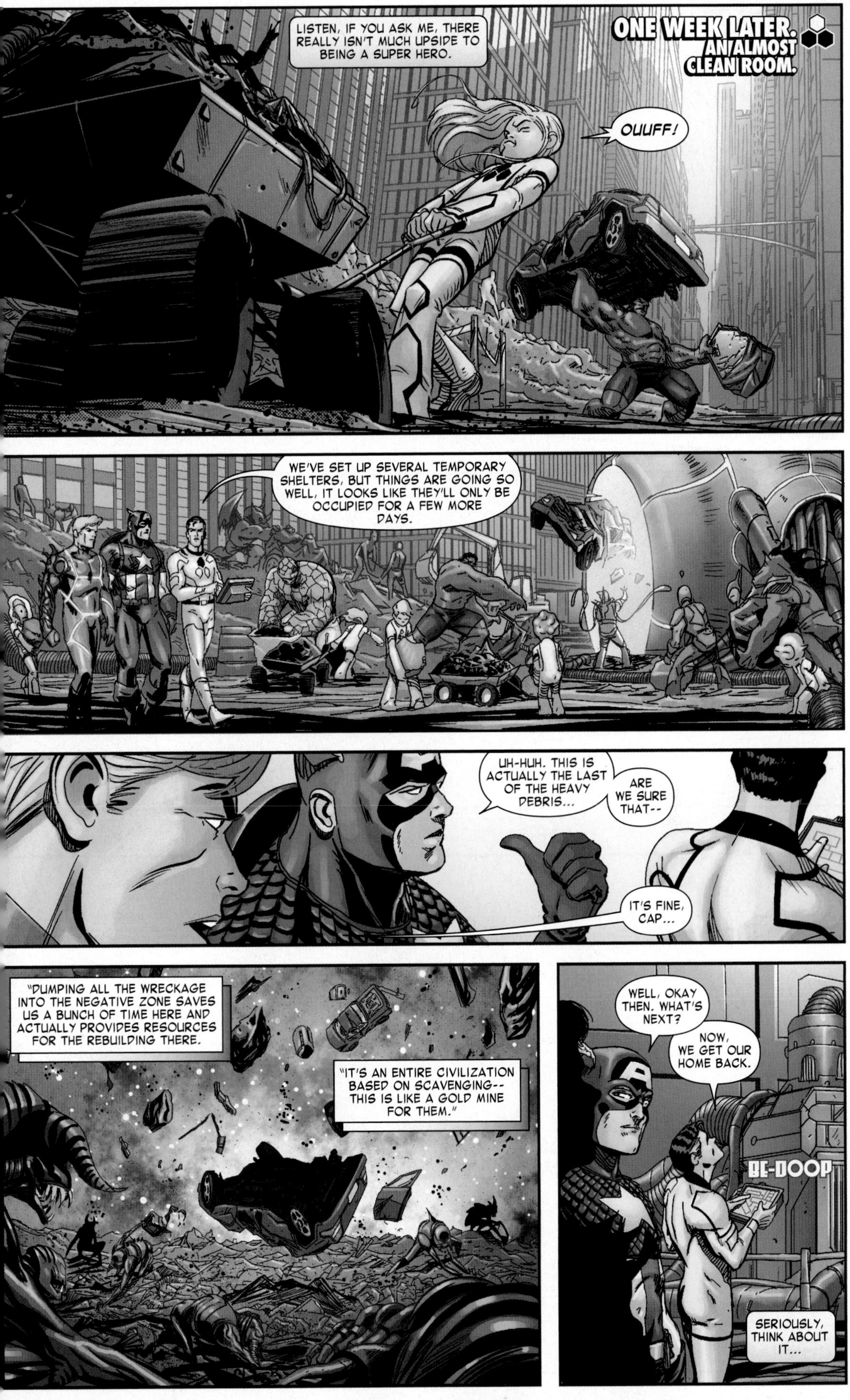
ONE WEEK LATER. AN ALMOST CLEAN ROOM.
LISTEN, IF YOU ASK ME, THERE REALLY ISN'T MUCH UPSIDE TO BEING A SUPER HERO.
OUUFF!
WE'VE SET UP SEVERAL TEMPORARY SHELTERS, BUT THINGS ARE GOING SO WELL, IT LOOKS LIKE THEY'LL ONLY BE OCCUPIED FOR A FEW MORE DAYS.
UH-HUH. THIS IS ACTUALLY THE LAST OF THE HEAVY DEBRIS...
ARE WE SURE THAT--
IT'S FINE, CAP...
"DUMPING ALL THE WRECKAGE INTO THE NEGATIVE ZONE SAVES US A BUNCH OF TIME HERE AND ACTUALLY PROVIDES RESOURCES FOR THE REBUILDING THERE.
"IT'S AN ENTIRE CIVILIZATION BASED ON SCAVENGING-- THIS IS LIKE A GOLD MINE FOR THEM."
WELL, OKAY THEN. WHAT'S NEXT?
NOW, WE GET OUR HOME BACK.
BE-DOOP
SERIOUSLY, THINK ABOUT IT...

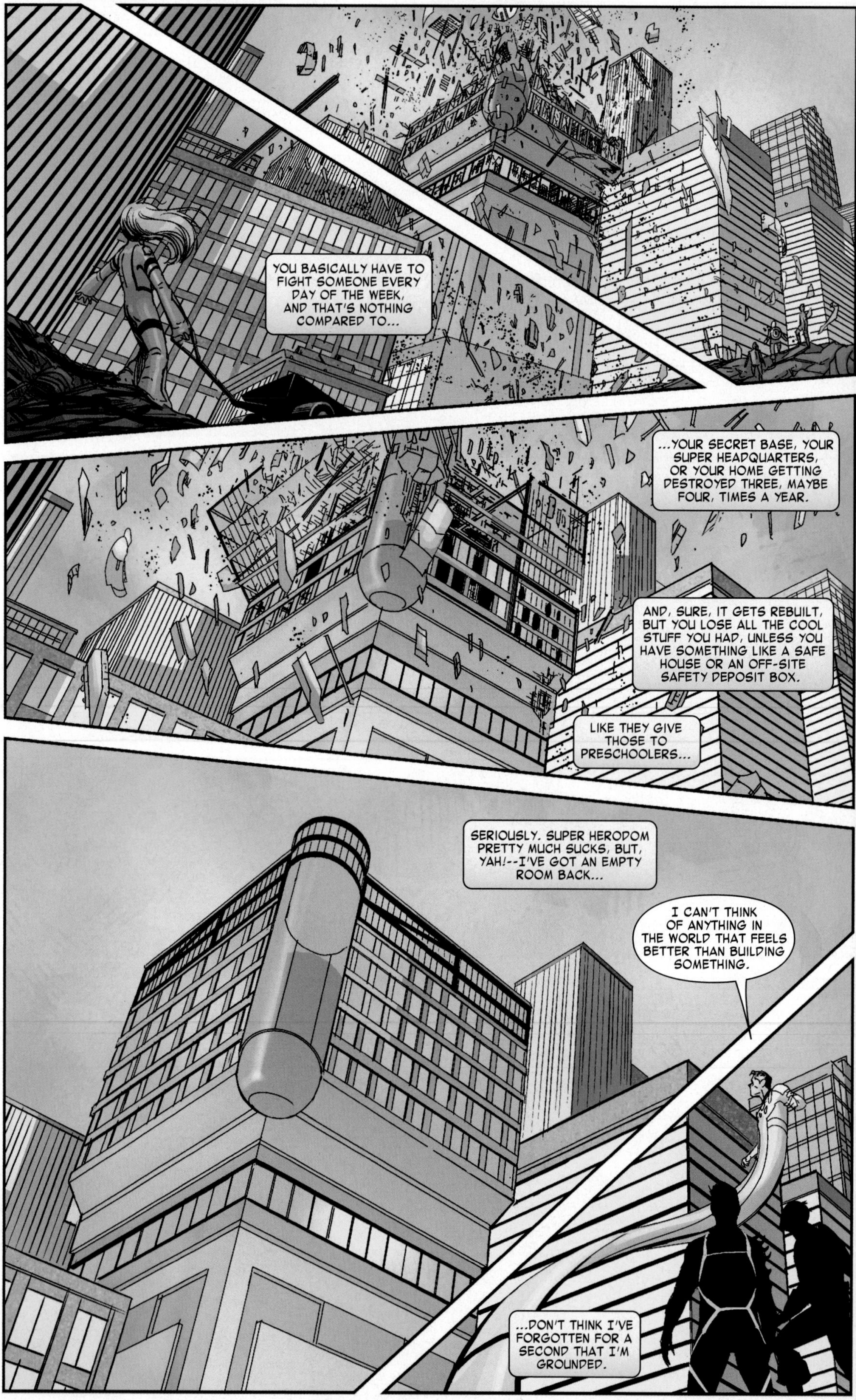
YOU BASICALLY HAVE TO FIGHT SOMEONE EVERY DAY OF THE WEEK, AND THAT'S NOTHING COMPARED TO...
...YOUR SECRET BASE, YOUR SUPER HEADQUARTERS, OR YOUR HOME GETTING DESTROYED THREE, MAYBE FOUR, TIMES A YEAR.
AND, SURE, IT GETS REBUILT, BUT YOU LOSE ALL THE COOL STUFF YOU HAD, UNLESS YOU HAVE SOMETHING LIKE A SAFE HOUSE OR AN OFF-SITE SAFETY DEPOSIT BOX.
LIKE THEY GIVE THOSE TO PRESCHOOLERS...
SERIOUSLY. SUPER HERODOM PRETTY MUCH SUCKS, BUT, YAH!--I'VE GOT AN EMPTY ROOM BACK...
I CAN'T THINK OF ANYTHING IN THE WORLD THAT FEELS BETTER THAN BUILDING SOMETHING.
...DON'T THINK I'VE FORGOTTEN FOR A SECOND THAT I'M GROUNDED.

OKAY, SO...

WE'VE CHANGED A FEW THINGS.

EACH OF YOU WILL HAVE YOUR OWN, MORE PERSONALIZED QUARTERS.

UNTIL THE BUILDING GETS DESTROYED AGAIN. COUNTDOWN READS: THREE MONTHS, TWENTY-SIX DAYS UNTIL IT ALL FALLS DOWN.

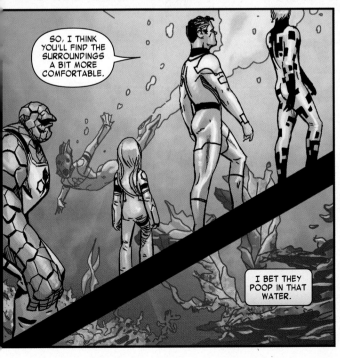

SO, I THINK YOU'LL FIND THE SURROUNDINGS A BIT MORE COMFORTABLE.

I BET THEY POOP IN THAT WATER.

THE LAYOUT HAS CHANGED, SO AS SOON AS YOU GET THE CHANCE, PLEASE FAMILIARIZE YOURSELF WITH THE UPDATED FLOORPLAN.

WE DON'T WANT ANYONE MISSING DINNER BECAUSE THEY GOT STUCK IN THE ZERO GRAVITY ROOM.

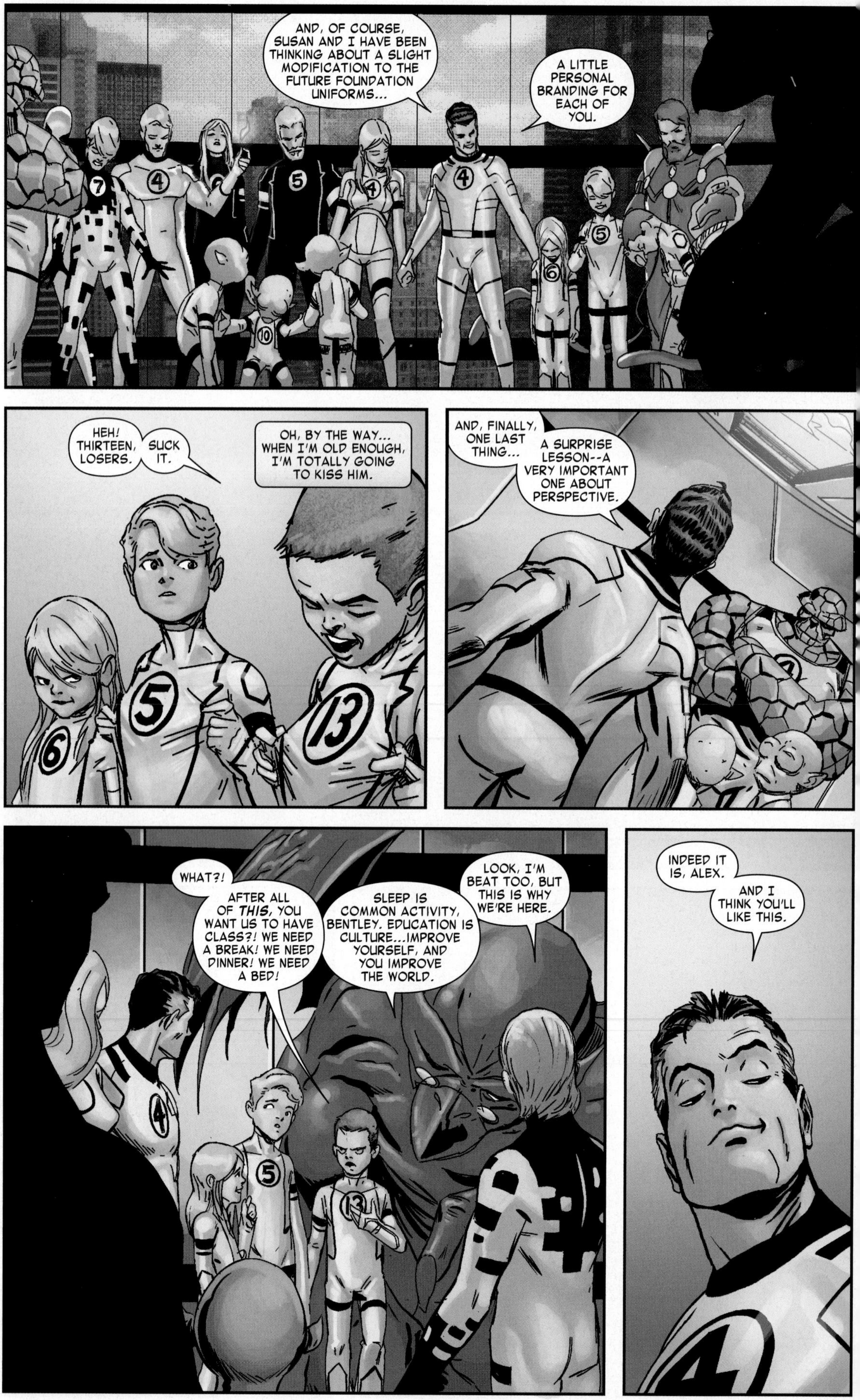
AND, OF COURSE, SUSAN AND I HAVE BEEN THINKING ABOUT A SLIGHT MODIFICATION TO THE FUTURE FOUNDATION UNIFORMS...
A LITTLE PERSONAL BRANDING FOR EACH OF YOU.
HEH! THIRTEEN, LOSERS.
SUCK IT.
OH, BY THE WAY... WHEN I'M OLD ENOUGH, I'M TOTALLY GOING TO KISS HIM.
AND, FINALLY, ONE LAST THING...
A SURPRISE LESSON--A VERY IMPORTANT ONE ABOUT PERSPECTIVE.
WHAT?!
AFTER ALL OF THIS, YOU WANT US TO HAVE CLASS?! WE NEED A BREAK! WE NEED DINNER! WE NEED A BED!
SLEEP IS COMMON ACTIVITY, BENTLEY. EDUCATION IS CULTURE...IMPROVE YOURSELF, AND YOU IMPROVE THE WORLD.
LOOK, I'M BEAT TOO, BUT THIS IS WHY WE'RE HERE.
INDEED IT IS, ALEX.
AND I THINK YOU'LL LIKE THIS.

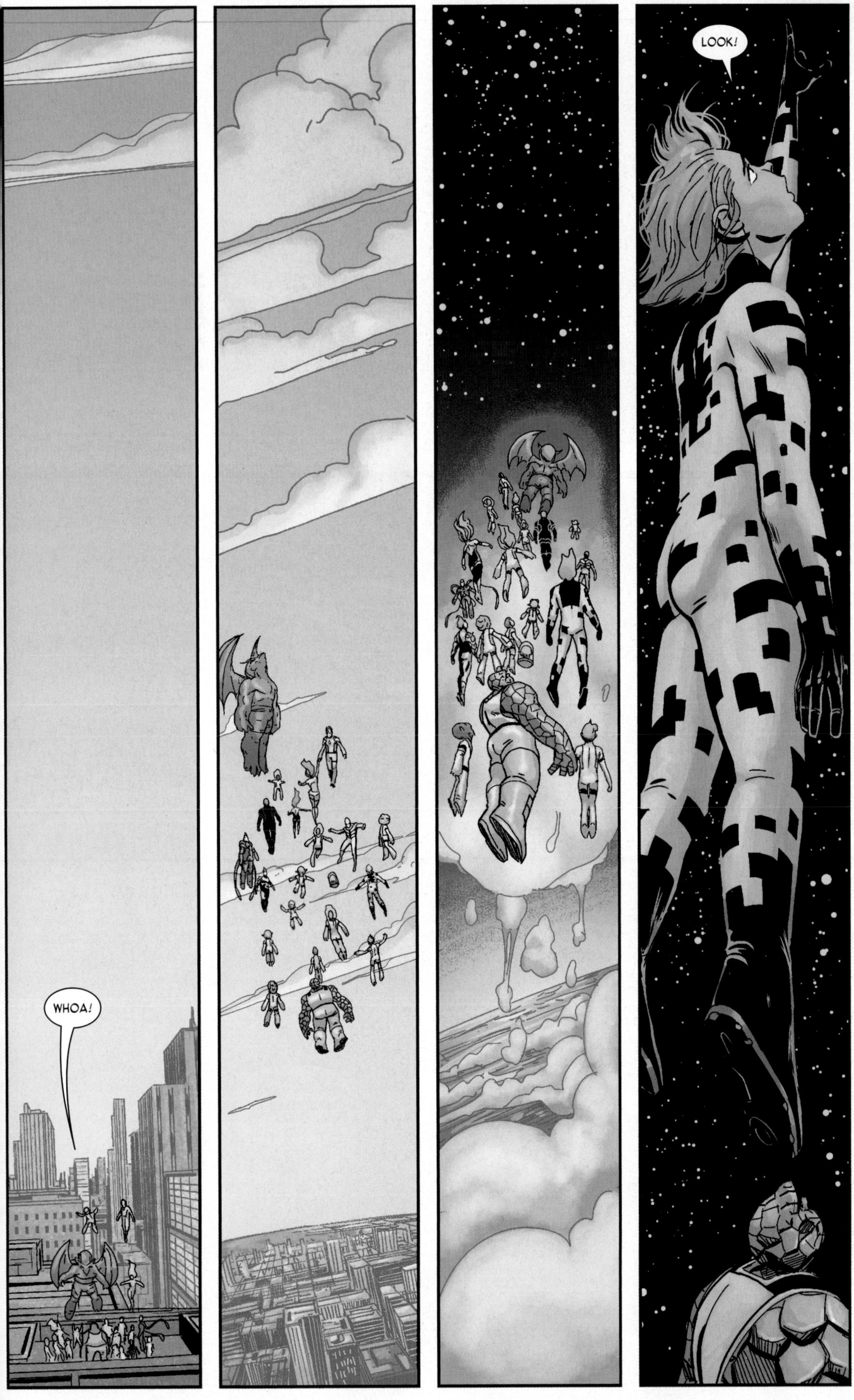

WHOA!
LOOK!

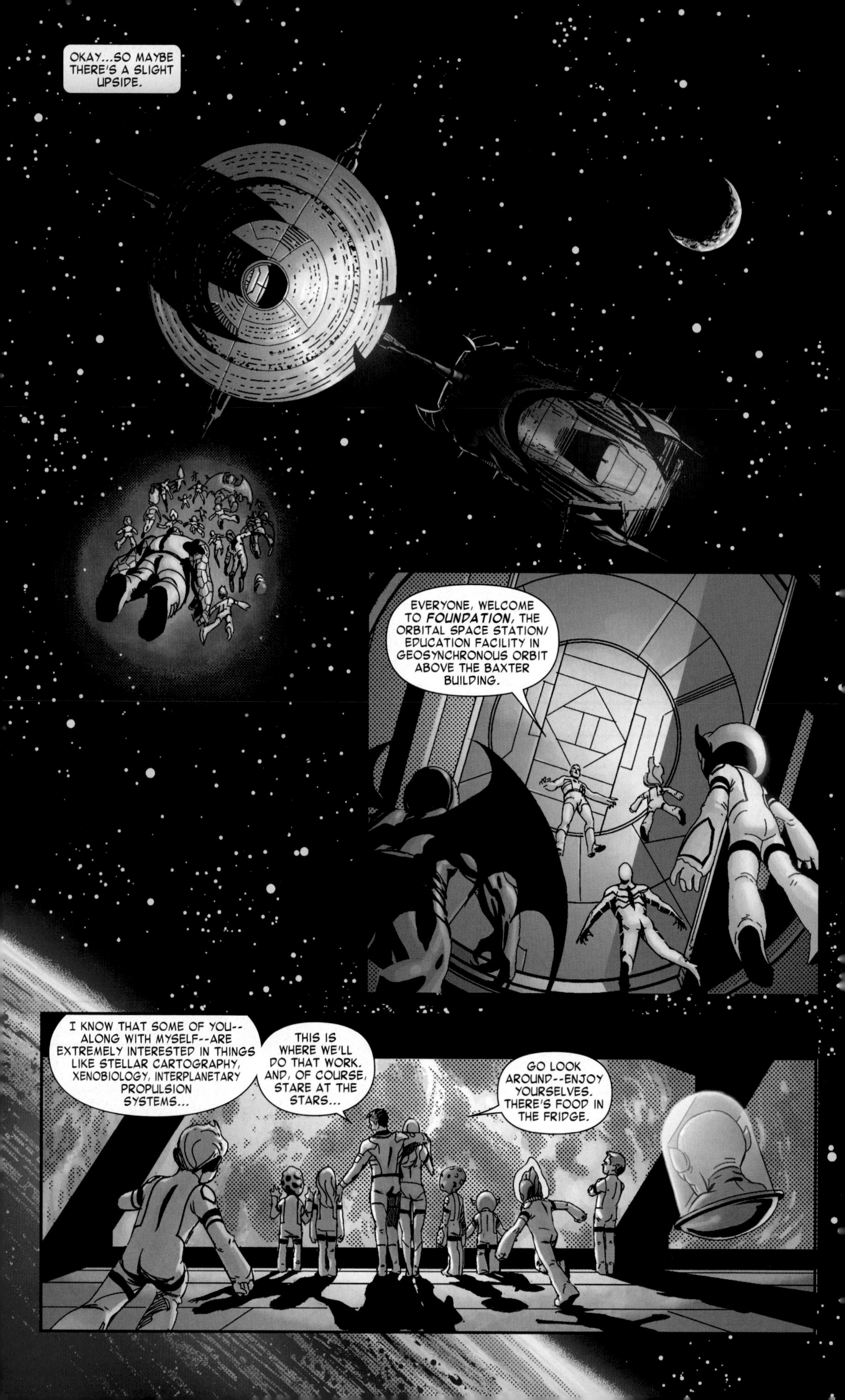
OKAY...SO MAYBE THERE'S A SLIGHT UPSIDE.
EVERYONE, WELCOME TO *FOUNDATION*, THE ORBITAL SPACE STATION/ EDUCATION FACILITY IN GEOSYNCHRONOUS ORBIT ABOVE THE BAXTER BUILDING.
I KNOW THAT SOME OF YOU-- ALONG WITH MYSELF--ARE EXTREMELY INTERESTED IN THINGS LIKE STELLAR CARTOGRAPHY, XENOBIOLOGY, INTERPLANETARY PROPULSION SYSTEMS...
THIS IS WHERE WE'LL DO THAT WORK. AND, OF COURSE, STARE AT THE STARS...
GO LOOK AROUND--ENJOY YOURSELVES. THERE'S FOOD IN THE FRIDGE.

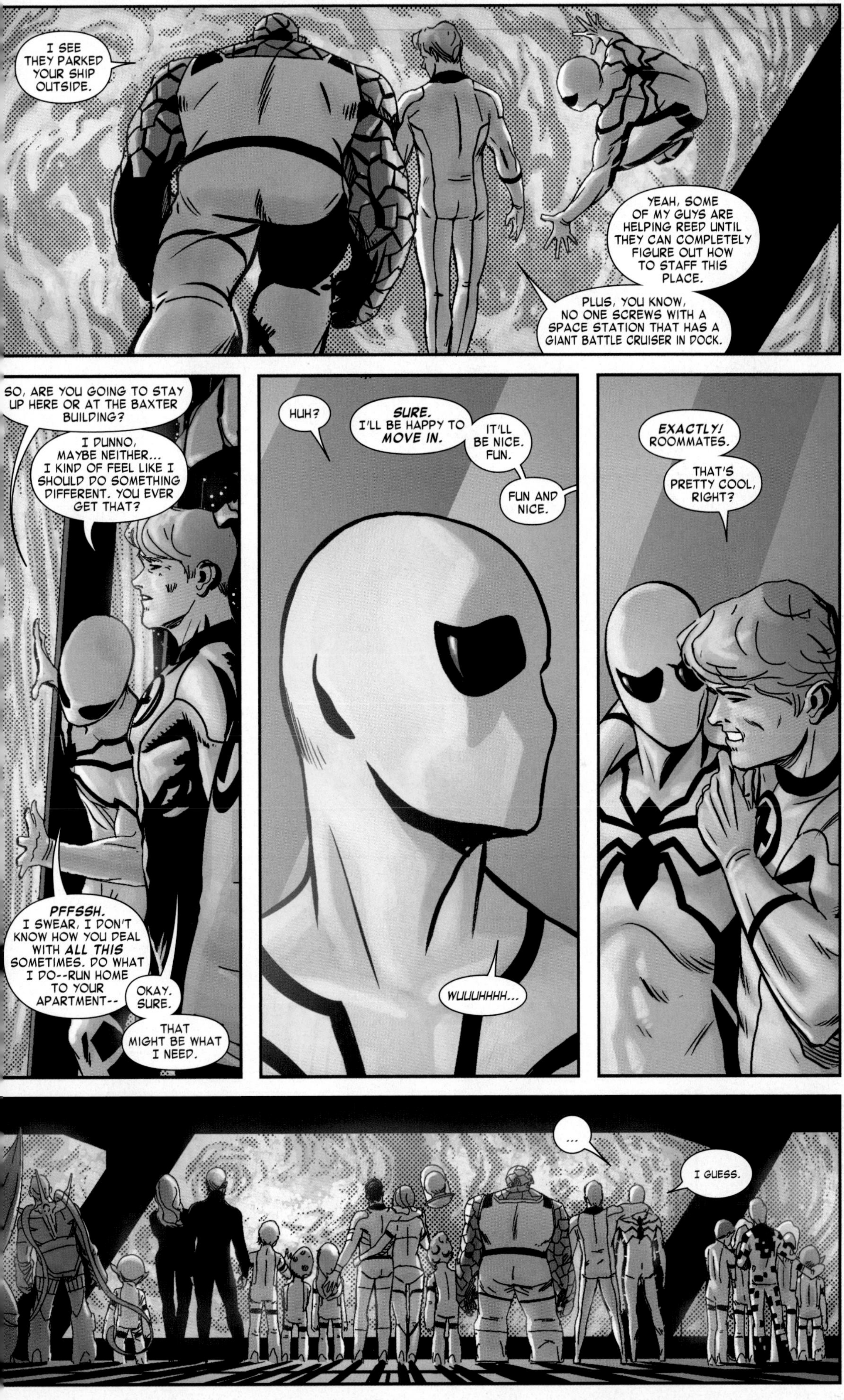
I SEE THEY PARKED YOUR SHIP OUTSIDE.
YEAH, SOME OF MY GUYS ARE HELPING REED UNTIL THEY CAN COMPLETELY FIGURE OUT HOW TO STAFF THIS PLACE.
PLUS, YOU KNOW, NO ONE SCREWS WITH A SPACE STATION THAT HAS A GIANT BATTLE CRUISER IN DOCK.
SO, ARE YOU GOING TO STAY UP HERE OR AT THE BAXTER BUILDING?
I DUNNO, MAYBE NEITHER... I KIND OF FEEL LIKE I SHOULD DO SOMETHING DIFFERENT. YOU EVER GET THAT?
PFFSSH. I SWEAR, I DON'T KNOW HOW YOU DEAL WITH ALL THIS SOMETIMES. DO WHAT I DO--RUN HOME TO YOUR APARTMENT--
OKAY. SURE.
THAT MIGHT BE WHAT I NEED.
HUH?
SURE. I'LL BE HAPPY TO MOVE IN.
IT'LL BE NICE. FUN.
FUN AND NICE.
WUUUHHHH...
EXACTLY! ROOMMATES.
THAT'S PRETTY COOL, RIGHT?
...
I GUESS.

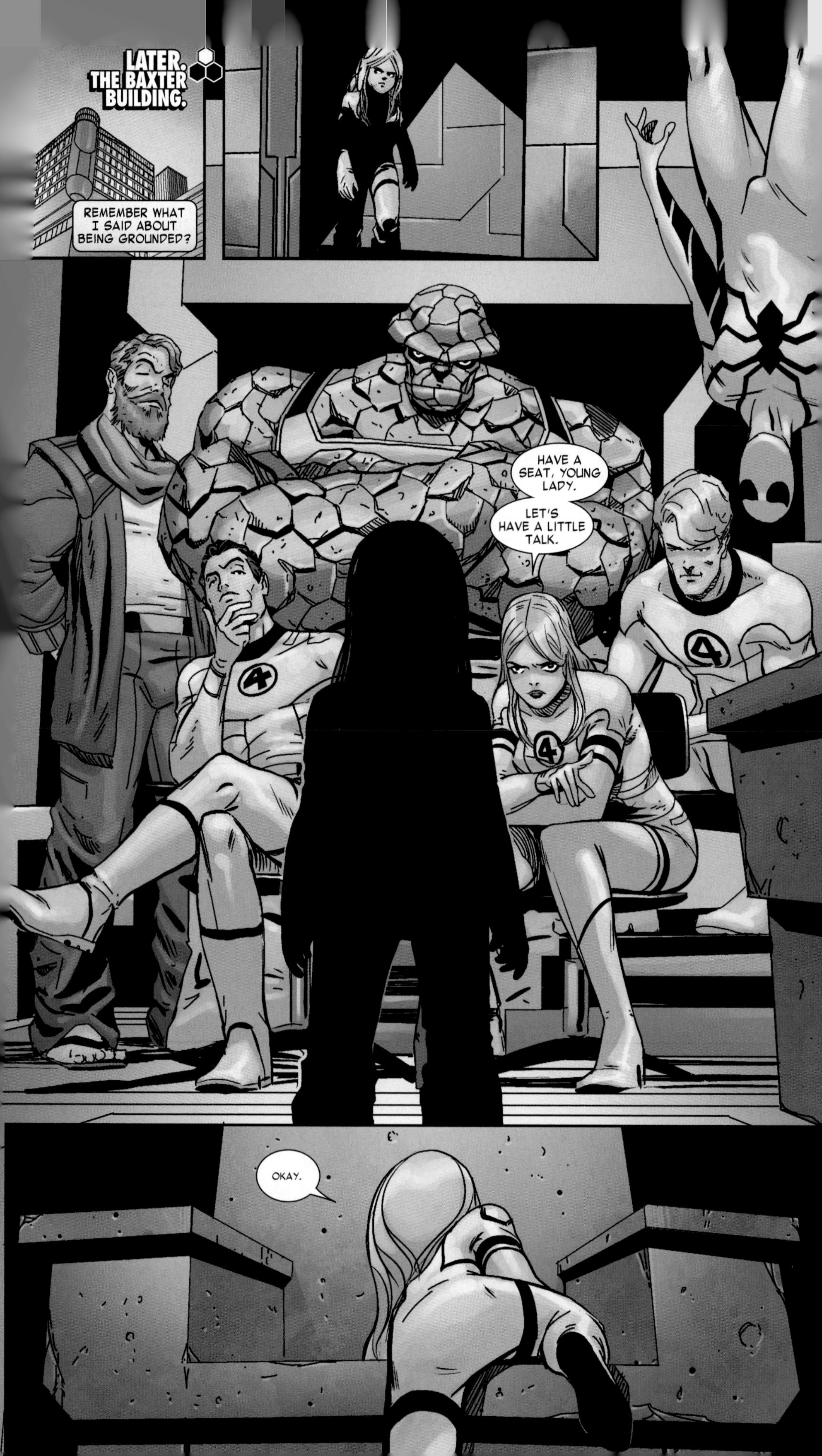

LATER. THE BAXTER BUILDING.
REMEMBER WHAT I SAID ABOUT BEING GROUNDED?
HAVE A SEAT, YOUNG LADY.
LET'S HAVE A LITTLE TALK.
OKAY.

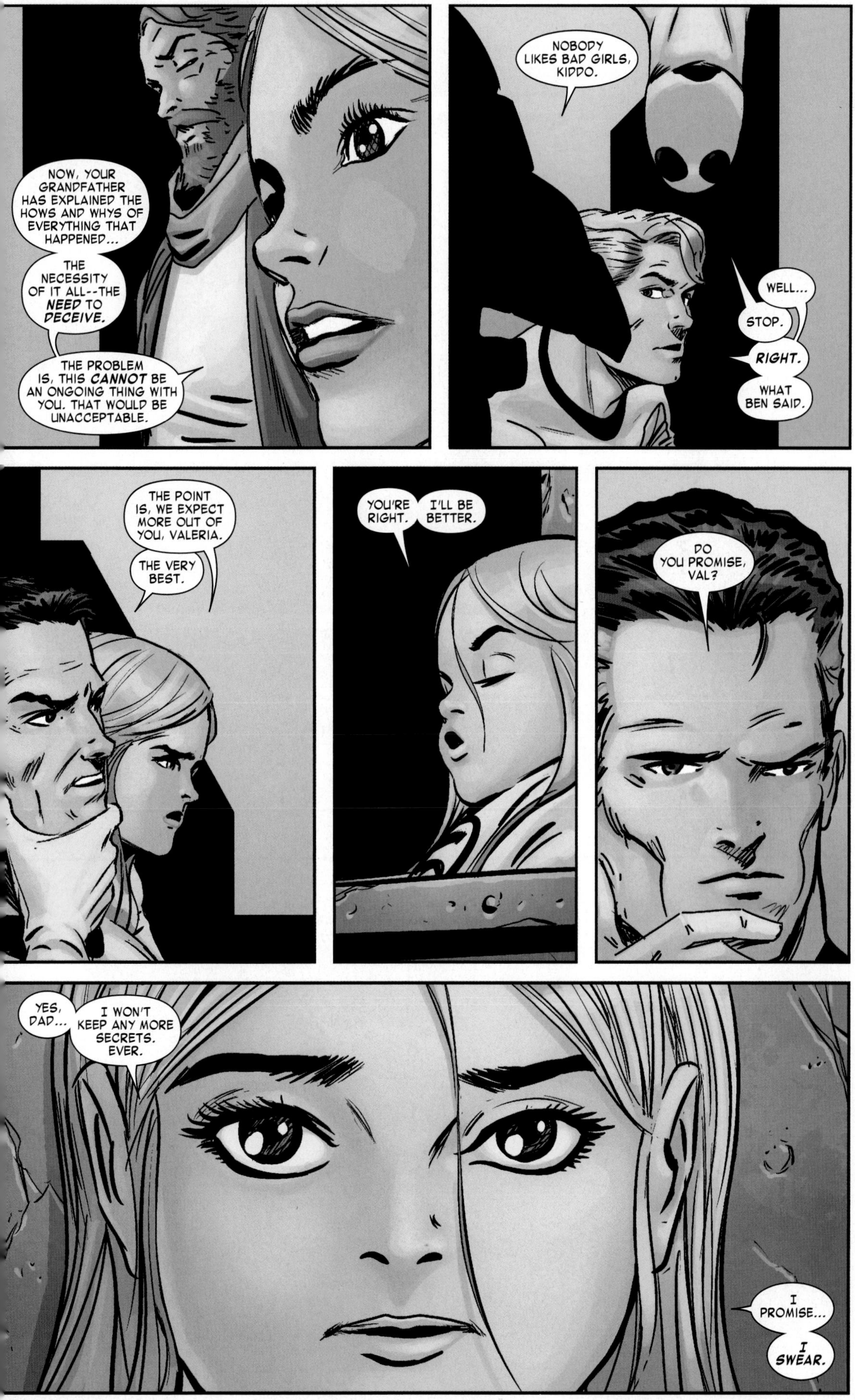

NOW, YOUR GRANDFATHER HAS EXPLAINED THE HOWS AND WHYS OF EVERYTHING THAT HAPPENED...
THE NECESSITY OF IT ALL--THE NEED TO DECEIVE.
THE PROBLEM IS, THIS CANNOT BE AN ONGOING THING WITH YOU. THAT WOULD BE UNACCEPTABLE.
NOBODY LIKES BAD GIRLS, KIDDO.
WELL...
STOP.
RIGHT.
WHAT BEN SAID.
THE POINT IS, WE EXPECT MORE OUT OF YOU, VALERIA.
THE VERY BEST.
YOU'RE RIGHT.
I'LL BE BETTER.
DO YOU PROMISE, VAL?
YES, DAD...
I WON'T KEEP ANY MORE SECRETS. EVER.
I PROMISE...
I SWEAR.

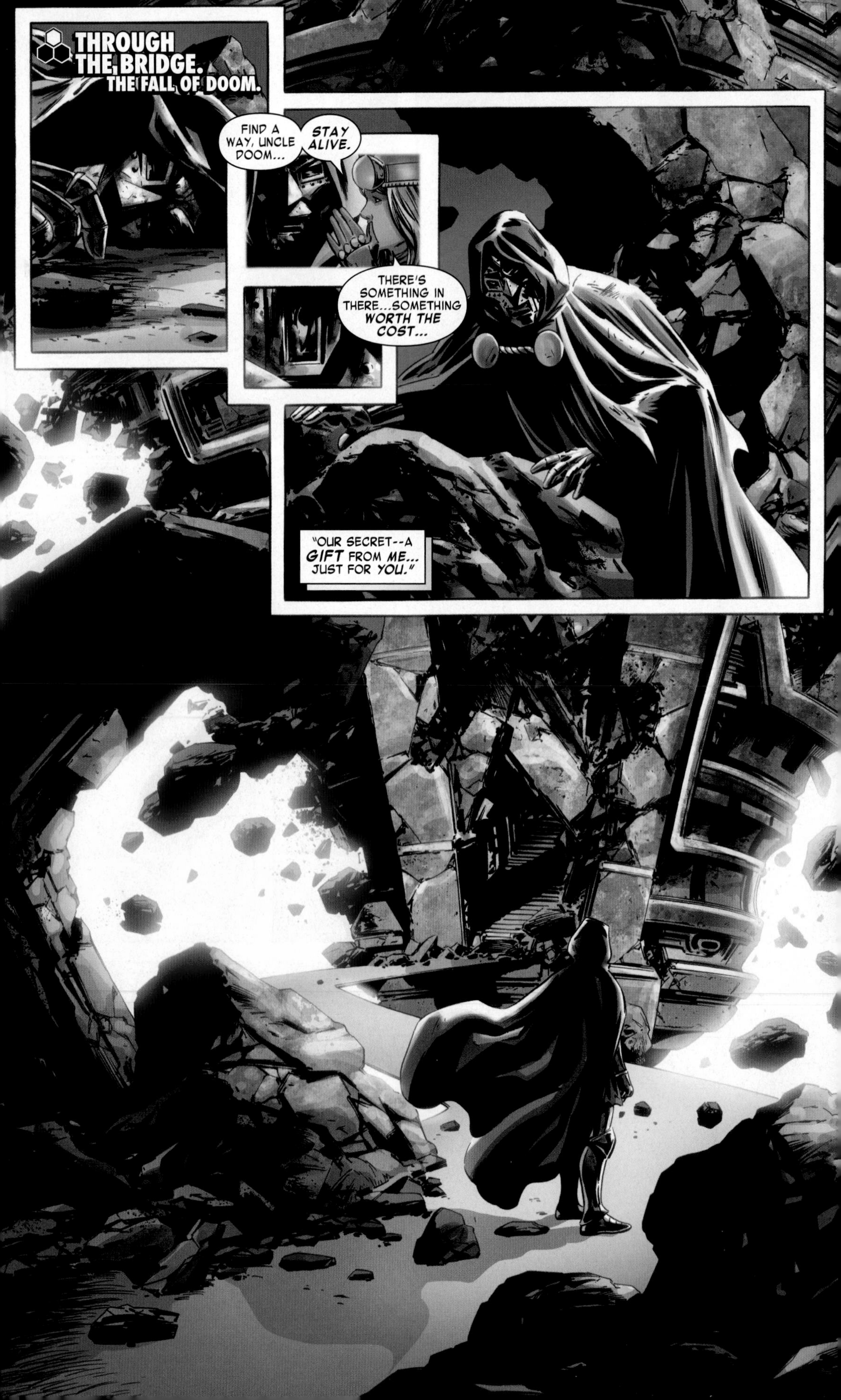
THROUGH THE BRIDGE.
THE FALL OF DOOM.
FIND A WAY, UNCLE DOOM...
STAY ALIVE.
THERE'S SOMETHING IN THERE...SOMETHING WORTH THE COST...
"OUR SECRET--A GIFT FROM ME... JUST FOR YOU."

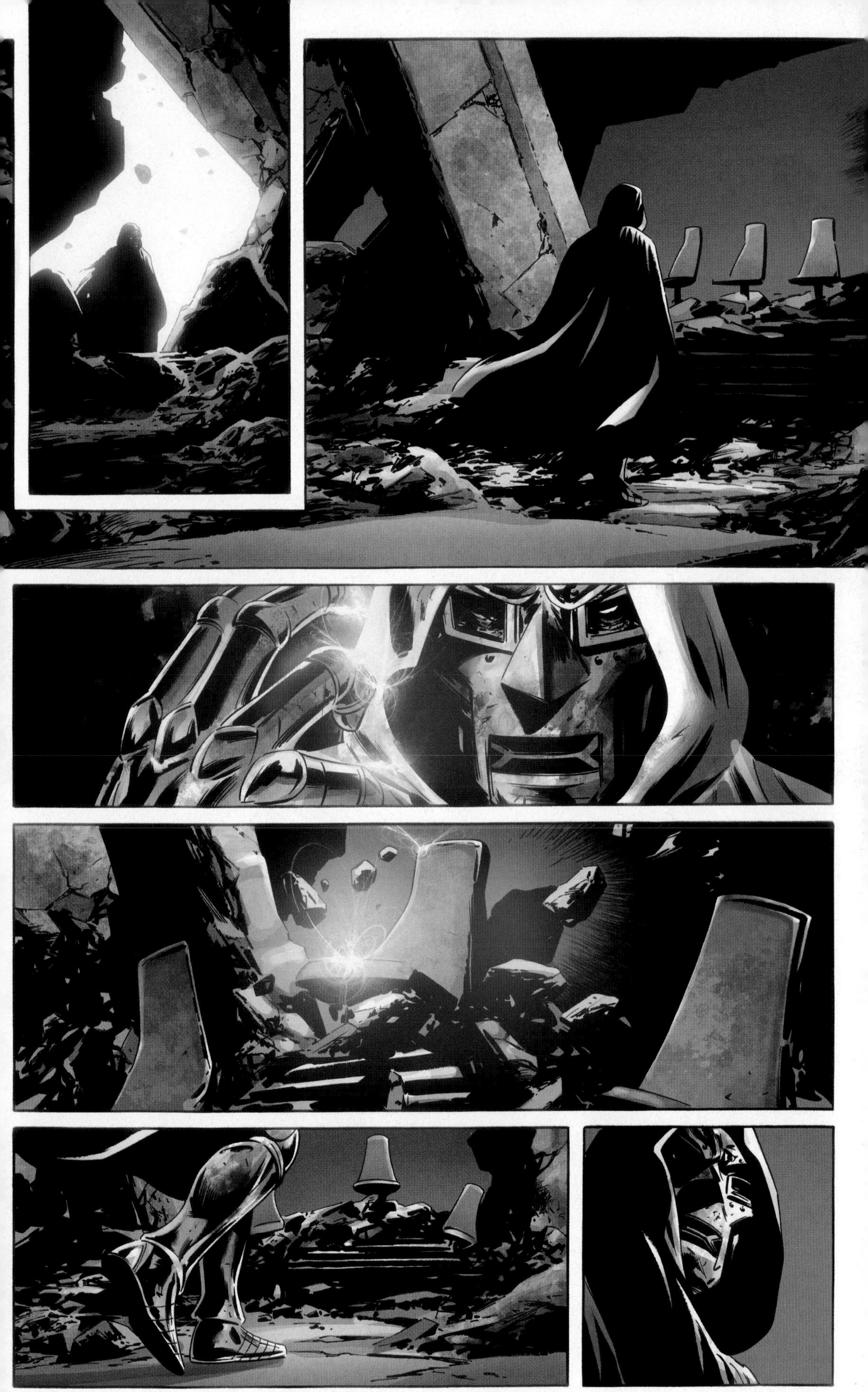

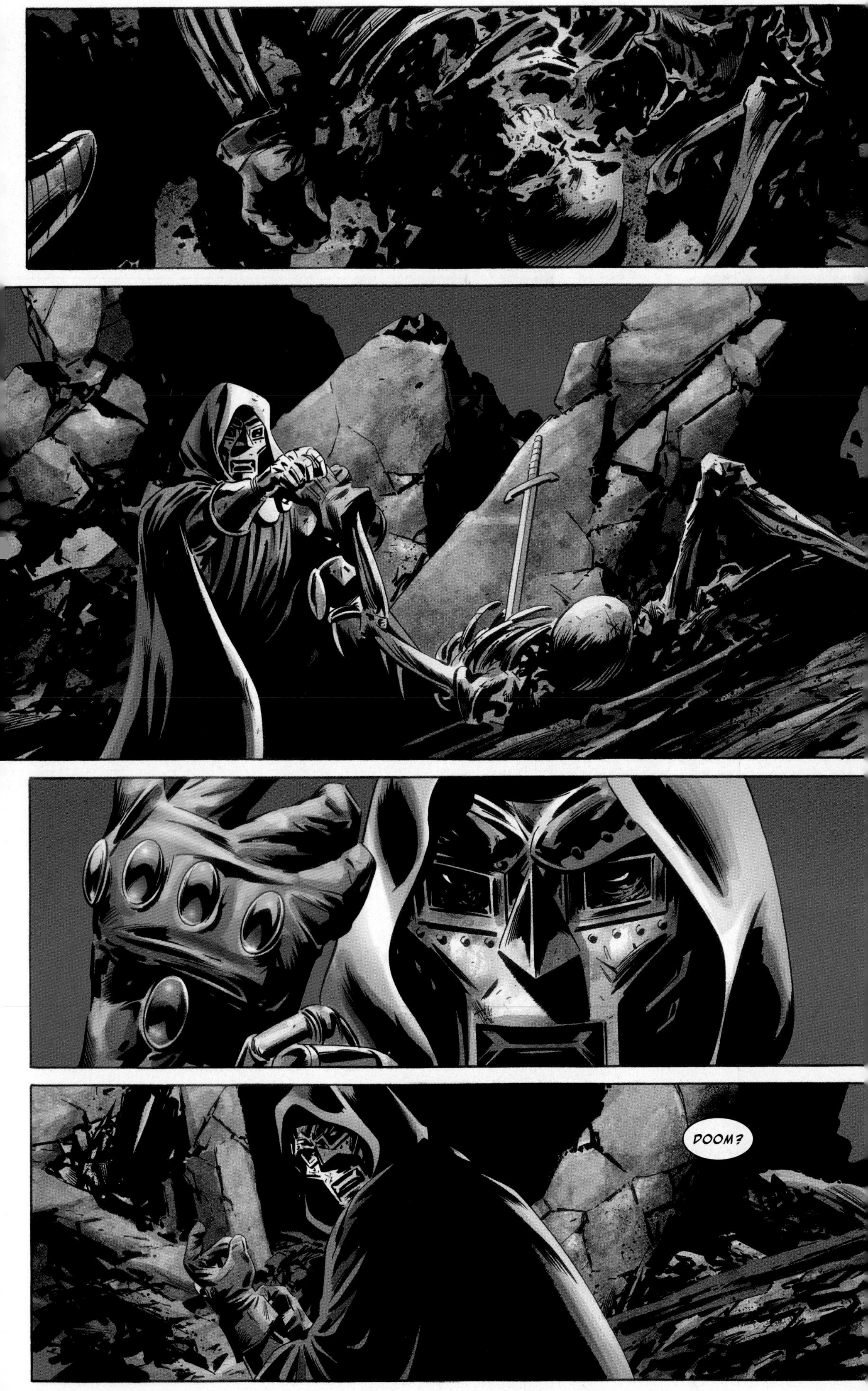
DOOM?

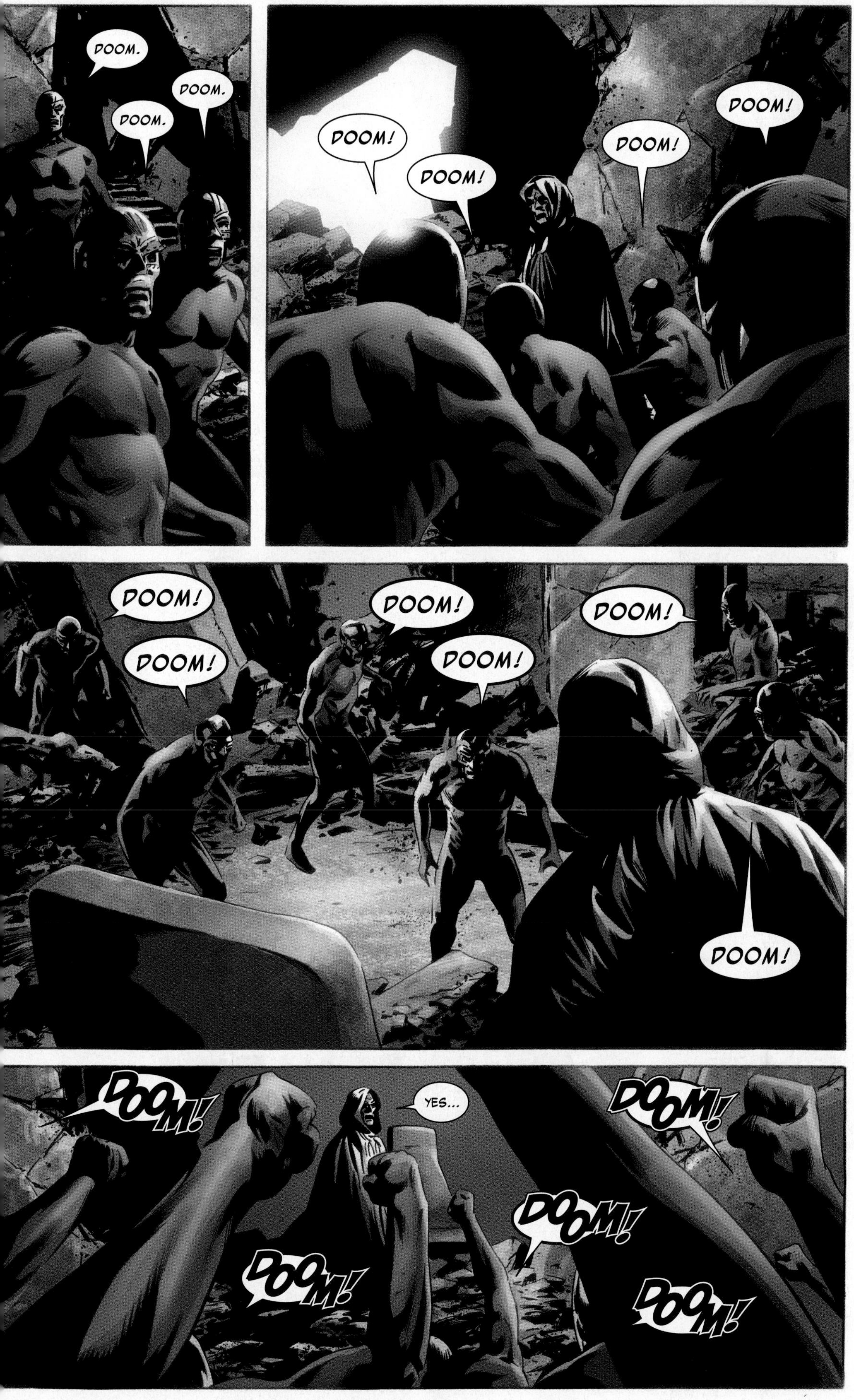

DOOM.
DOOM.
DOOM.
DOOM!
DOOM!
DOOM!
DOOM!
DOOM!
DOOM!
DOOM!
DOOM!
DOOM!
DOOM!
DOOM!
YES...
DOOM!
DOOM!
DOOM!
DOOM!

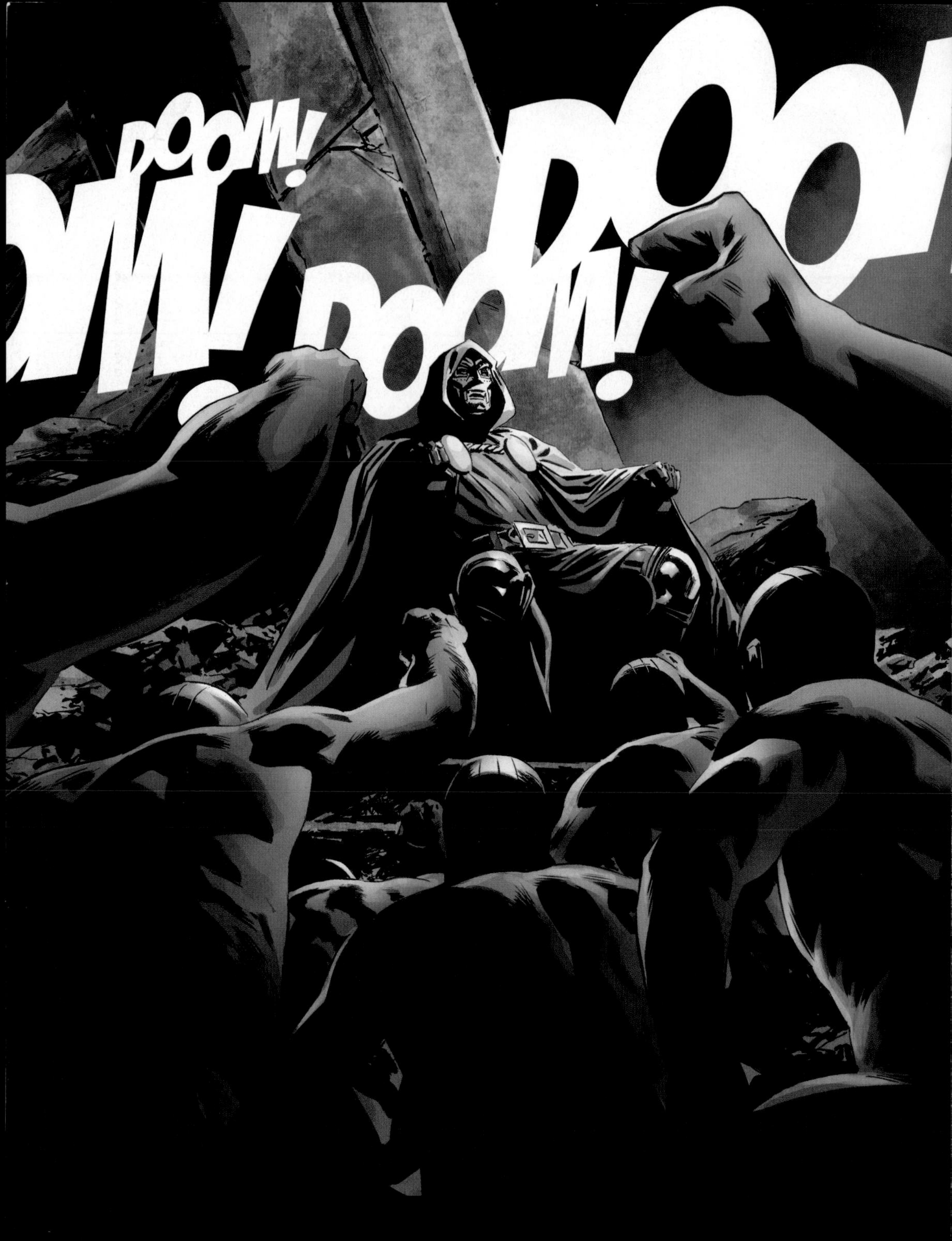
DOOM!
DOOM!

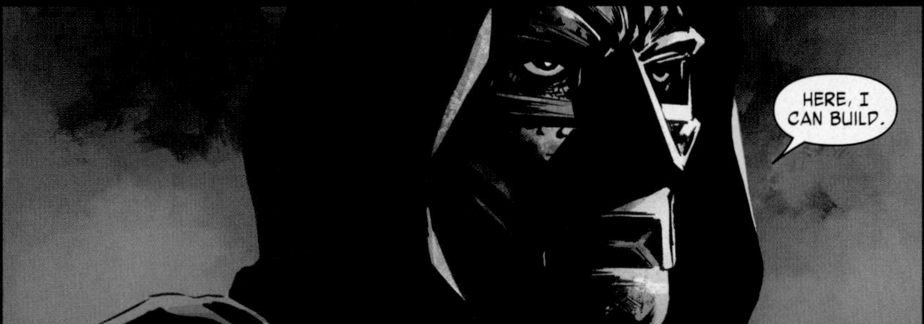
HERE, I CAN BUILD.

THE PARLIAMENT OF DOOM

COVER GALLERY

#12 COVER: **STEVE EPTING**

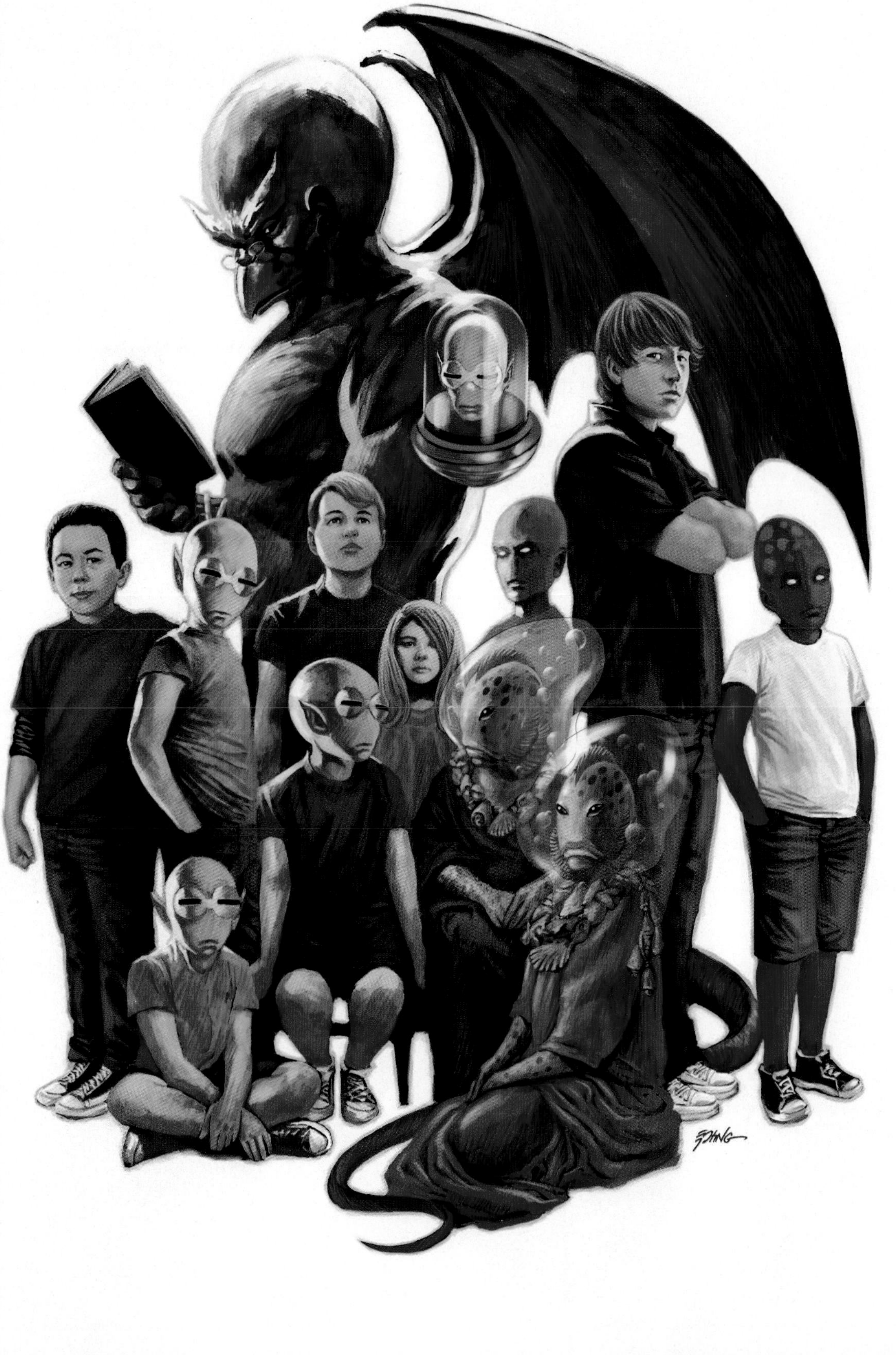

#13 COVER. MIKE CHOI & GURU-eFX

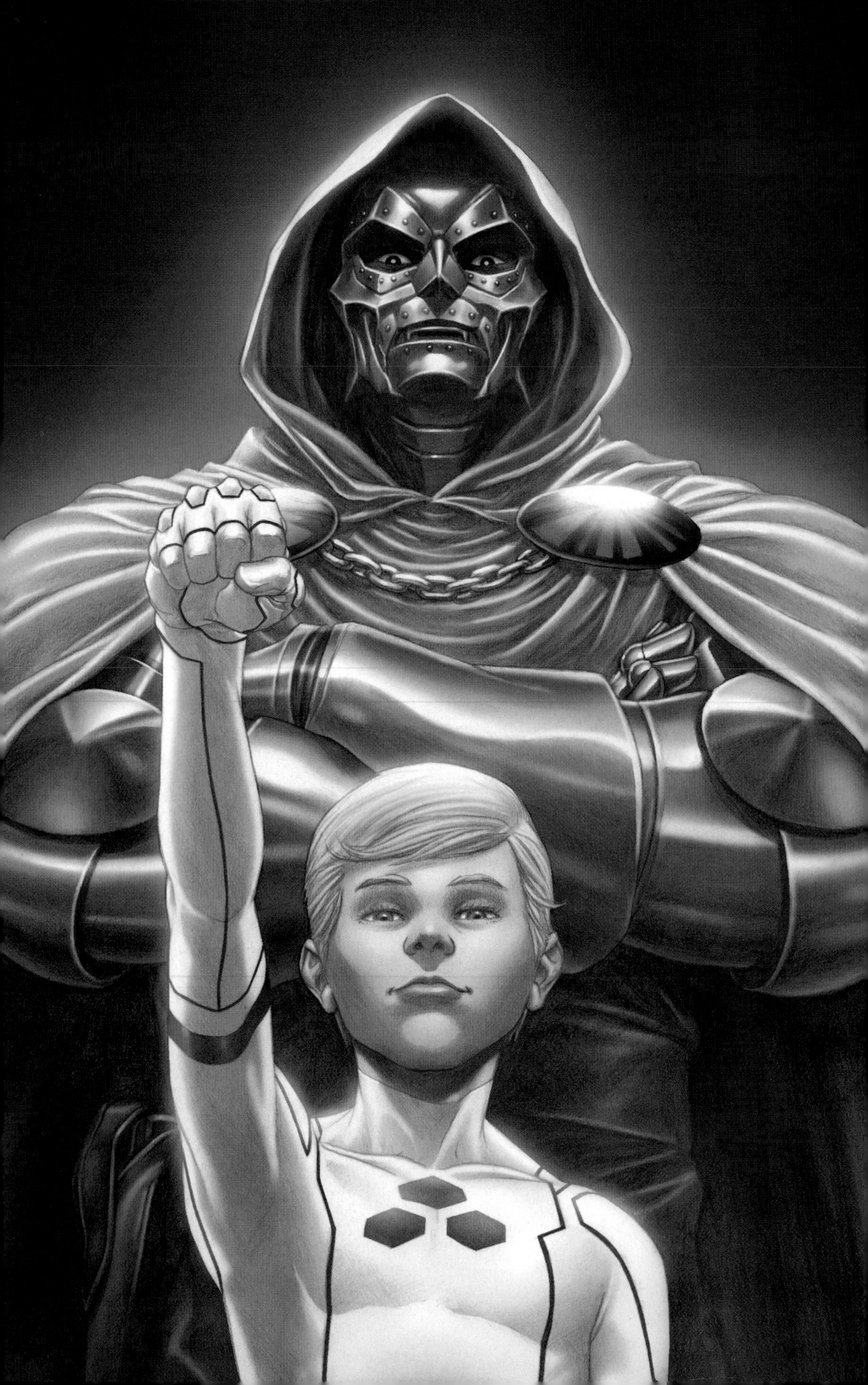

#14 COVER: MIKE CHOI & GURU-eFX

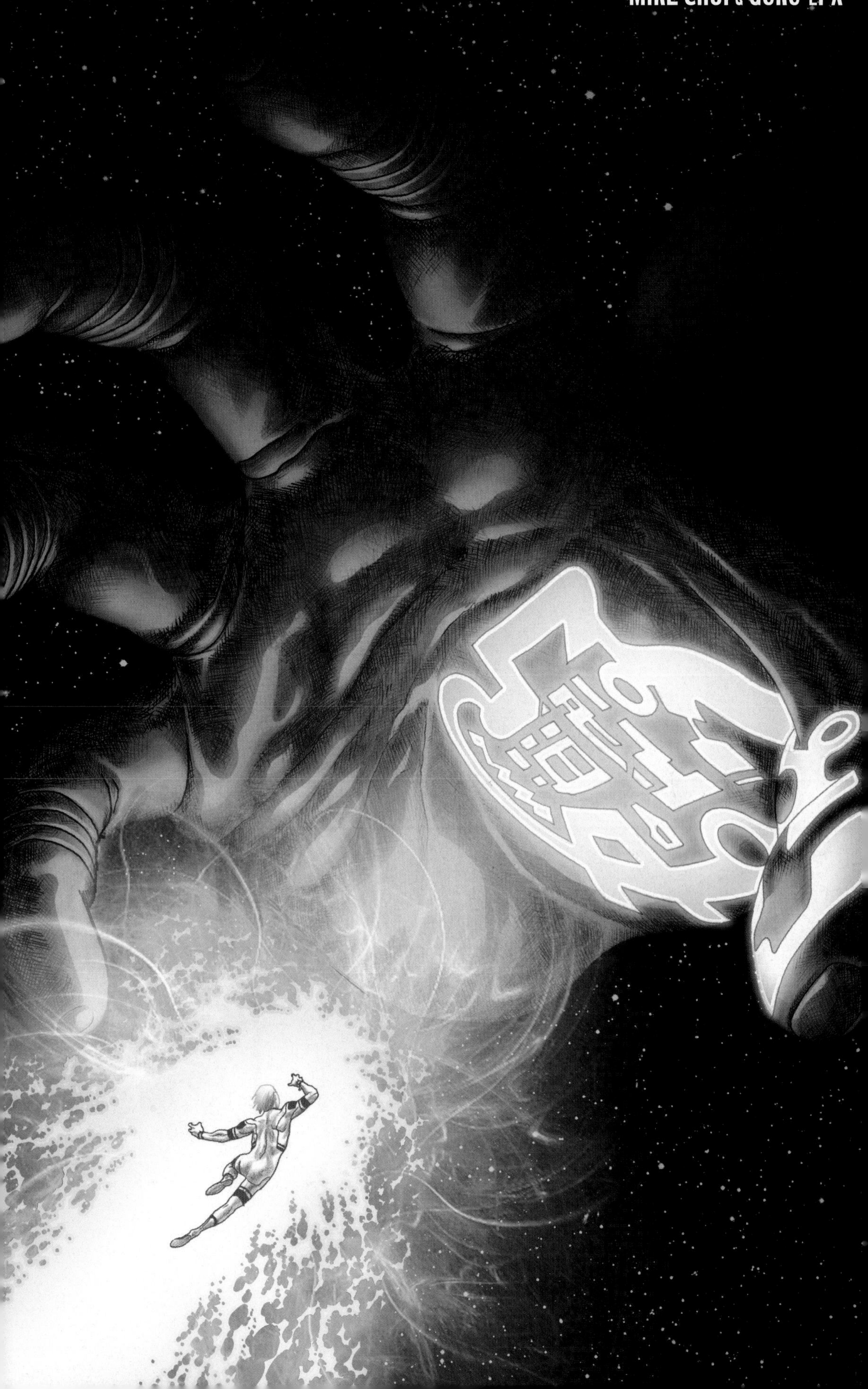

#15 COVER: MIKE CHOI & GURU-eFX

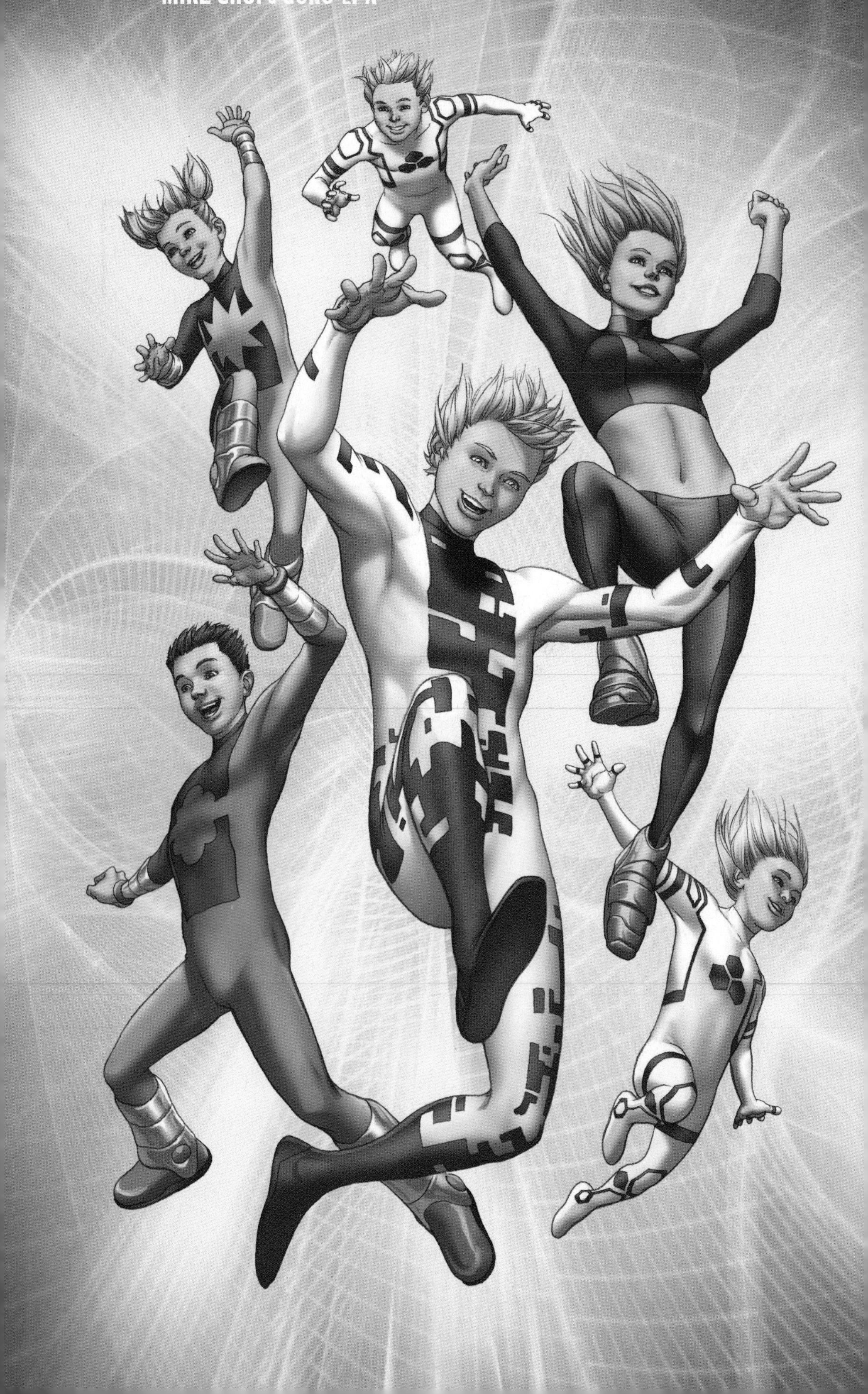

#16 COVER: MIKE CHOI & GURU-eFX

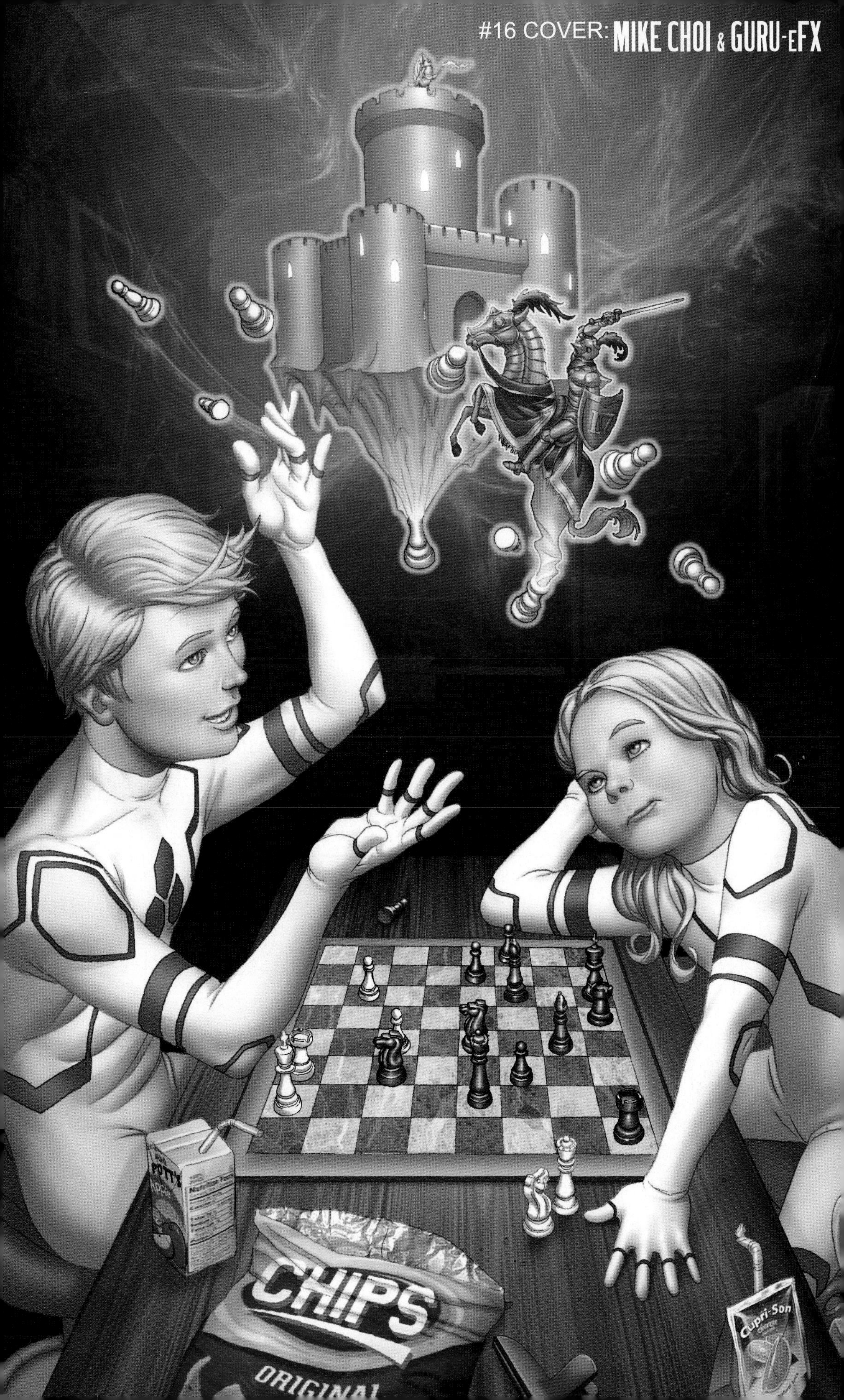
CHIPS
ORIGINAL
Cupri-Son

#12 FANTASTIC FOUR 50TH ANNIVERSARY VARIANT: **SKOTTIE YOUNG**

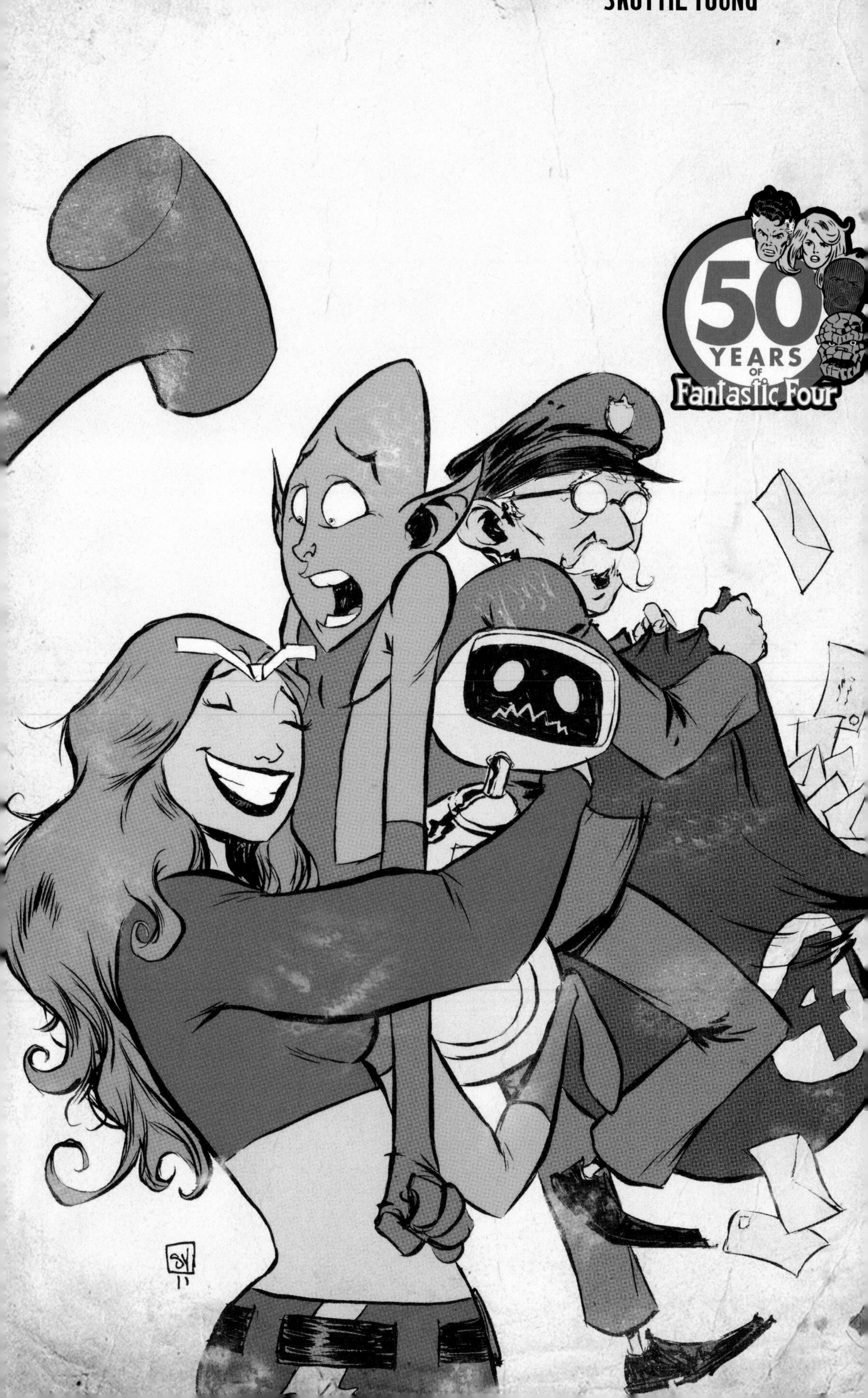

50
YEARS
OF
Fantastic Four

#12 VARIANT: GABRIELE DELL'OTTO

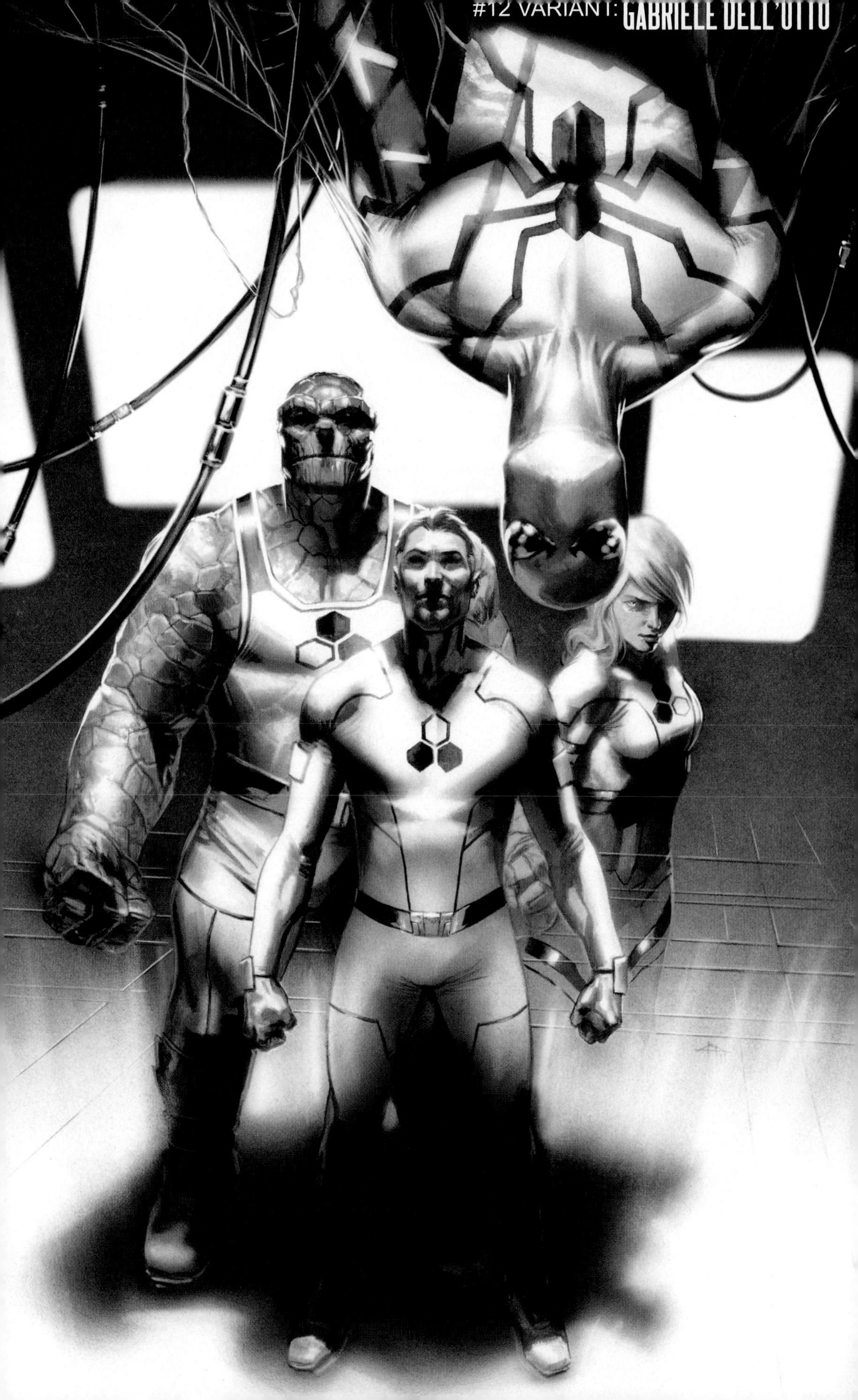

FANTASTIC FOUR #601 & FF #13 COMBINED VARIANTS: GIUSEPPE CAMUNCOLI &MARTE GRACIA

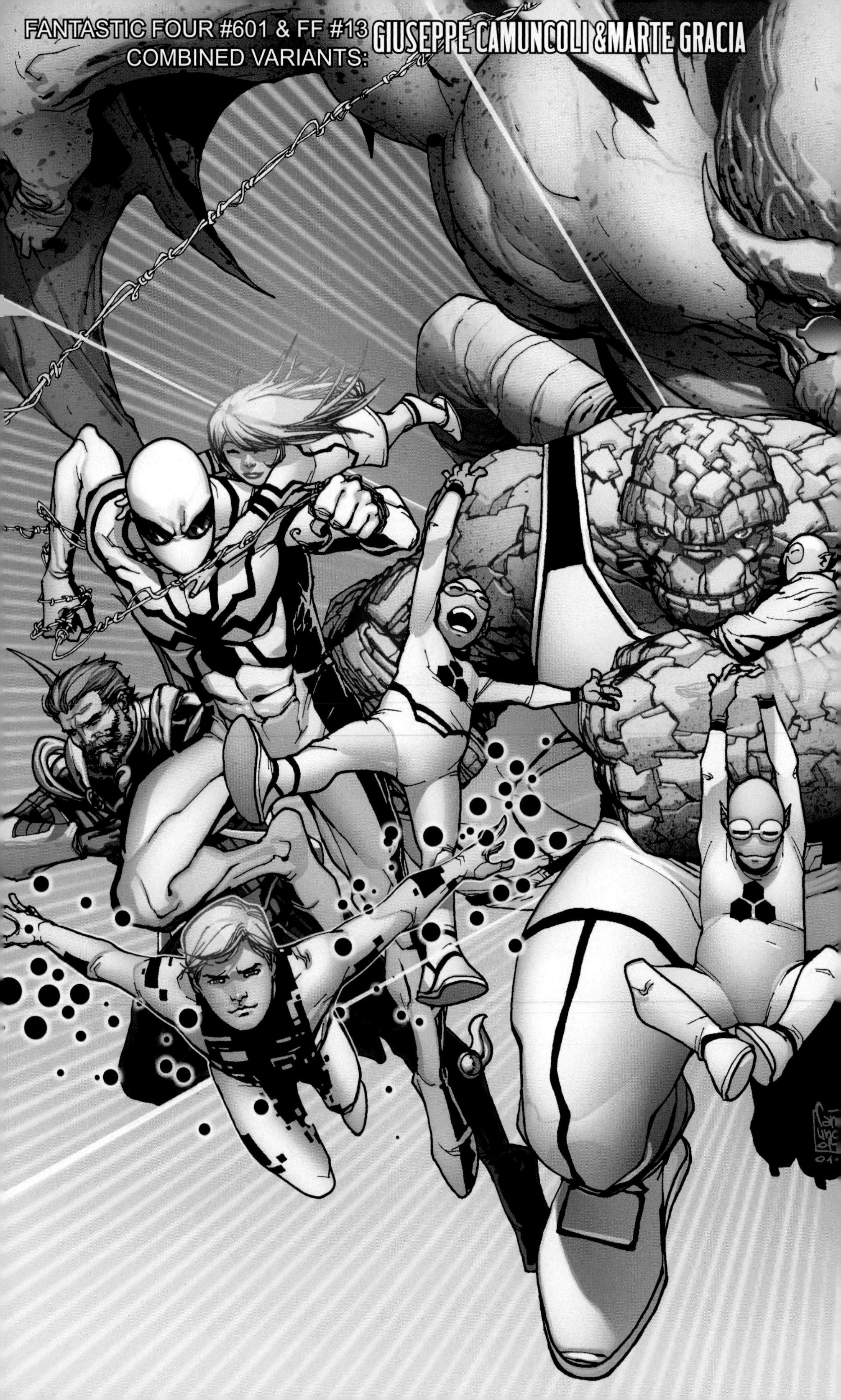

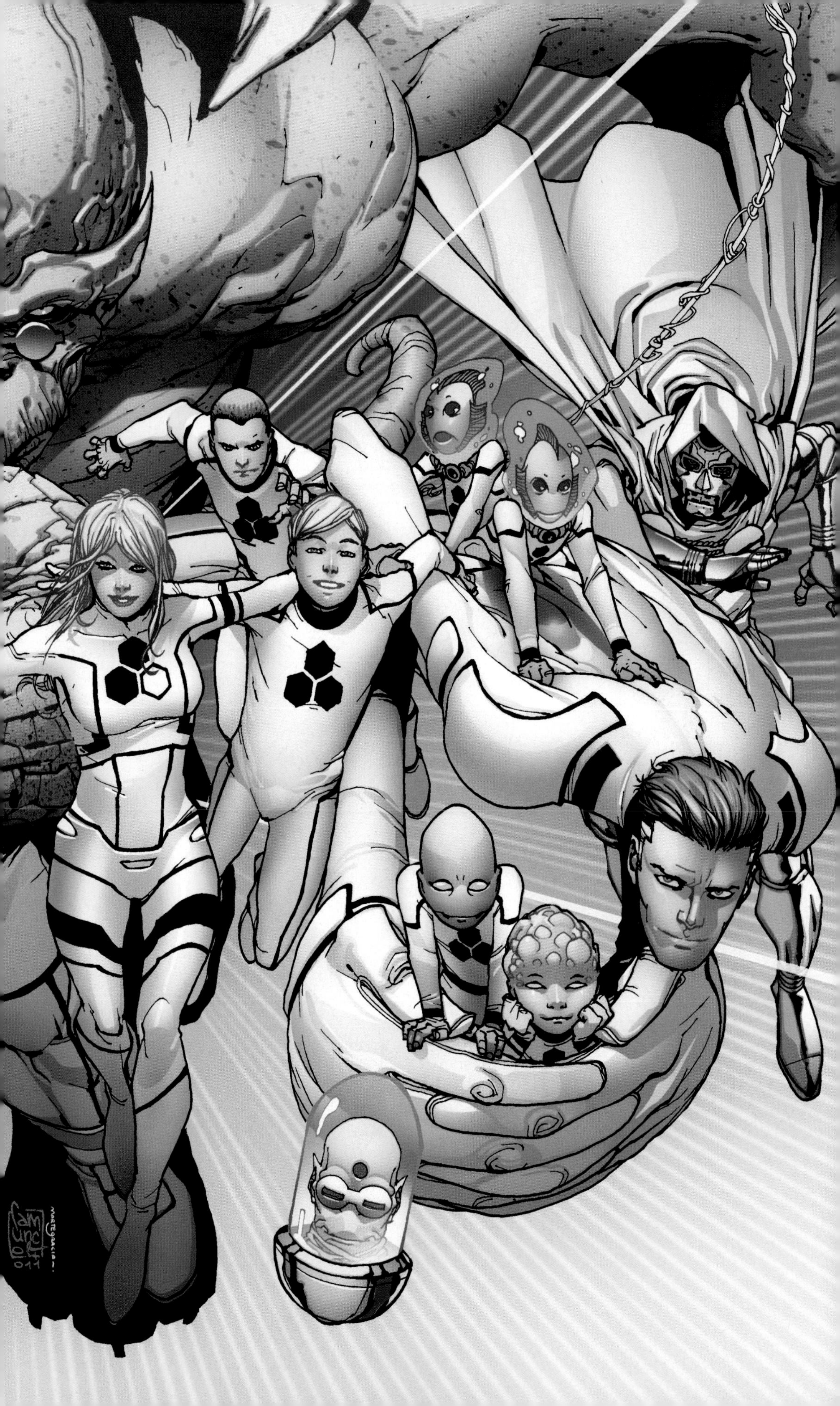

#14 VENOM VARIANT: **MICHAEL RYAN & CHRIS SOTOMAYOR**

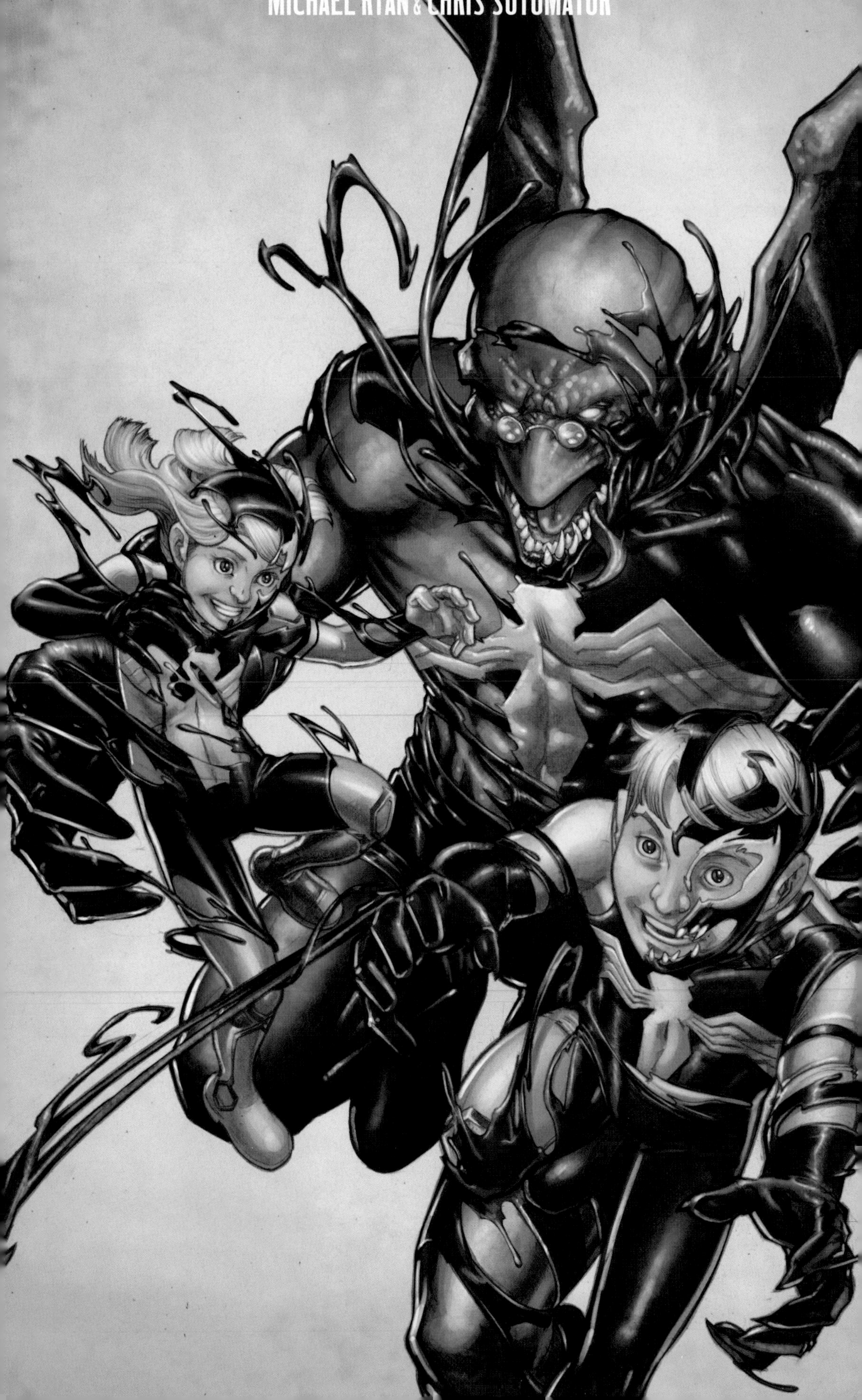

#15 VARIANT: JUNE BRIGMAN, ROY RICHARDSON & CHRISTINA STRAIN

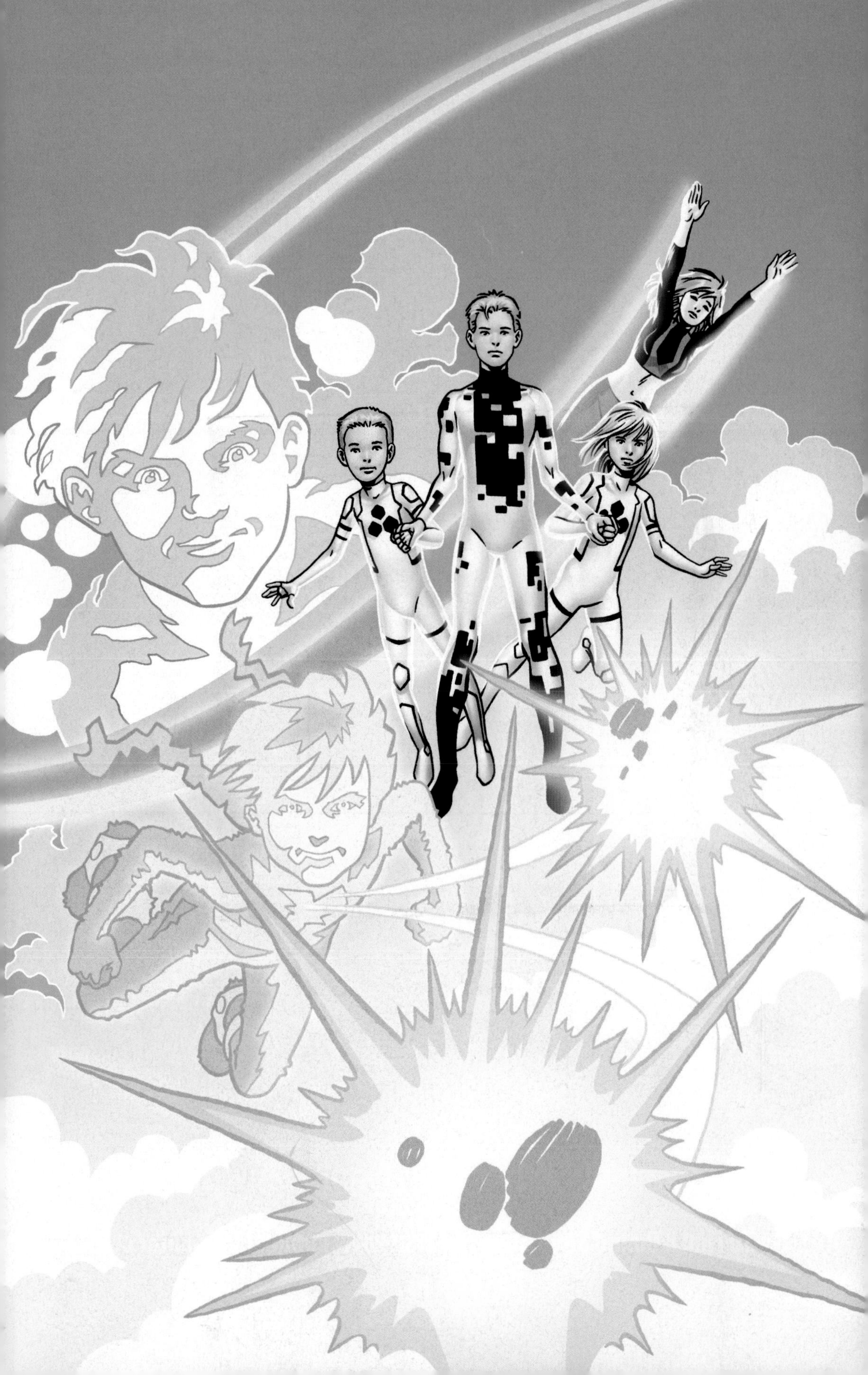

"HICKMAN SEEKS TO REVITALIZE THE TITLE BY BRINGING IT BAC
TO WHAT ALWAYS MADE IT WORK...HE'S SUCCEEDING." – *IGN*

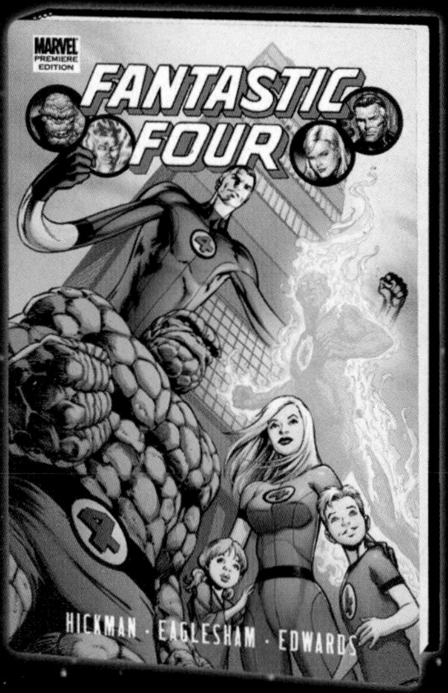
MARVEL PREMIERE EDITION
FANTASTIC FOUR
HICKMAN · EAGLESHAM · EDWARDS

FANTASTIC FOUR BY JONATHAN HICKMAN
VOL. 1 PREMIERE HC
978-0-7851-4317-8

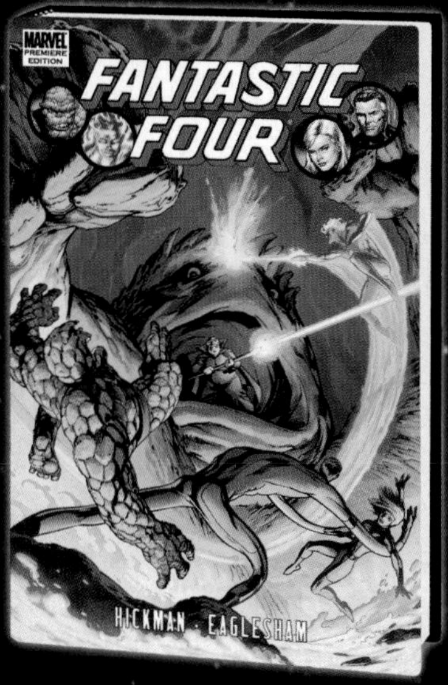
MARVEL PREMIERE EDITION
FANTASTIC FOUR
HICKMAN · EAGLESHAM

FANTASTIC FOUR BY JONATHAN HICKMAN
VOL. 2 PREMIERE HC
978-0-7851-4716-9

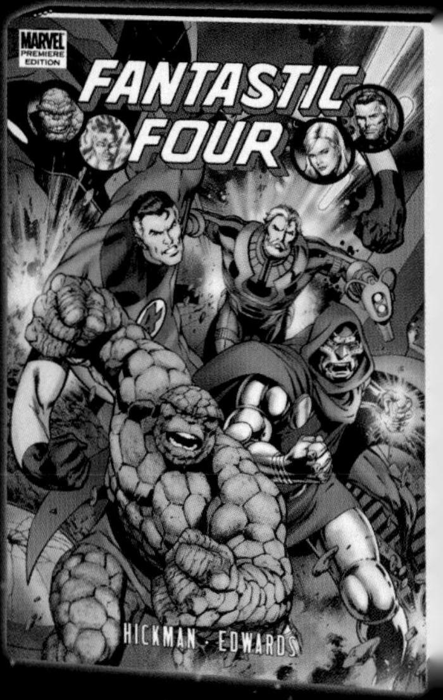
MARVEL PREMIERE EDITION
FANTASTIC FOUR
HICKMAN · EDWARDS

FANTASTIC FOUR BY JONATHAN HICKMAN
VOL. 3 PREMIERE HC
978-0-7851-4717-6

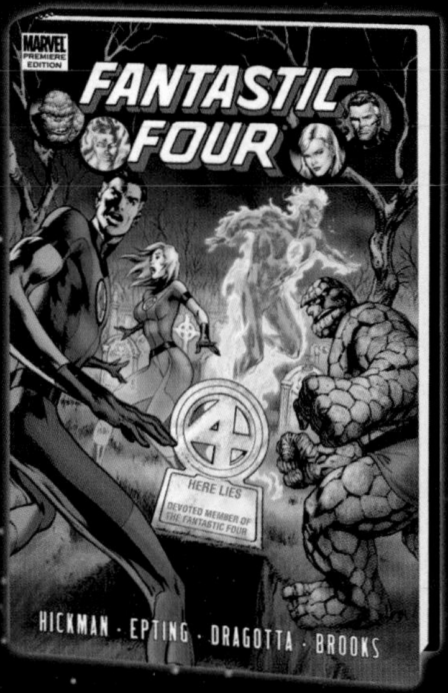
MARVEL PREMIERE EDITION
FANTASTIC FOUR
HERE LIES
DEVOTED MEMBER OF THE FANTASTIC FOUR
HICKMAN · EPTING · DRAGOTTA · BROOKS

FANTASTIC FOUR BY JONATHAN HICKMAN
VOL. 4 PREMIERE HC
978-0-7851-4891-3

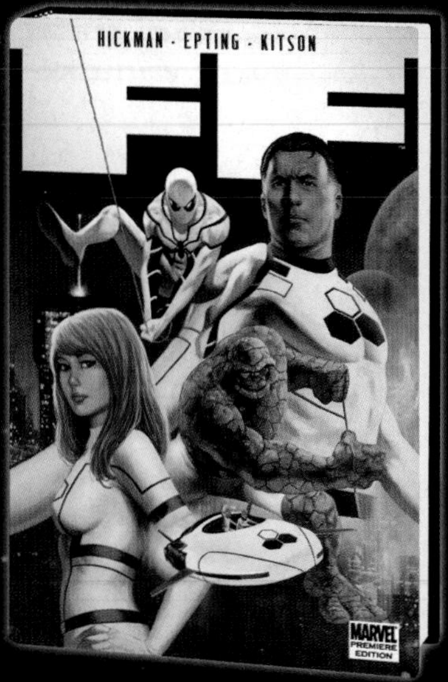
HICKMAN · EPTING · KITSON
FF
MARVEL PREMIERE EDITION

FF BY JONATHAN HICKMAN
VOL. 1 PREMIERE HC
978-0-7851-5144-9

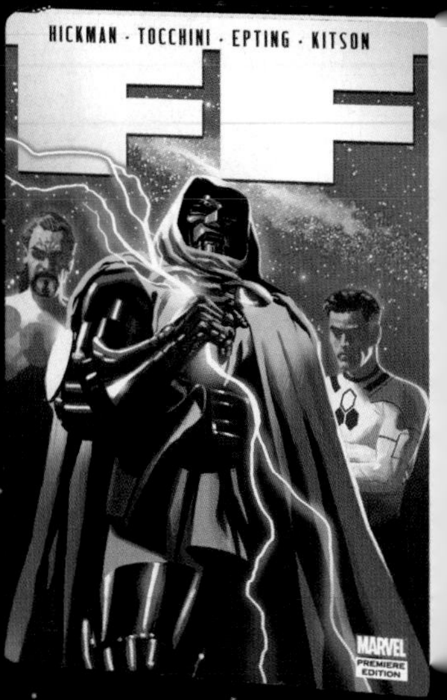
HICKMAN · TOCCHINI · EPTING · KITSON
FF
MARVEL PREMIERE EDITION

FF BY JONATHAN HICKMAN
VOL. 2 PREMIERE HC
978-0-7851-5769-4

Available Wherever Books Are Sold

To Find A Comic Shop Near You Visit www.comicshoplocator.com